TITANIC BELFAST

Edited by

Dr Claude-Bernard Costecade

John Paul Doherty

SOUVENIR GUIDEBOOK

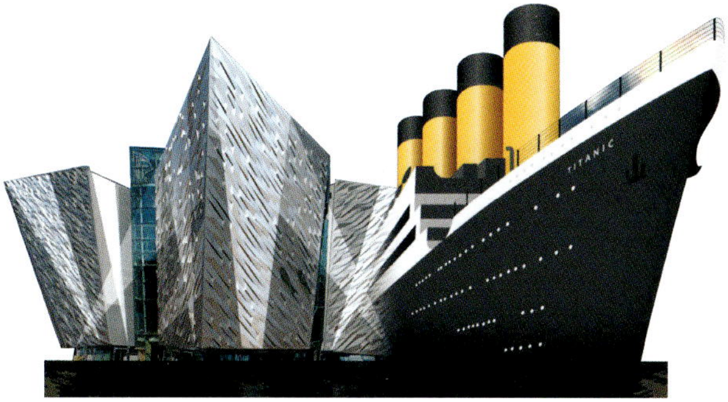

TITANIC BELFAST PUBLICATIONS

CAD OLUX®

Contents

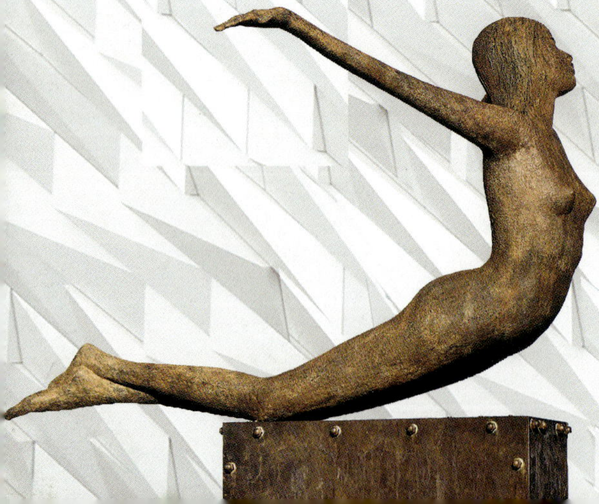

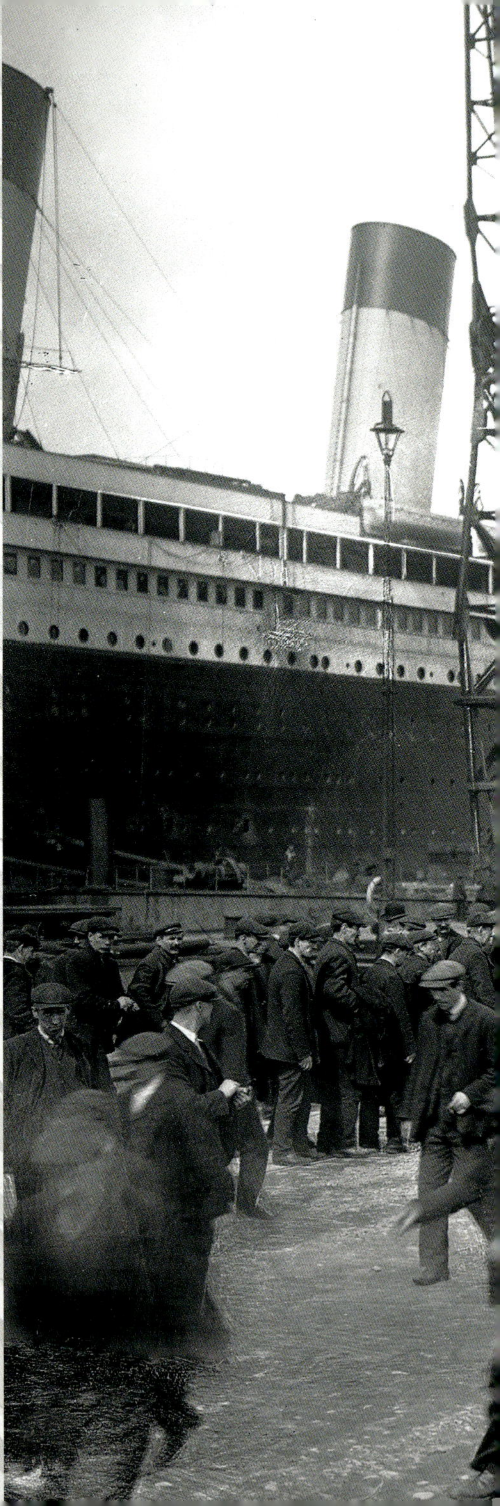

NATIONAL MUSEUMS NI

RIGHT: Harland & Wolff workmen with *Olympic* in Thompson Dry Dock

LEFT: A bronze sculpture, *Titanica* by Rowan Gillespie, greets visitors to Titanic Belfast

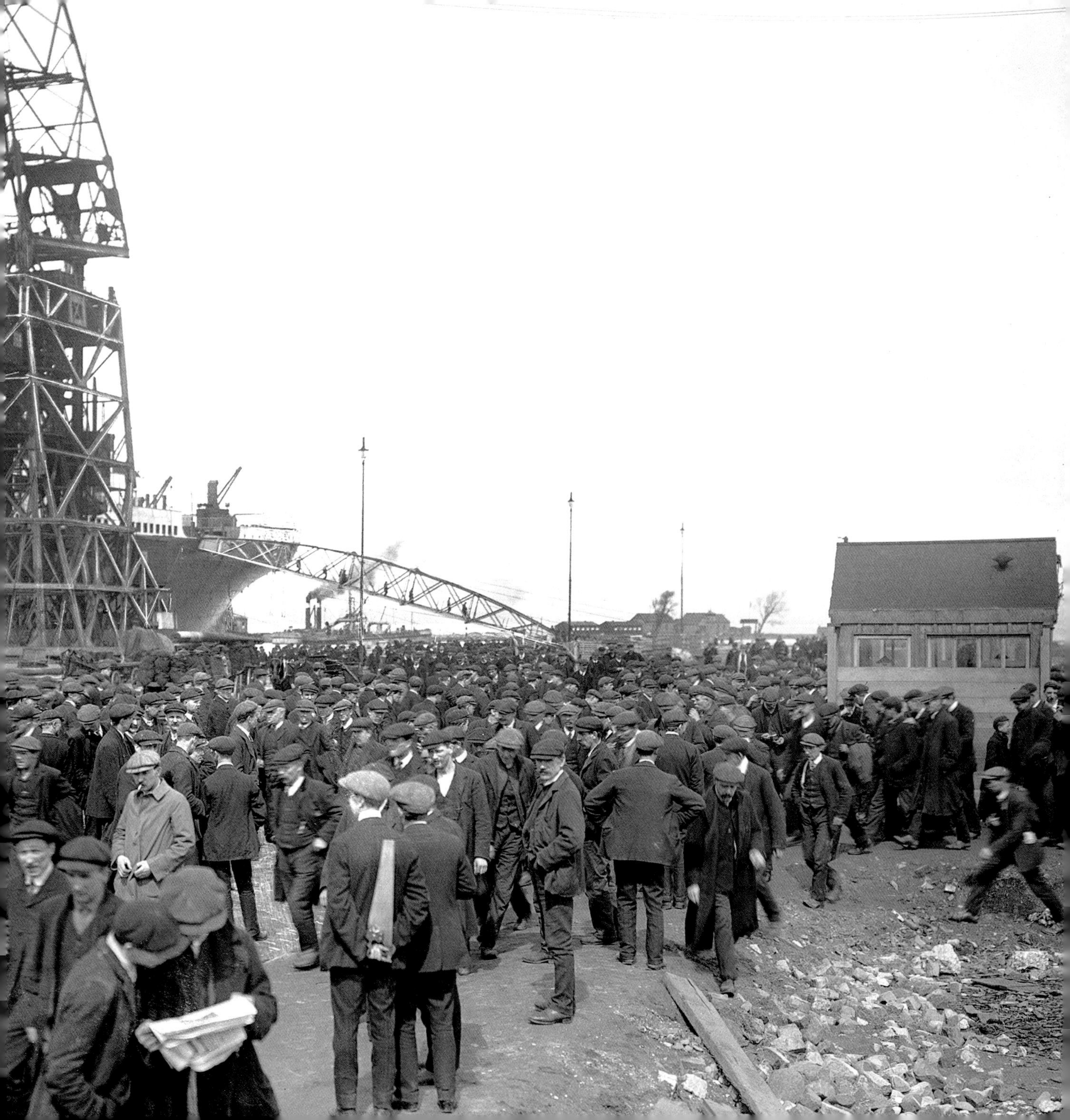

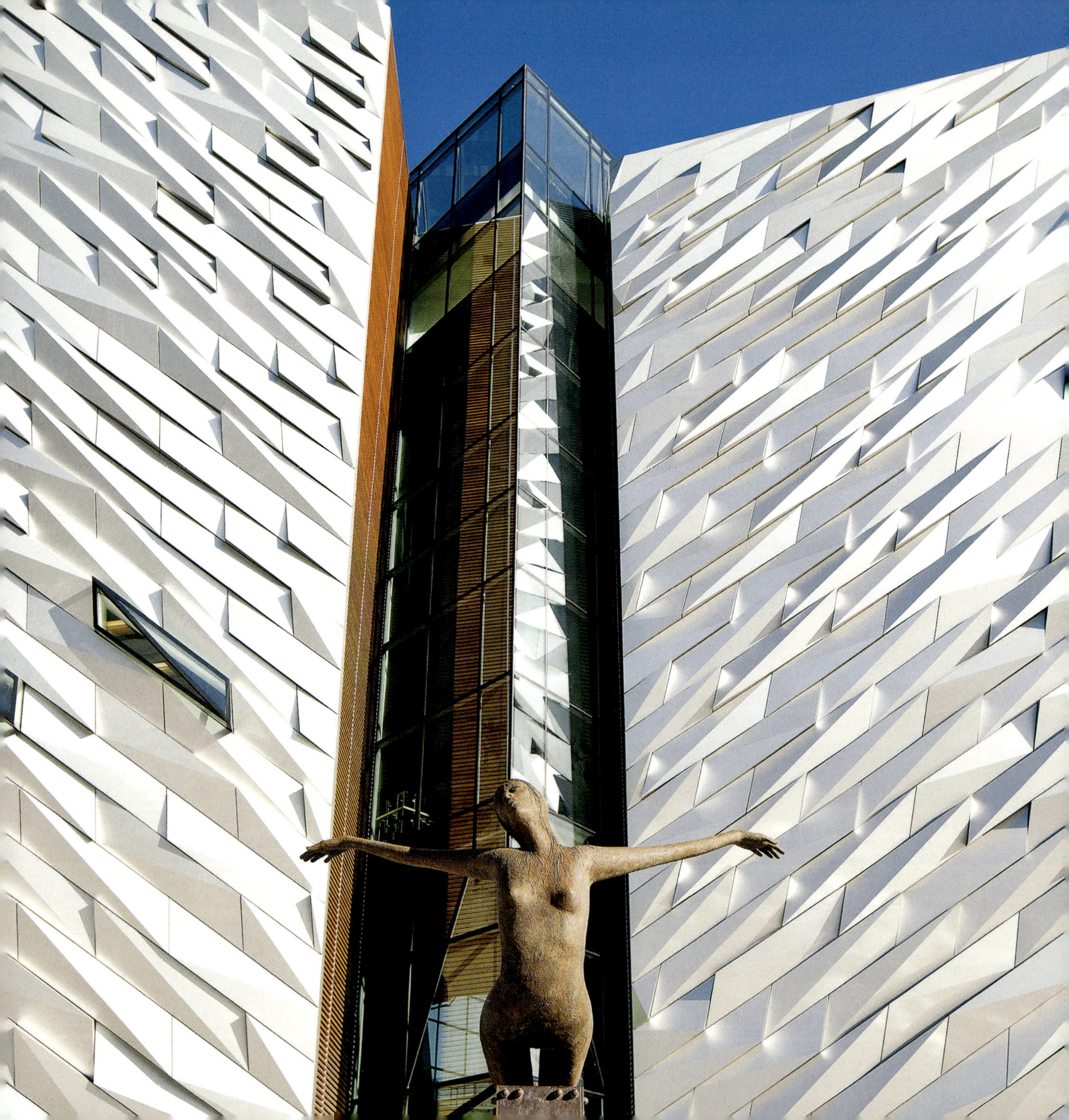

FROM VISION TO REALITY

Titanic Belfast is the culmination of the vision and collective efforts of many people. It represents the best of what can be achieved when we work together.

It also represents the true impact of political will such as that expressed by the entire NI Executive and Belfast City Council who invested their political capital and cash into a project that has put Belfast on the international map for all the right reasons.

The legacy of this collective investment of time, money and effort has been redeployed directly back into Belfast and the wider Northern Ireland community under the stewardship and trusteeship of the Maritime Belfast Trust with its charitable and educational remit.

I am proud to have played a part in bringing the project to fruition. As someone who has spent a lifetime in construction, I can appreciate craftsmanship.

Northern Ireland should be proud of the huge amount of local craftsmanship and skills that are still available here and which are unbeatable in terms of standards.

I hope that as people walk through and wonder at Titanic Belfast, both from within and without, that they appreciate the craftsmanship and skills of the many tradesmen and professionals who by their collective abilities and skills rendered this operation so successful.

The landscape of Belfast is changing, and the city, through its array of beautiful architecture both old and new, where once the proud boast was that we built ships, we now build communities.

Communities built on shared space, where young people are educated together at places like the Belfast Metropolitan College, where people live together at the ARC, where people work together at the Science Park and, of course, where people play together at the Odyssey and Titanic Belfast.

My decision to invest in Belfast was originally based on my belief that Belfast had a future and was a place to do business. I am even more committed to that now than back then.

I am most grateful to the tenacious and passionate people of this city who built Titanic Belfast. We have created something to be proud of.

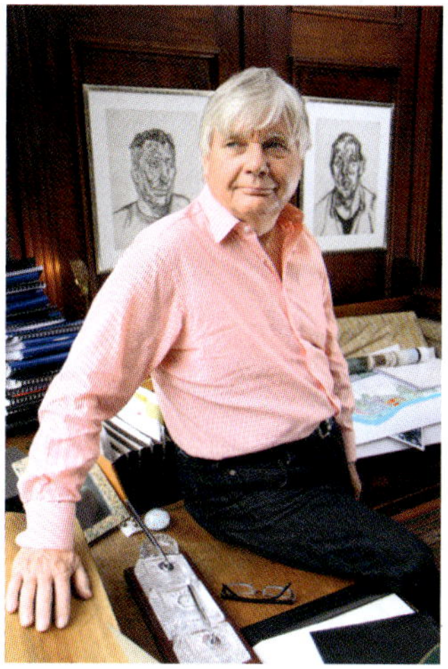

Pat Doherty OBE
Chairman of Titanic Belfast
and Harcourt Developments

THE BIRTH OF TITANIC BELFAST

There are rare moments in the world where men and women assemble to build something for the ages ... such is the birth of Titanic Belfast.

Already at work on the Master Plan for Titanic Quarter, we sought a place to position a structure that would welcome the world to its threshold: its first plans were sketched on the very site where Harland & Wolff's Plating Works stood. Aligned with the hallowed slipways where RMS *Titanic* and RMS *Olympic* were built, opposite the Drawing Office where they were planned, greeting the working neighbourhoods of those who built her, and towering over the River Lagan where she was launched over one hundred years ago ... this icon honours her legacy.

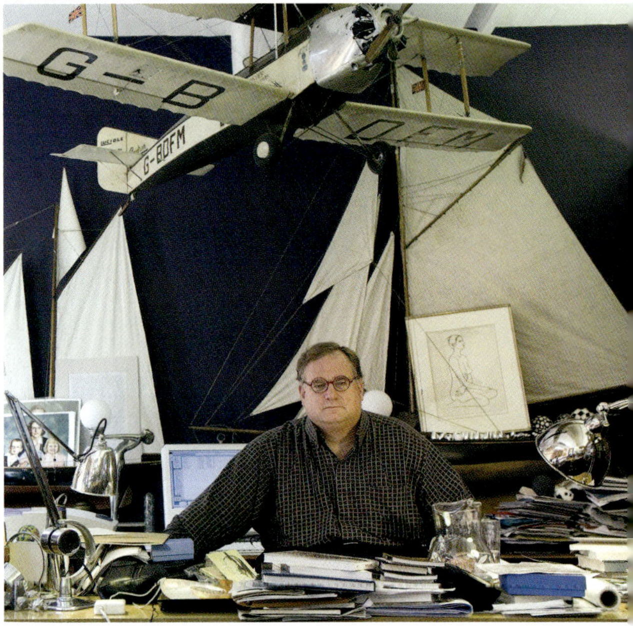

Eric Kuhne, AIA, architect
CivicArts, design architects for Titanic Belfast

Outside and in, this building had to capture the collective imagination. It had to inspire others to continue to tell the story of both *Titanic* and Belfast as centrepieces of invention and innovation in shipbuilding. Titanic Belfast is a touchstone for four centuries of Belfast's maritime legacy and commemorates those many thousands who built the great ships of Belfast.

It takes great courage to build something the world can't imagine. The modern partnerships between the City of Belfast's leaders are no different than those forged between the men and women who straightened the Lagan and built Queen's Island over 150 years ago. Belfast has risen to the challenge to redeem her leadership among the world's active waterfronts.

A century ago, Ismay, Pirrie, Carlisle, Andrews and Morgan defied precedent; they conceived, designed, financed and built the Olympic-class of ships to which *Titanic* belonged. One hundred years later, a new defiant team prevails. Look at what we've created. Stand inside our work and get a sense of the vibrant life of this shipbuilding yard at its peak. Listen and you may hear the sounds of the workers and machinery that forged *Titanic*. Behold the deep history of her story and the wider story of Belfast's maritime legacy and remember that Titanic Belfast does more than teach us about its heritage, for it also teaches us about ourselves.

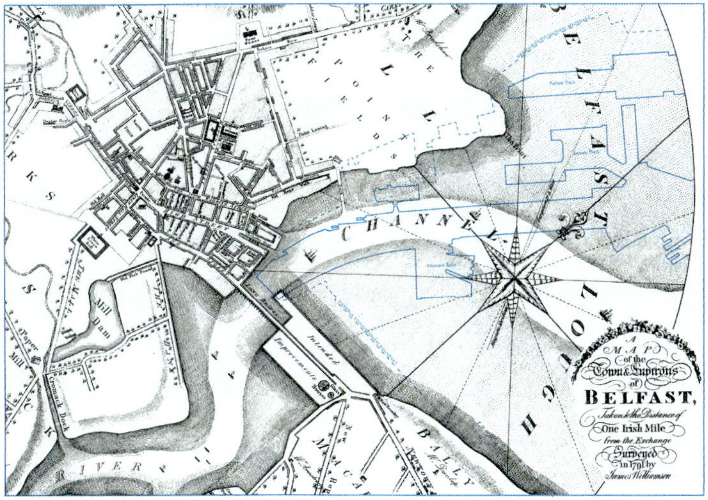

Evolution comes full circle

The compass rose of Williamson's map of 1791 aligns almost perfectly with Titanic Belfast's plan. Over two centuries have elapsed between them, but now that compass rose has become the new 'Star of the Northland', and Titanic Belfast finds itself embedded even further in the history and cartography of Queen's Island.

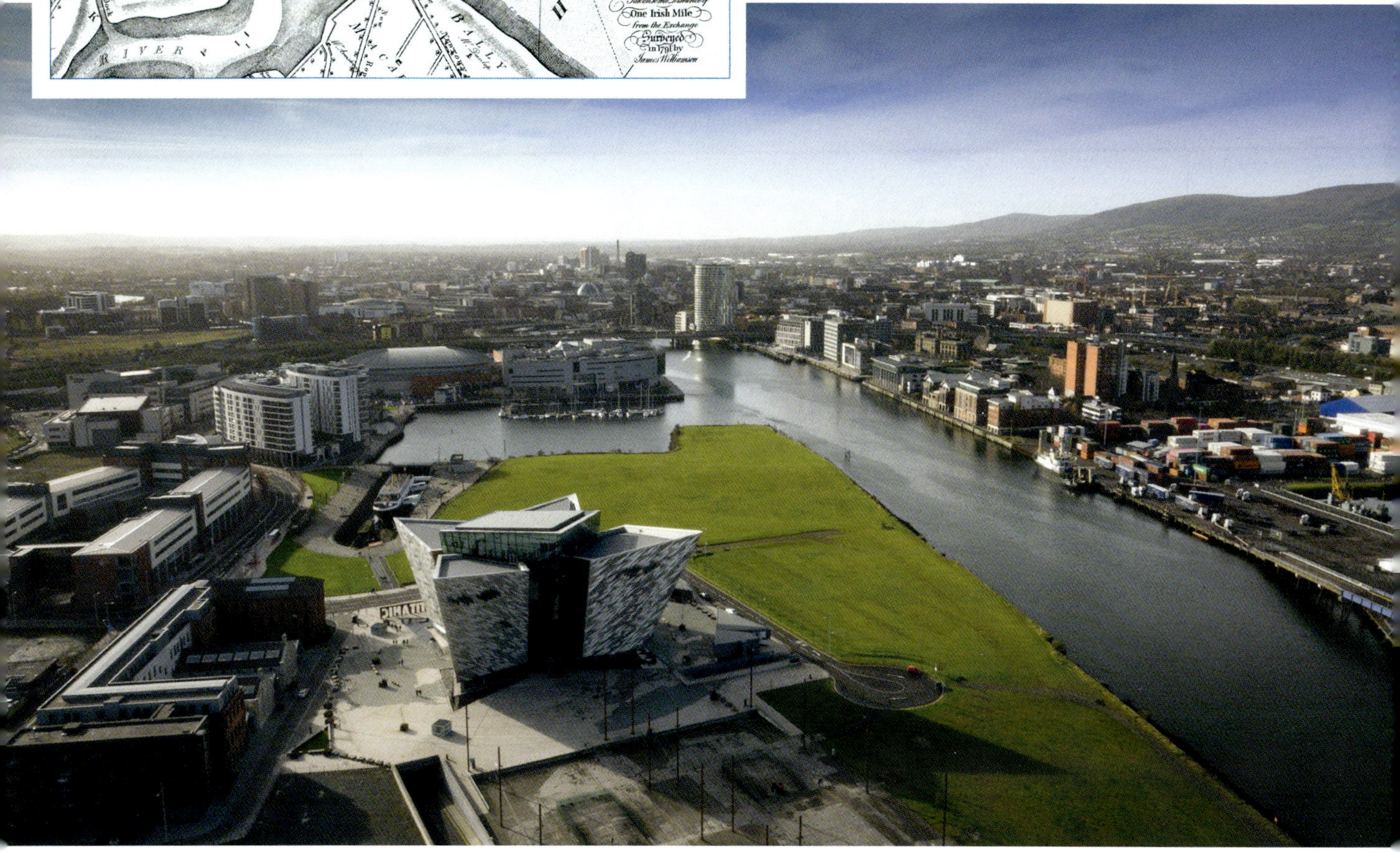

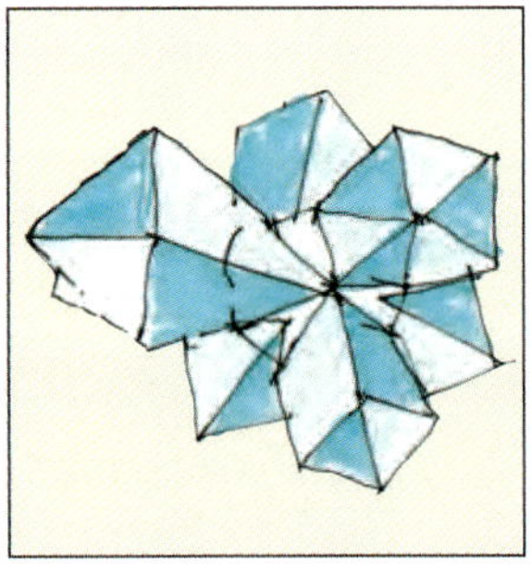 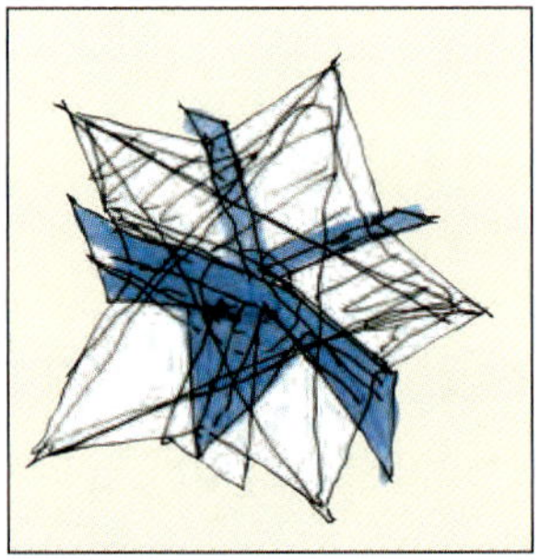 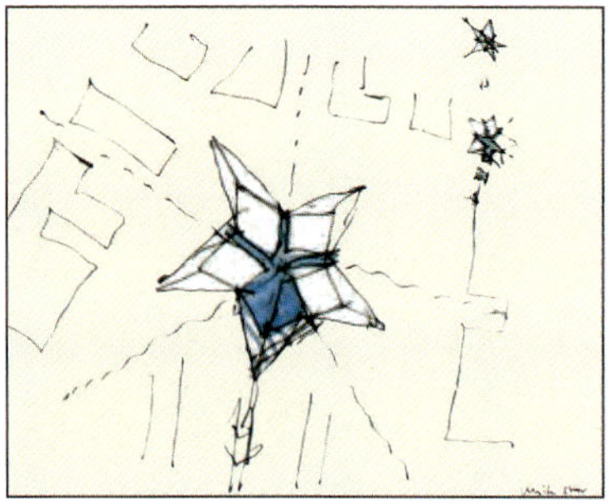

Crystal, Iceberg, White Star, Ships

DESIGNING TITANIC BELFAST

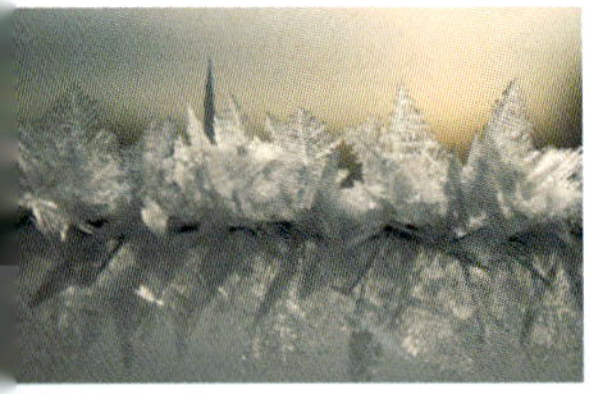

Titanic Belfast's distinctive shape has been inspired by many images that connect the city of Belfast and *Titanic* to the sea. The final form captures the diversity of elements to be found in both ships and sea.

The icy conditions in the North Atlantic provided the point of departure for the design process. Exploring crystal structures led inevitably to solid ice, and the berg that played the fateful part in *Titanic*'s story. Titanic Belfast's architectural form has reached a balance between the informality of nature's frozen giants and the design formality found within shipyards.

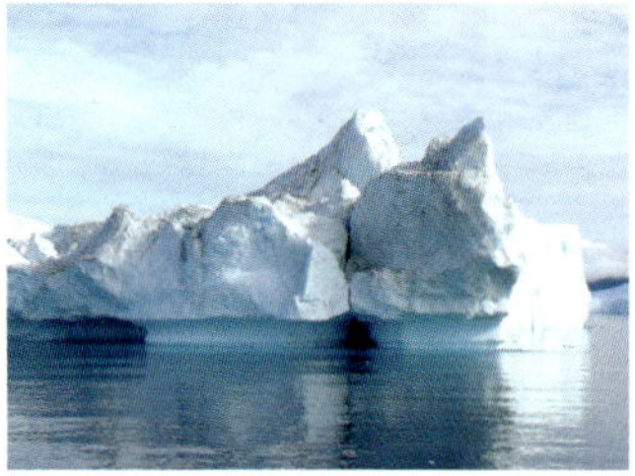

The construction sites of Harland & Wolff are symbols of Belfast as a great centre of innovation and invention, its

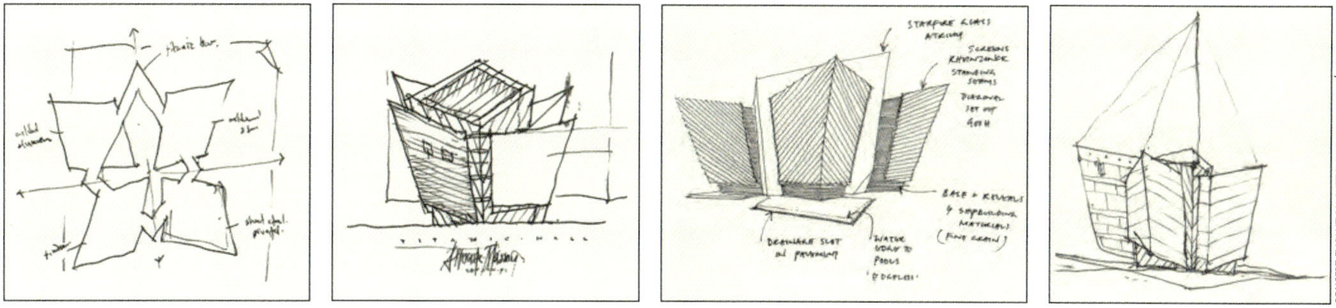

CONCEPT EVOLUTION SKETCHES BY CIVICARTS / ERIC R. KUHNE & ASSOCIATES

& The Ages of Shipbuilding In Titanic Belfast

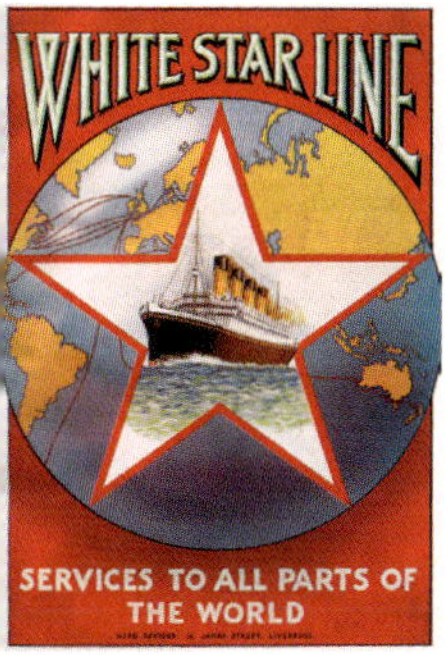

ships opening up the world through ocean travel. Uniting the White Star with the ship's hulls forever connects the determination of J Bruce Ismay and the shipbuilding skills of William Pirrie. The fifth point of the White Star logo soon became a glass shard, pointing down the former slipways between the lines of *Olympic* and *Titanic*; it then drew back into the centre, protected by four hulls that radiate like a compass rose.

The four ages of shipbuilding in Belfast – Wood, Iron, Steel and Aluminium – are now celebrated by the four hulls of the building, inspired by the archive image of diverging hulls laid upon the North Yard's slipways, hidden in their wooden scaffolds. The monumental scale of the Arrol Gantry and the construction of both *Olympic* and *Titanic* inspired a sense of grandeur.

Four plated hulls now ring the atrium, clothed in their faceted plates of aluminium, and the final form encompasses all that went before: water crystal, iceberg, star and bow.

Taken in 1898, this photograph shows *Afric*, Oceanic and Medic under construction where Titanic Belfast now stands

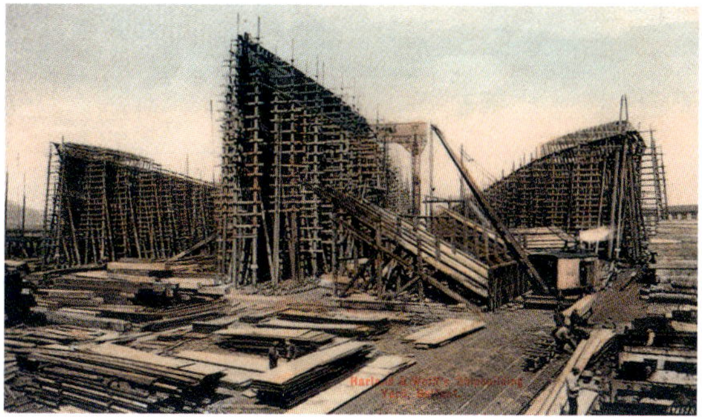

TITANIC BELFAST: AN ICON

The Atrium

The soaring central atrium creates a grand and evocative entrance hall to the building. Its tall, dark volume, lit by narrow shafts of light, echoes the dramatic intensity of the crowded void between the *Titanic* and *Olympic* hulls as they rested upon the slipways. The brass and stone lines of the central Compass Rose anchor the floor plan in the graphics of maritime maps, and incorporate the stirring words of Belfast poet, Thomas Carnduff:

O city of sound and motion!
O city of endless stir!
From the dawn of a misty morning,
To the fall of the evening air;
From the night of the moving shadows,
To the sound of the shipyard horn;
We hail thee Queen of the Northland,
We who are Belfast Born.

Men of Belfast
from *Songs of the Shipyards*, 1924

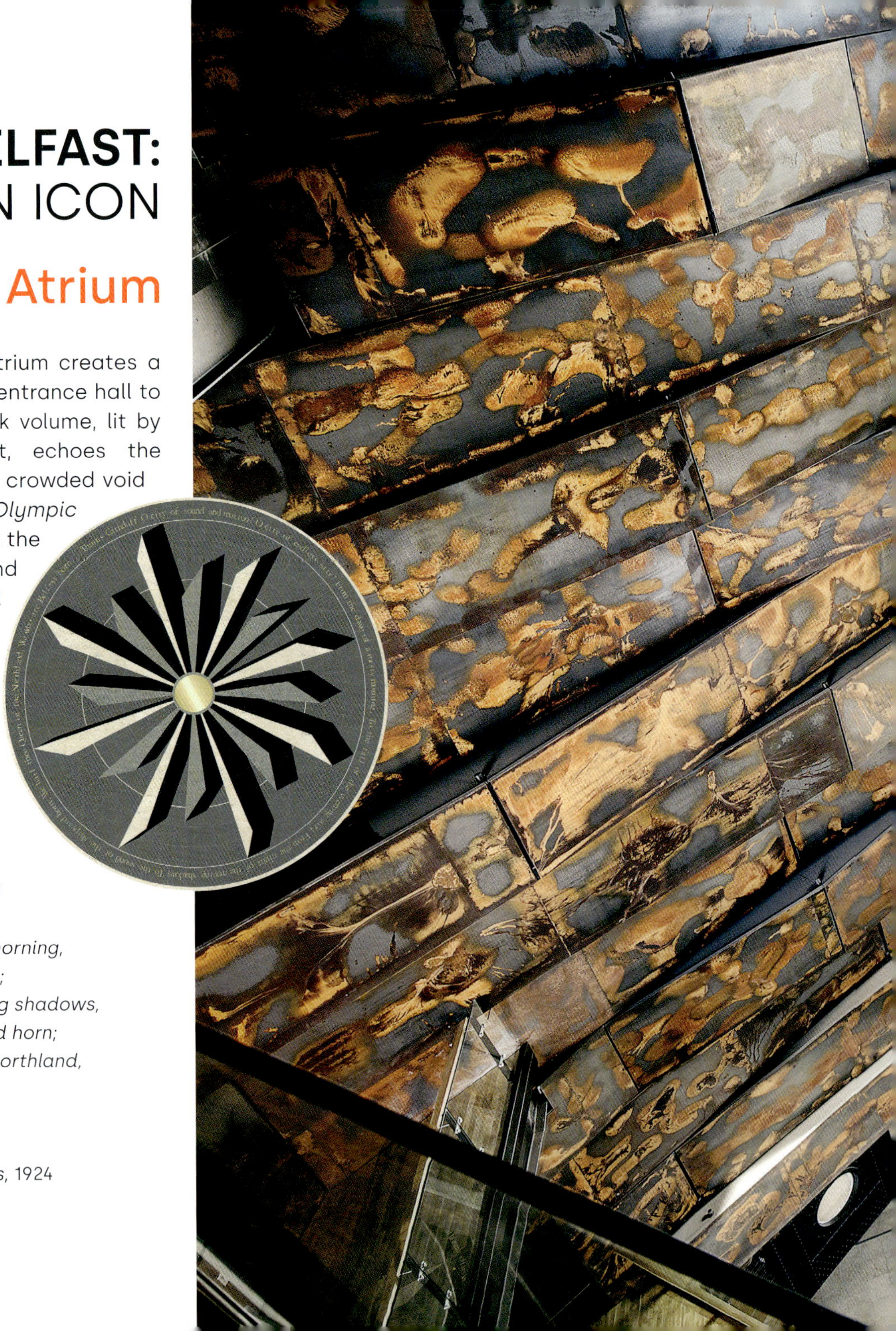

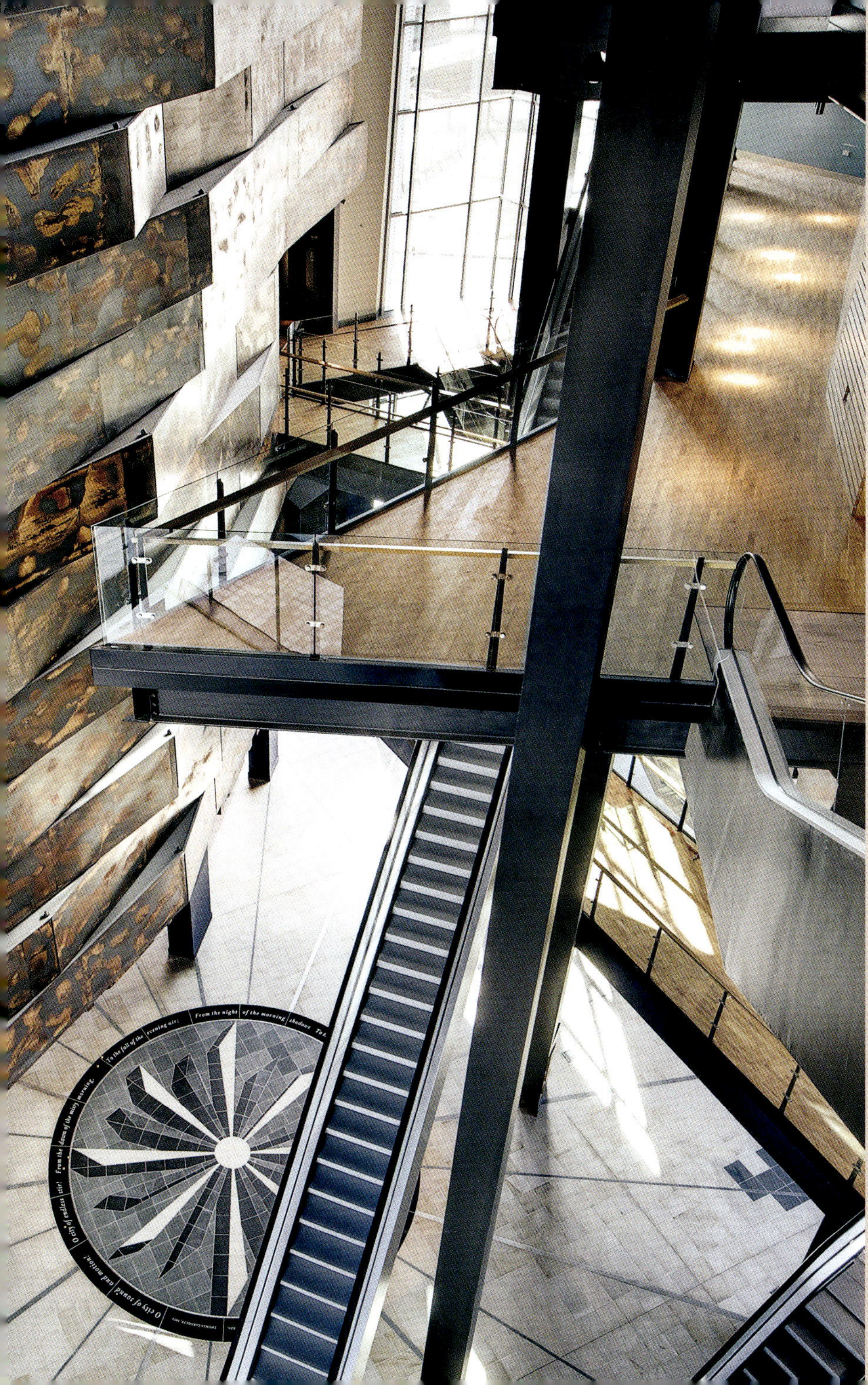

The long lines of the escalators are reminiscent of the labyrinth of gangways zigzagging through the Arrol Gantry, while the decoration of the galleries' outer walls capture the awesome scale of the steel plates from which the ships were constructed.

The atrium acts as a civic space connecting the building's functions from the Titanic Experience – the world leading visitor attraction, to the banqueting hall high above. Like ships' promenade decks, it offers a vantage point from which to view the city, the river, the historic shipyards... and the very ground upon which *Titanic* was built.

The Building

Stacked like nested deck plans, the arrangement of Titanic Belfast's floor plates mirrors those of the famous liners. Piercing up through five floors, the atrium recalls the awesome size of *Titanic*'s engine rooms: cathedral-like spaces, four decks in height whose hissing machinery formed the ship's beating heart.

While the Titanic Experience galleries themselves are controlled, light-secure volumes, the circulation spaces around the atrium allow visitors to experience some of the jostling, angular intensity of the shipyard in its heyday. Laid out above them are the banqueting hall and hospitality suites: contemporary staterooms and promenade decks filled with light and air, in which to host the best of Belfast functions.

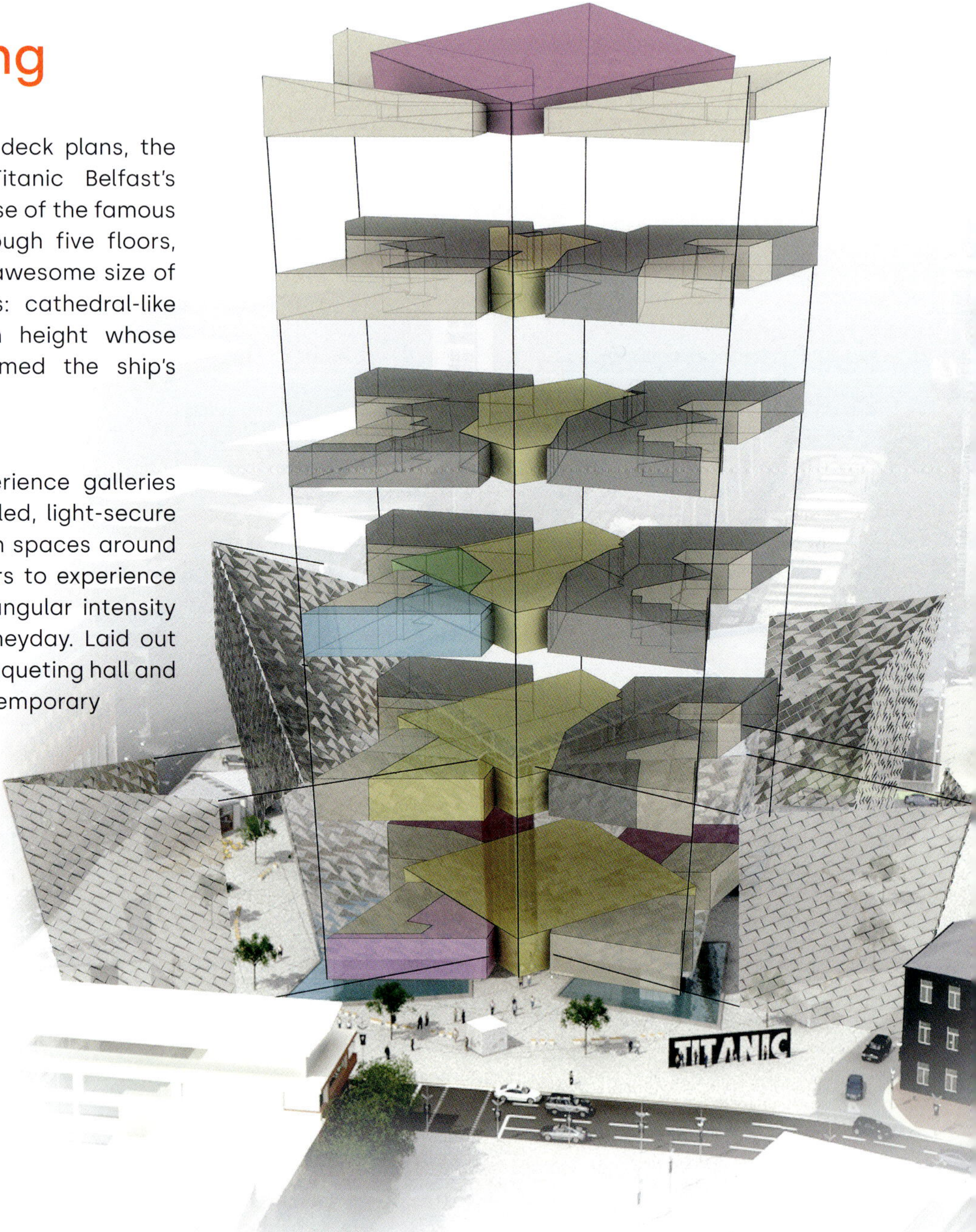

Fifth and Sixth Floors

The top two floors comprise an unparalleled range of private event spaces for any occasion; offering elegant surroundings in a unique design based on *Titanic*'s interiors. The extensive use of glass makes maximum use of the hall's vantage point, high above the slipways, transforming this glowing level into a panoramic observatory from which to survey the city; providing an outstanding conference and banqueting venue for Northern Ireland.

Third and Fourth Floor

The upper floors of the self-guided Titanic Experience contain immersive technology combined with original maritime heritage where guests discover the sights, sounds, smells and stories of the ship, as well as the people and city that made her.

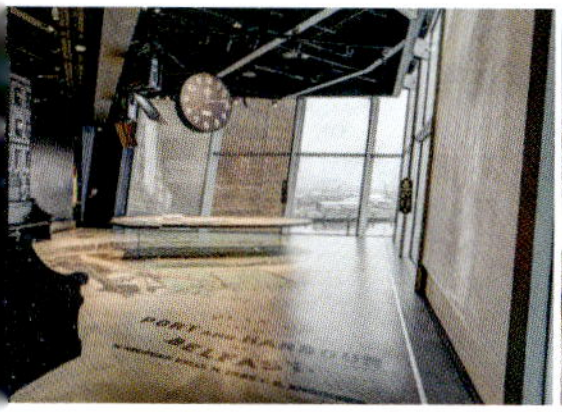

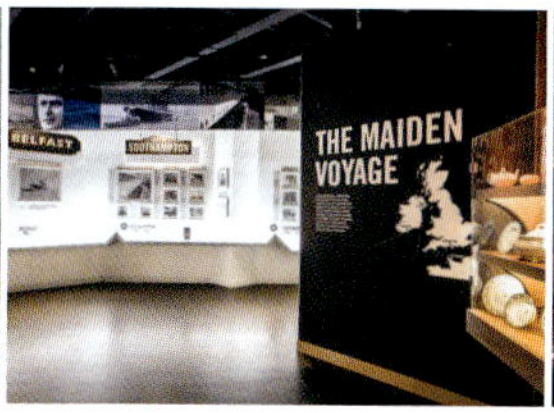

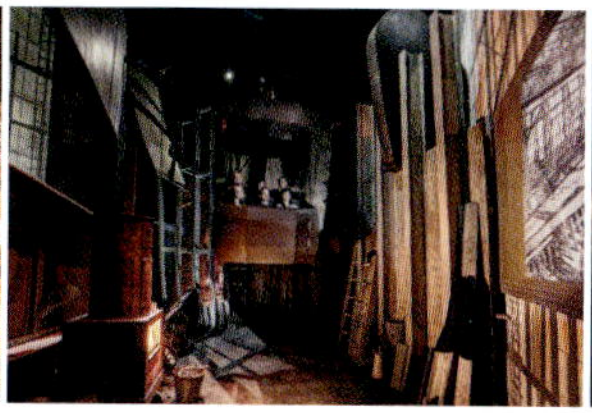

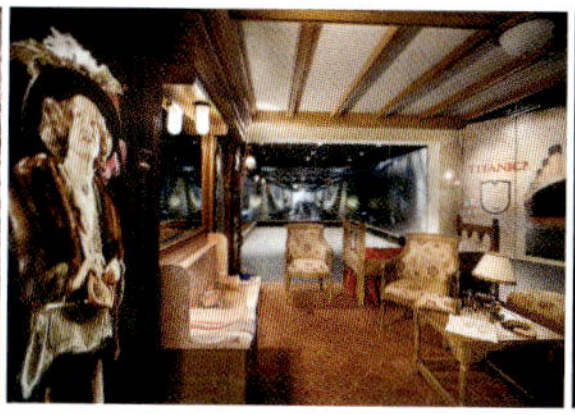

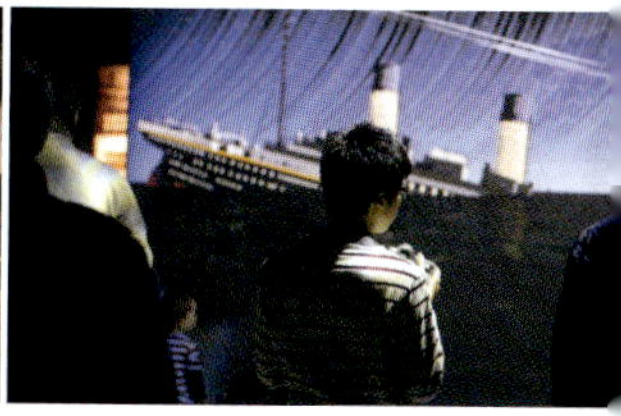

Second Floor

This floor includes the schools' education centre and The Andrews Gallery – a large space for hosting regularly-renewed art exhibitions and events.

First Floor

The Titanic Experience begins on the first floor, connected by timber-decked balcony walkways beside walls inscribed with the names of former Harland & Wolff vessels; building the maritime experience before guests have even stepped inside.

Ground Floor

A cathedral-like, public space, open to all, the ground floor acts as grand entrance and welcome hall. A café, restaurant, gift shop, and ticket office ring the atrium, making Titanic Belfast a lively, vibrant hub for local residents and visitors.

Basement Levels

The convenient underground car park connects directly to the ground floor entrance with its generous array of amenities.

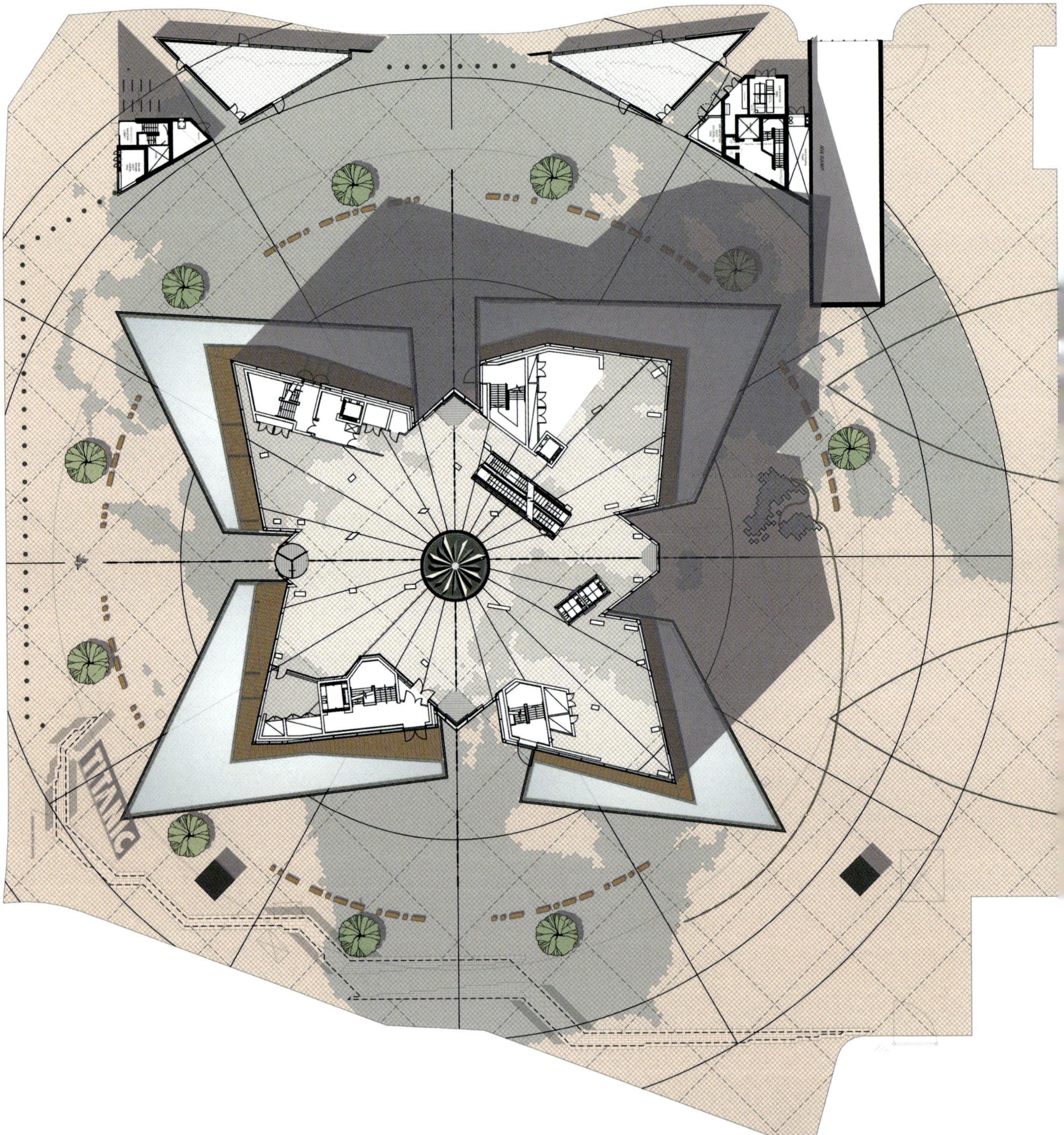

The Plaza

A subtle, sweeping map of the northern hemisphere is picked out in the pavers of the surrounding public plaza, with markers plotting the course of *Titanic*'s maiden voyage so that visitors may retrace its fateful journey.

The map is orientated so the United Kingdom and the route of *Titanic* are on the northern part of the plaza, closest to the slipways where she was built.

Cities relevant to *Titanic* are identified on the map: Belfast, Southampton, Cherbourg, Cobh (Queenstown), New York, Halifax.

A halo of dot and dashed shaped benches ring the building, spelling out *Titanic*'s infamous Morse code distress call – SOS CQD – together with *Titanic*'s own call sign DE MGY. Trees shade these symbolic benches providing places of contemplation for those who visit this hallowed site to reflect upon the wider narrative laid out before them.

Reflection pools bring water to the foot of the building, strengthening the allusions to naval architecture and providing rippling patterns of reflected light at night.

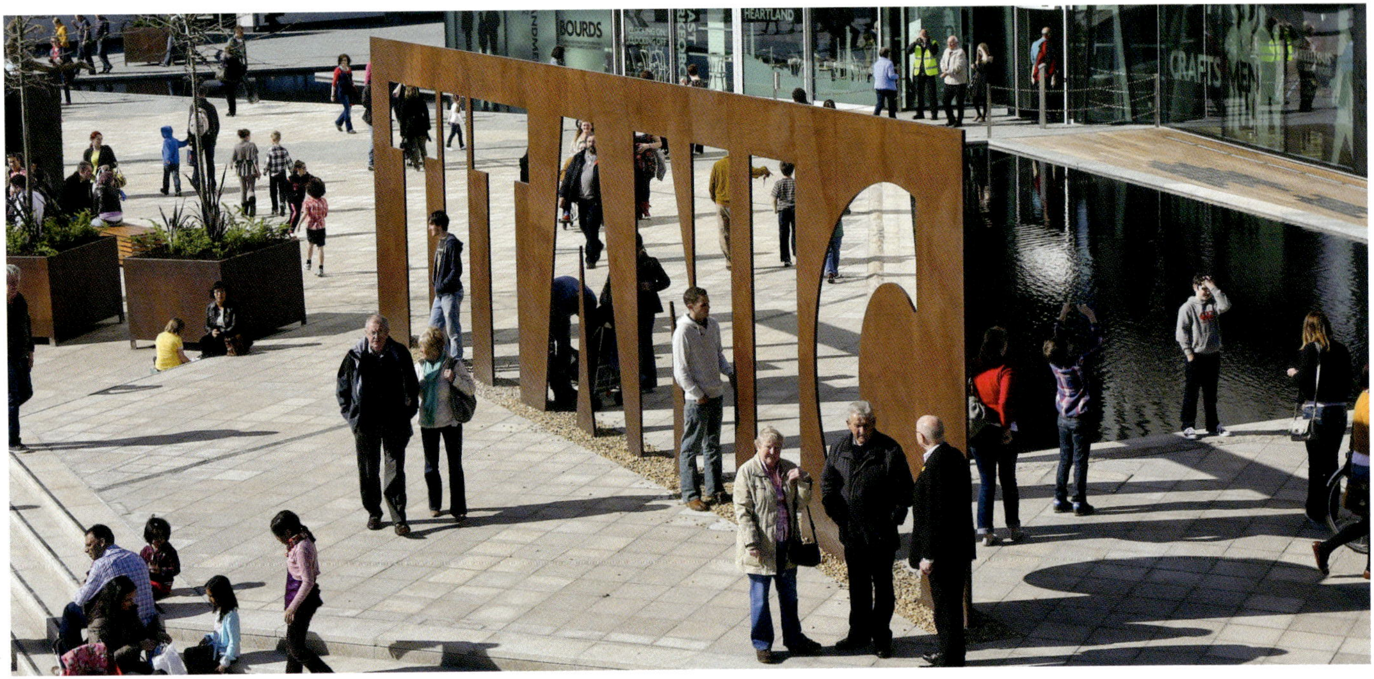

The *Titanic* Sign

Cut from the same 2.5 cm (1 inch) steel plate used to construct the great ship herself, this entry sign announces TITANIC to the world. Three metres tall, and twelve metres long, the letters are large enough to allow guests to step 'into character' for a memorable photograph, and open enough to frame striking views of the building behind. At night the building comes to life...and the sign becomes a dark lattice around glowing letters, evoking the mysteries and stories within the Titanic Experience. This subtractive approach to letter making also acts as a subtle tribute to the missing.

Capturing the scale, solidity and strength of the immense components that emerged from the Plating Sheds that once stood here, this bold sign is a steely tribute to the thousands of workers who laboured on those great ships.

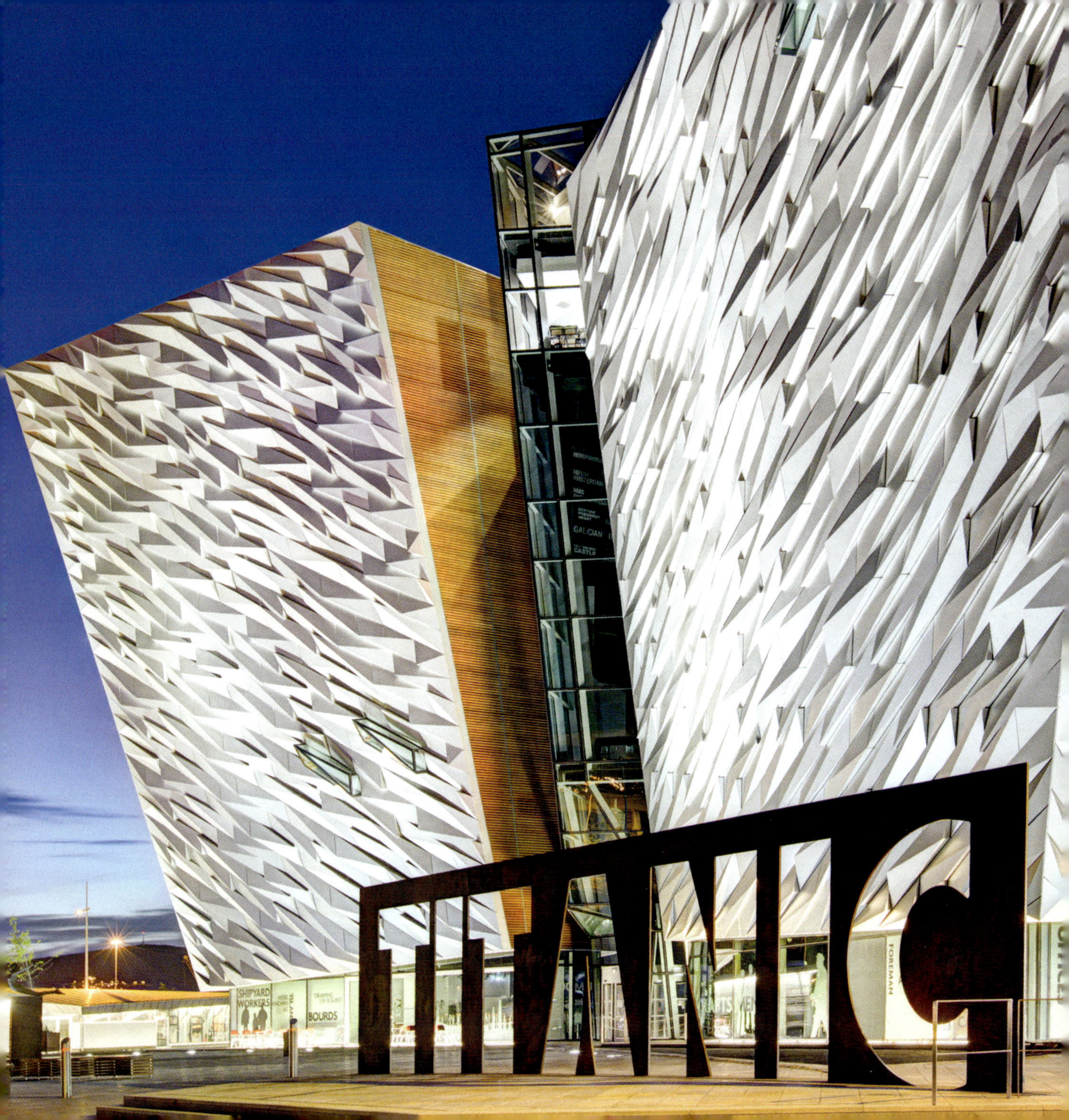
SHIPYARD WORKERS
FOREMAN

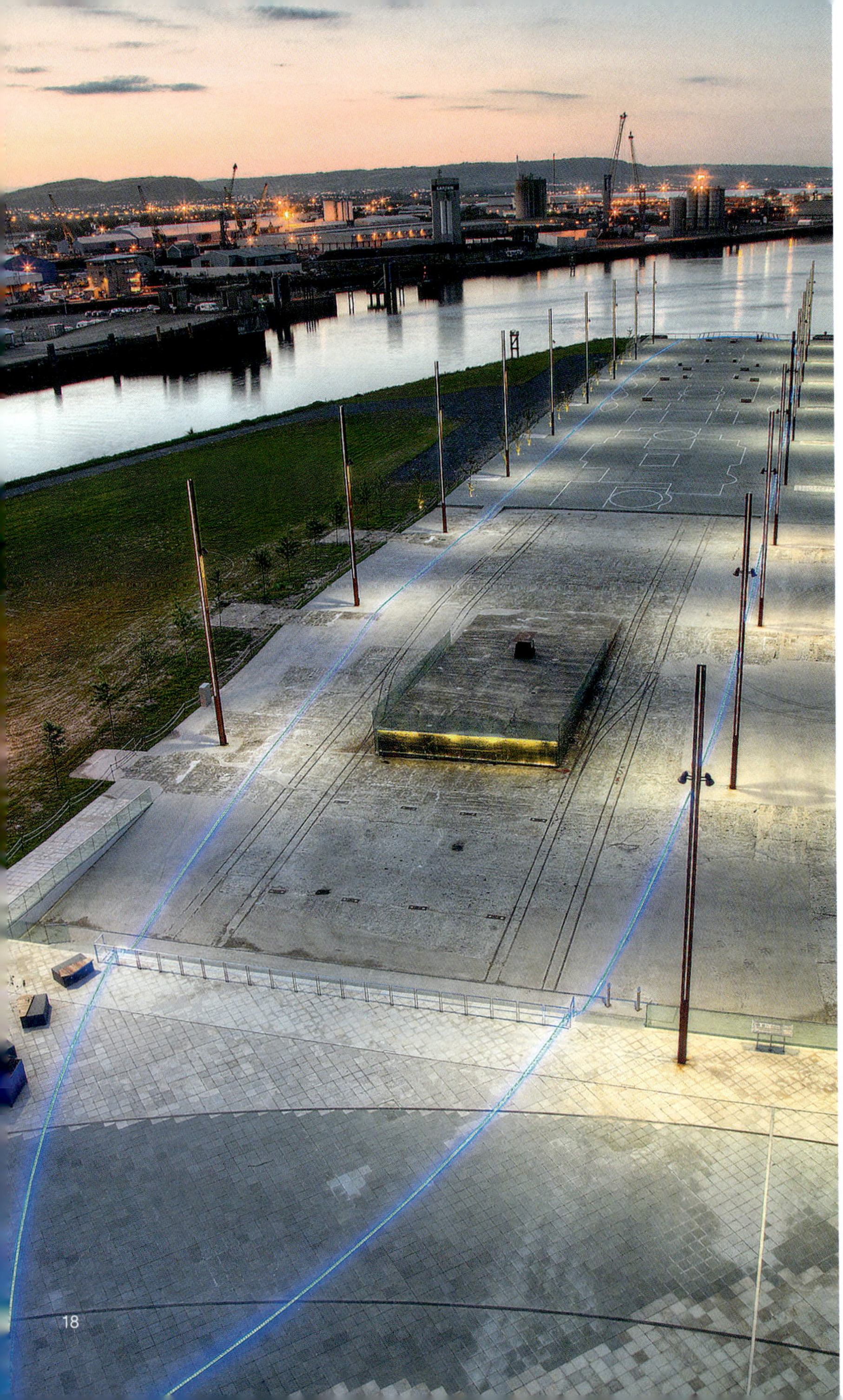

HEBER-PERCY & PARKER ARCHITECTS

The Slipways

Today, embedded in the slipways is a continuous strip of blue lit glass that defines at full size the whole outline of *Titanic* and *Olympic* in the positions they were built.

On the left, the *Olympic* slipway comprises four lawns alternating with four timber decks relating to the proportions of those lost in the *Titanic* tragedy (lawns) and those who were saved (decks) in each of the three travel classes of passengers and crew. Their respective names are set in glass panels fixed to the vertical faces of the concrete wedges.

On the right, inlaid white stones trace the main deck plan of *Titanic*, echoing the original blueprint.

Modern benches have been positioned in the same location as the benches on the ship.

The stanchions of the former Arrol Gantry are depicted by steel lamp posts with inset vertical lights introducing a third dimension. Together with the footprints, they reference the scale and structure of the ships, and the sense of adventure of its passengers and crew.

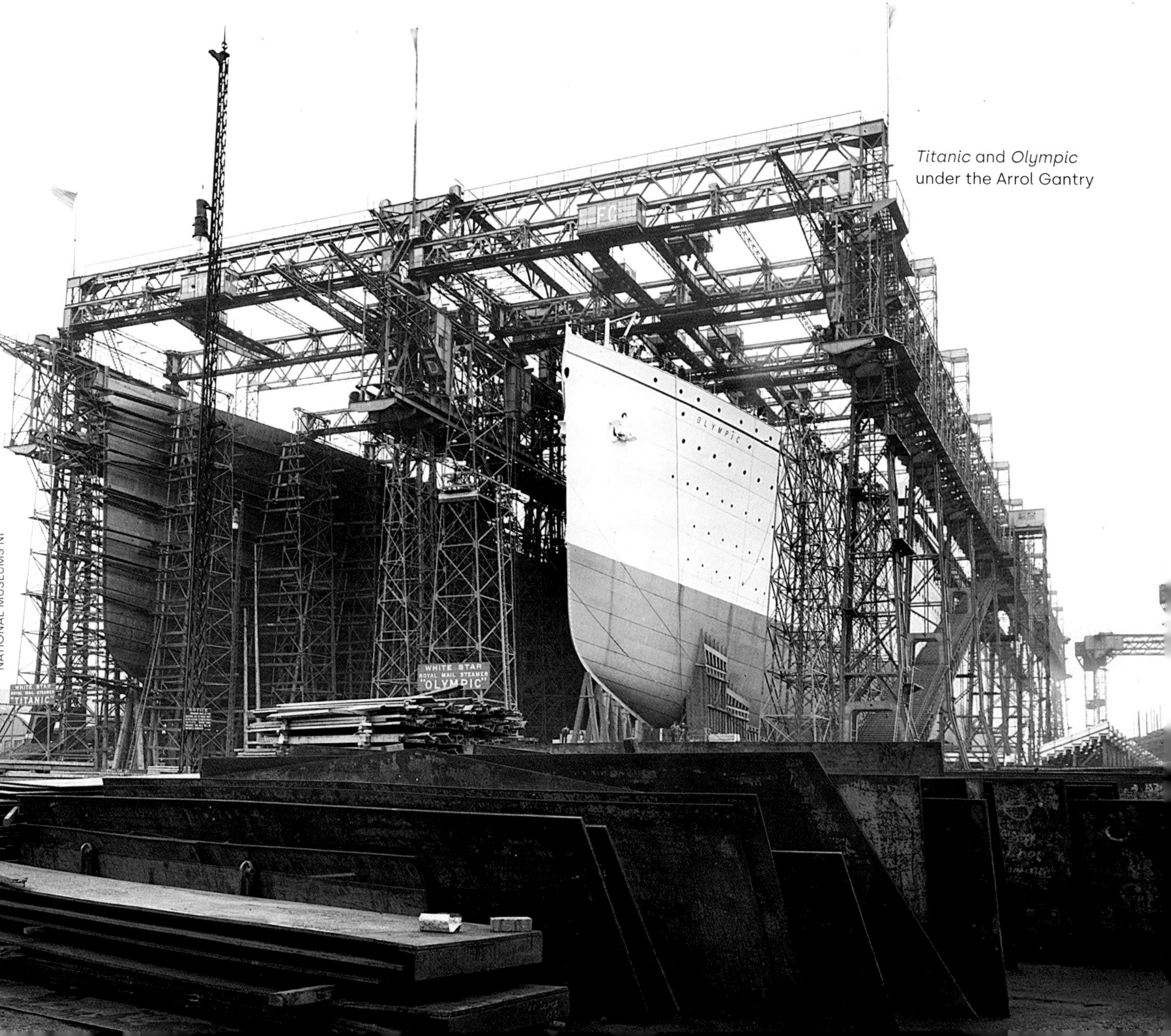

Titanic and *Olympic* under the Arrol Gantry

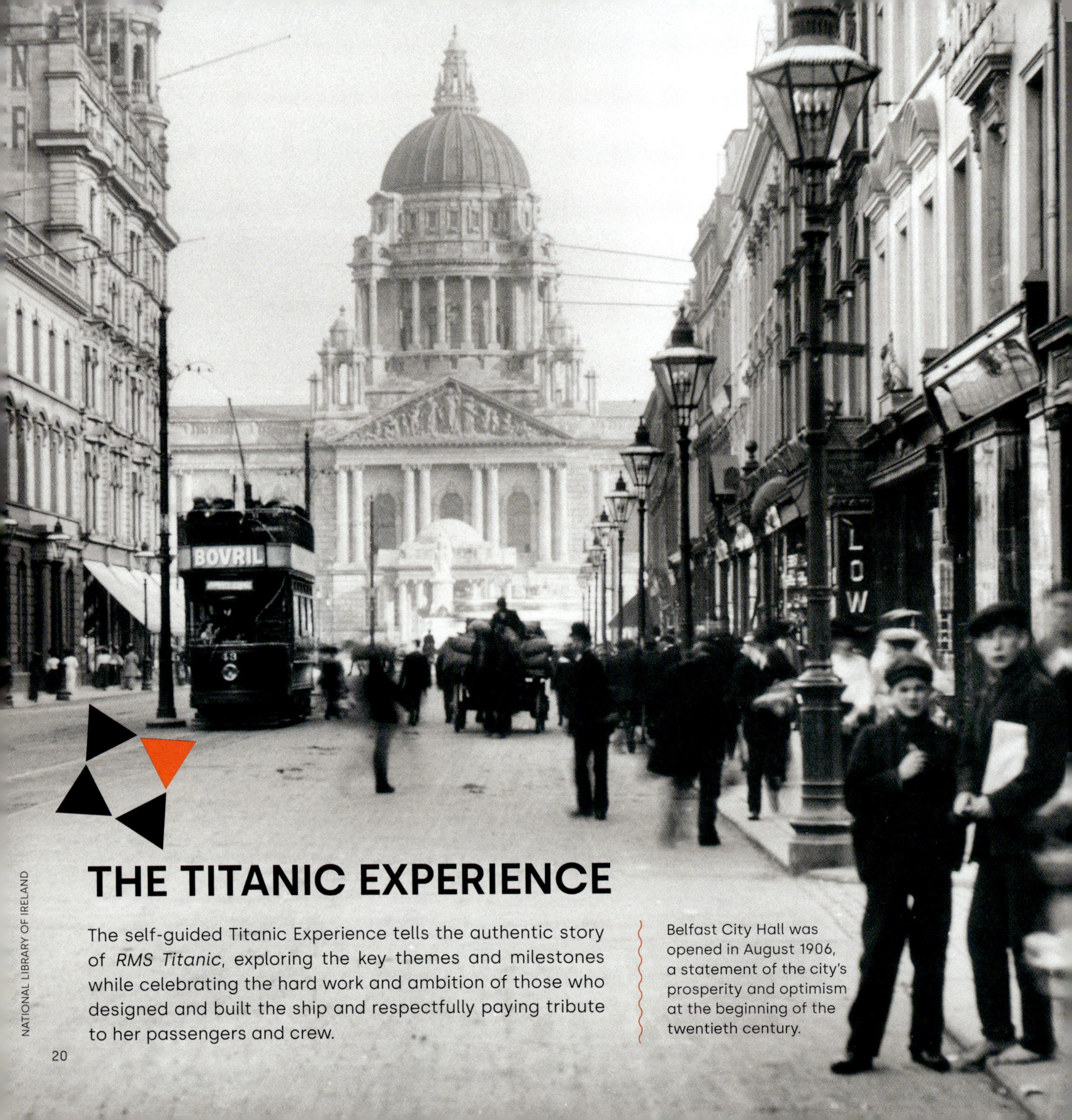

NATIONAL LIBRARY OF IRELAND

THE TITANIC EXPERIENCE

The self-guided Titanic Experience tells the authentic story of *RMS Titanic*, exploring the key themes and milestones while celebrating the hard work and ambition of those who designed and built the ship and respectfully paying tribute to her passengers and crew.

Belfast City Hall was opened in August 1906, a statement of the city's prosperity and optimism at the beginning of the twentieth century.

Boomtown Belfast

The world was changing rapidly in the late 19th century. After the Great Famine that ravaged Ireland in the 1840s, people flooded into Belfast to find work in the new linen mills, the docks, the shipyards, and a range of successful and interconnected industries that employed large workforces. The decline of the rural economy coincided with growing prosperity in Belfast. Between 1851 and 1901, the city's population increased from 87,062 to 349,180. At the time, Belfast was the fastest growing city in the British Empire.

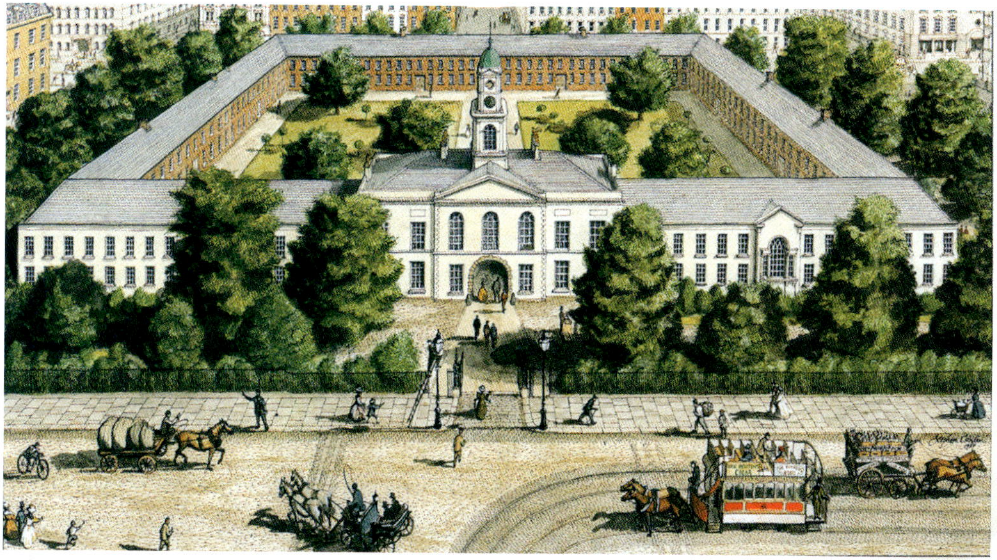

LINEN HALL LIBRARY

Situated on the site of the future City Hall the White Linen Hall was the centre of trading for bleached linen from 1784.

Belfast, the linen capital of the world

By 1900, Belfast was producing and exporting more linen than anywhere else in the world. The city's location did much to develop the linen industry. The River Lagan had tributaries that could drive the machinery and provided routes to collect linens. Finished products were exported through Belfast Docks.

With industrialisation, the linen trade began to be centred around Belfast. There was a ready supply of labour, and Belfast had the infrastructure to facilitate the growth of industry.

Flax

Fibres from the pale blue flax flower stem are used to make linen. Flax was sown in spring and harvested one hundred days later.

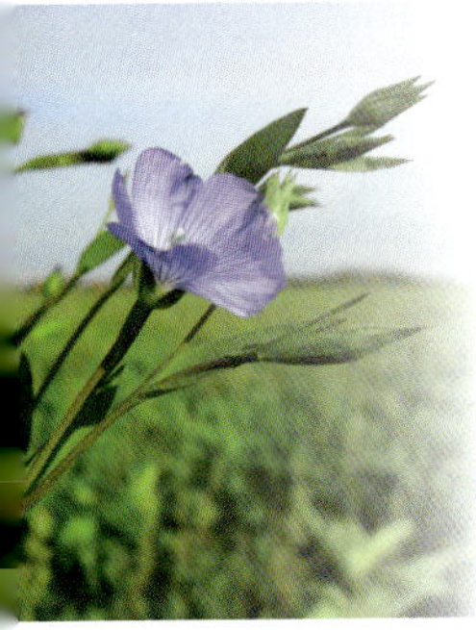

A cottage industry

Flax was grown in the countryside along with foodstuffs. Growing flax and turning it into linen was a long process with many stages. Traditionally, women and children prepared the flax and spun the fibres into thread. Men then wove the yarn into linen cloth. This work was carried out at home on spinning wheels and hand looms. Weavers and spinners worked long hours to make a living. Once the linen cloth was made, it would be taken to a brown linen market to be sold for finishing. The finished product was then exported, mainly to England. Irish linen was known for its fine quality.

The linen trade

Flax has been used to make linen for thousands of years. This involves a series of processes, many of which were carried out in the linen mills of Belfast.

Before industrialisation, the process of growing, harvesting and turning flax into linen took place in the countryside. By the 17th century, this was an important industry in the north of Ireland. During the early 19th century, linen production moved away from the countryside to the towns.

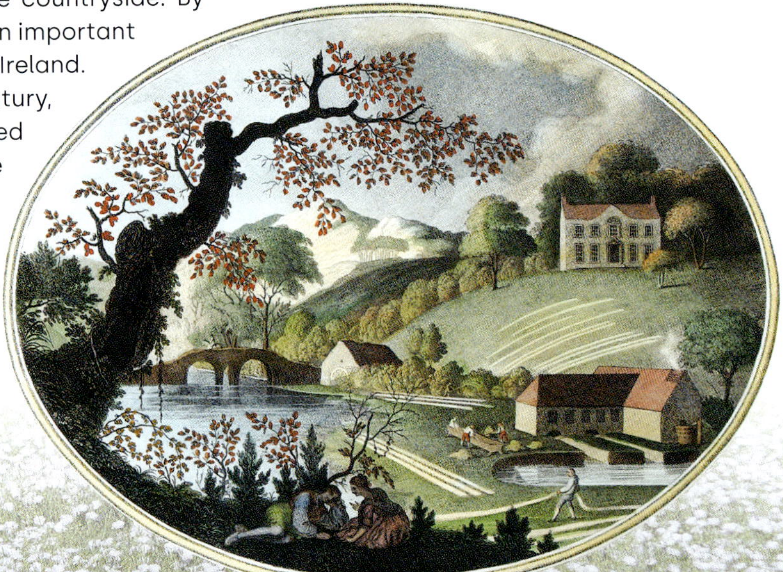

A print by William Hincks of Linen Hill House overlooking a bleach green and mill, 1783

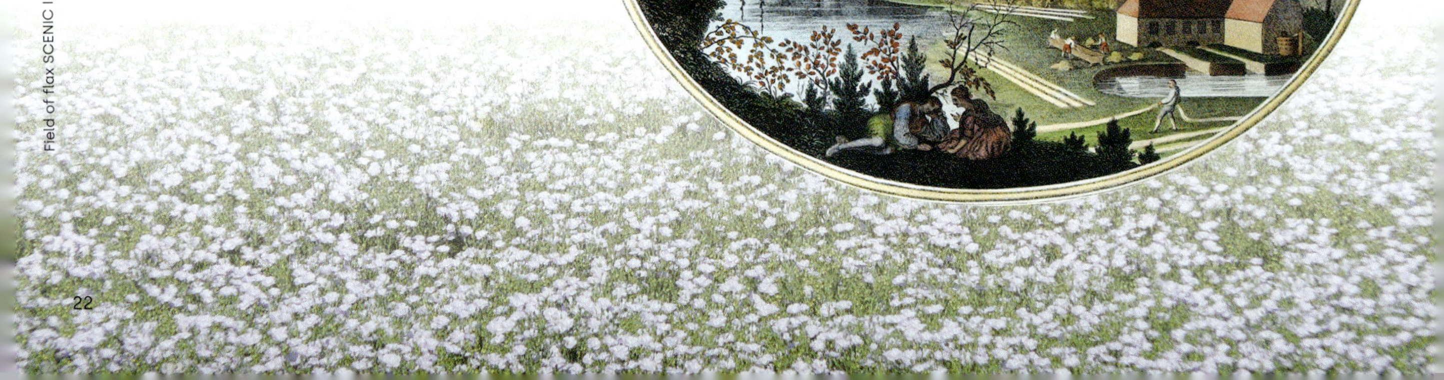

Field of flax SCENIC IRELAND

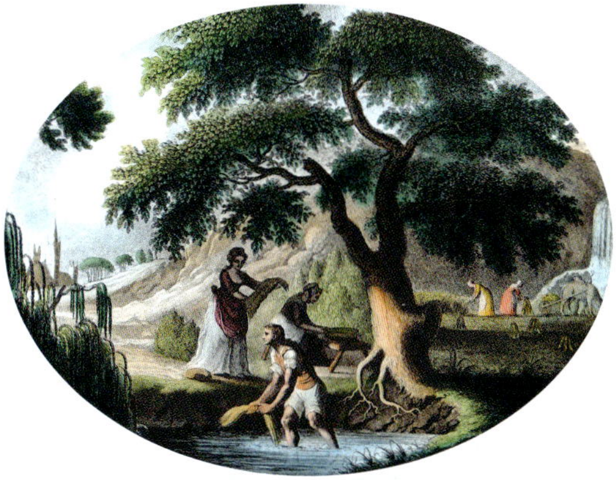

Harvesting flax

Flax was pulled rather than cut to ensure the fibres were undamaged and as long as possible. Flax was then rippled to remove the seeds from the stem. Retting rotted the stems so the fibres could be removed.

Linen Yarn

Flax was spun on a spinning wheel or machine to produce linen yarn. This Hincks print illustrates the cottage industry.

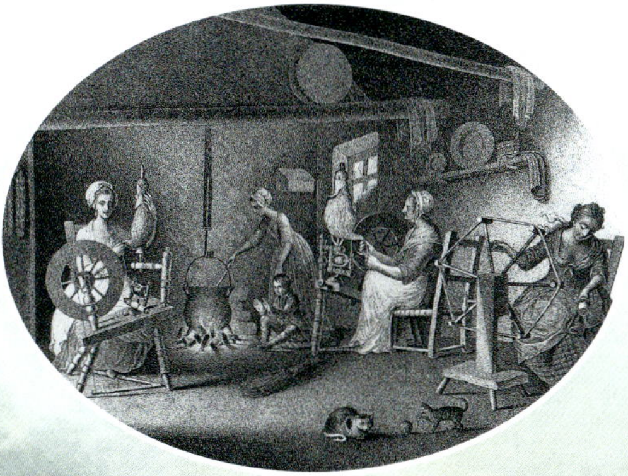

In 1828, Mulholland's cotton mill in Belfast burnt down and was rebuilt to spin flax. This was a success, and many other companies soon switched to spinning linen. The initial success of the linen industry in Belfast resulted in more linen firms starting up in the area. The York Street Flax Spinning and Weaving Company was the largest linen mill in the world.

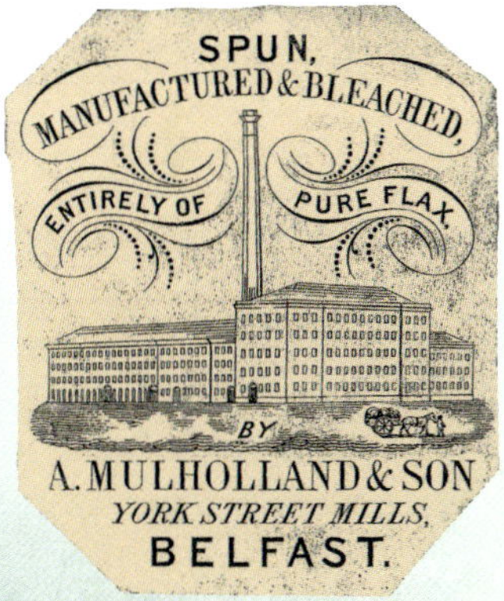

The industrialisation of the linen trade meant new inventions, expertise and investment; it transformed the way linen was produced. The introduction of mechanised wet spinning meant that yarn was produced to a high standard much more quickly and cheaply. Later, power looms were introduced that could weave fine Irish linens.

Mills and a variety of industries straddle the River Lagan up to Belfast Lough and the docks, so essential to trade.

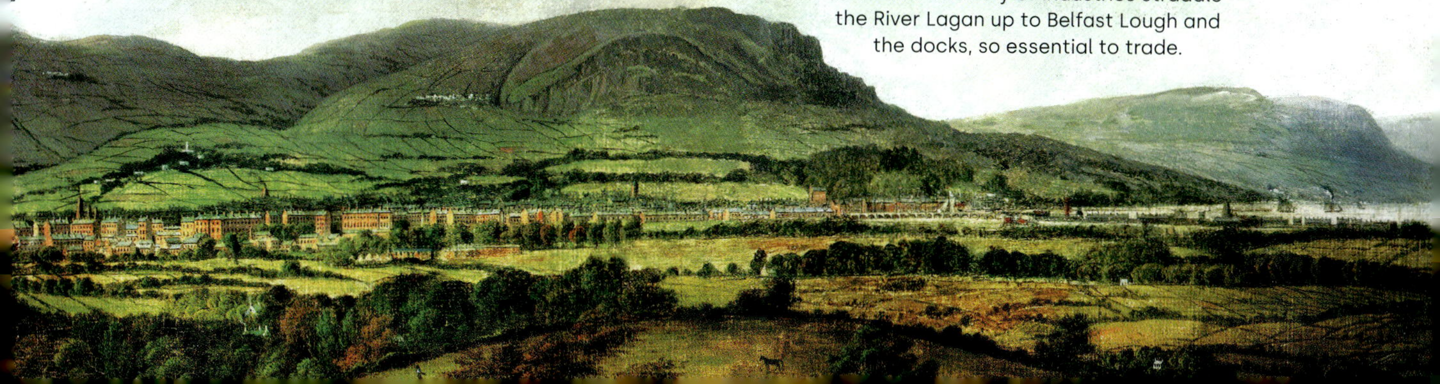

Linen mill workers and half-timers

The different processes that went into making linen meant a series of different jobs within the mills. Some were better paid, more skilled or had better working conditions than others. In 1900, 65,000 people worked in linen mills in Ireland. Most of these were in Belfast. Employees worked six days a week from 6.30am to 6.00pm for a low rate of pay. Most were women who often continued to work after marriage and during pregnancy, returning to work shortly after childbirth.

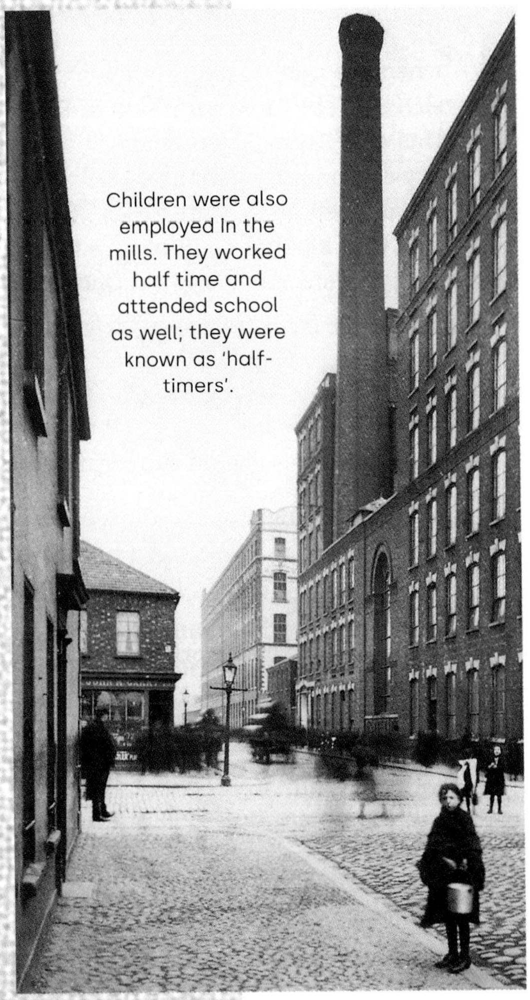

Children were also employed In the mills. They worked half time and attended school as well; they were known as 'half-timers'.

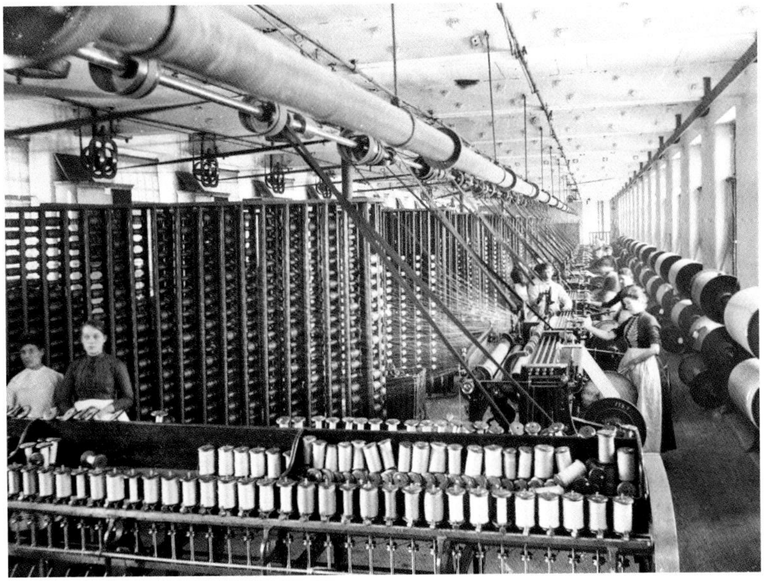

NATIONAL MUSEUMS NORTHERN IRELAND

Working conditions and health hazards varied from job to job. Dust inhaled when preparing flax triggered tuberculosis. The hot humid conditions needed for spinning and weaving caused chest infections. Working barefoot in water in the spinning rooms often led to painful foot conditions.

Throughout the mill there was the ever-present danger of serious injury or death from accidents with machinery.

The final stages of the process, such as embroidering, commanded low pay, but were carried out in healthier working environments and were regarded as socially superior.

'THE LARGEST AND MOST IMPORTANT PROSPEROUS COMMERCIAL AND MANUFACTURING CITY IN IRELAND'

Many of Belfast's industries were related to each other, for example, the ropeworks supplied the shipyards, and textile engineering firms supplied machinery to the linen mills.

The largest ropeworks in the world

As shipbuilding in Belfast grew, so did the need for a large and reliable supply of rope. The Belfast Ropework Company was established to meet this demand, replacing a number of smaller companies.

In the middle of Connswater, a working-class area in East Belfast, the ropeworks enjoyed a ready supply of labour. By 1900, the ropeworks was the largest in the world employing more than 2,000 people, and eventually the factory buildings covered over 40 acres. The company made a huge variety of ropes, cords, lines and twines from large cables to fine packing twine. These were used in many ways including shipbuilding, fishing, manufacturing and for domestic purposes. The ropeworks exported its goods worldwide and confidently claimed that there was probably no port in the world where their products were not well known.

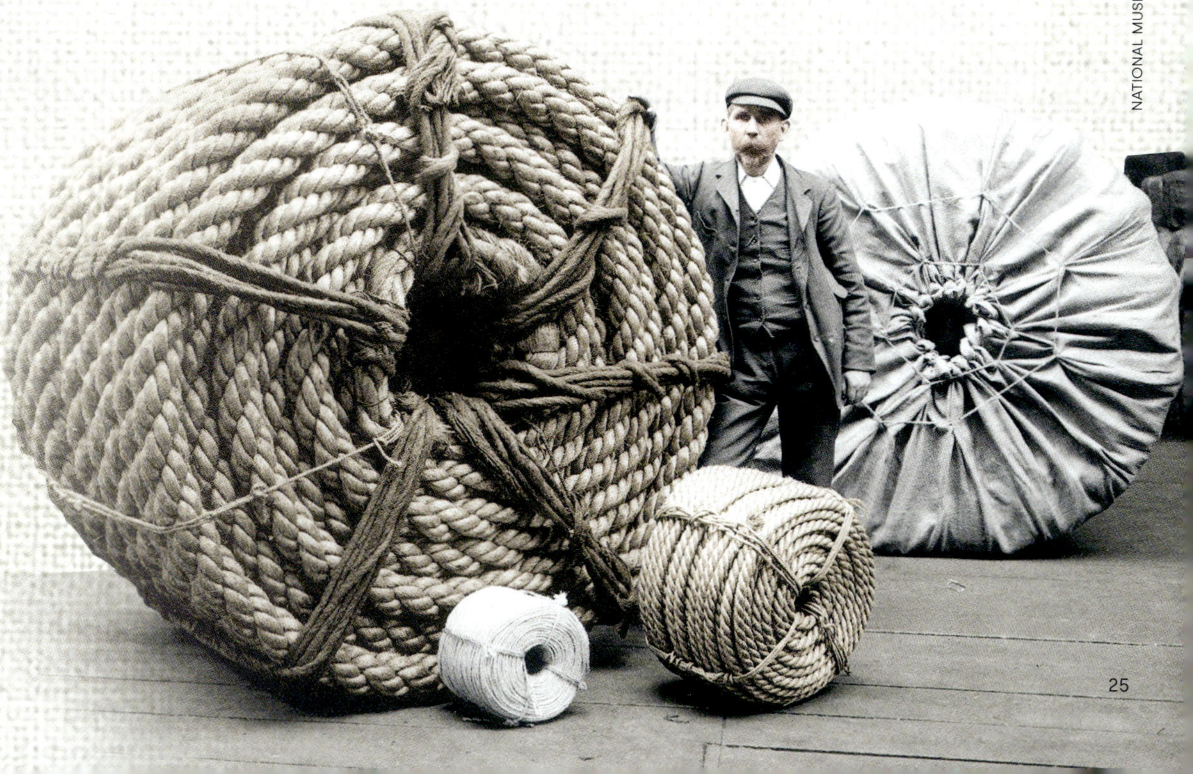

NATIONAL MUSEUMS NORTHERN IRELAND

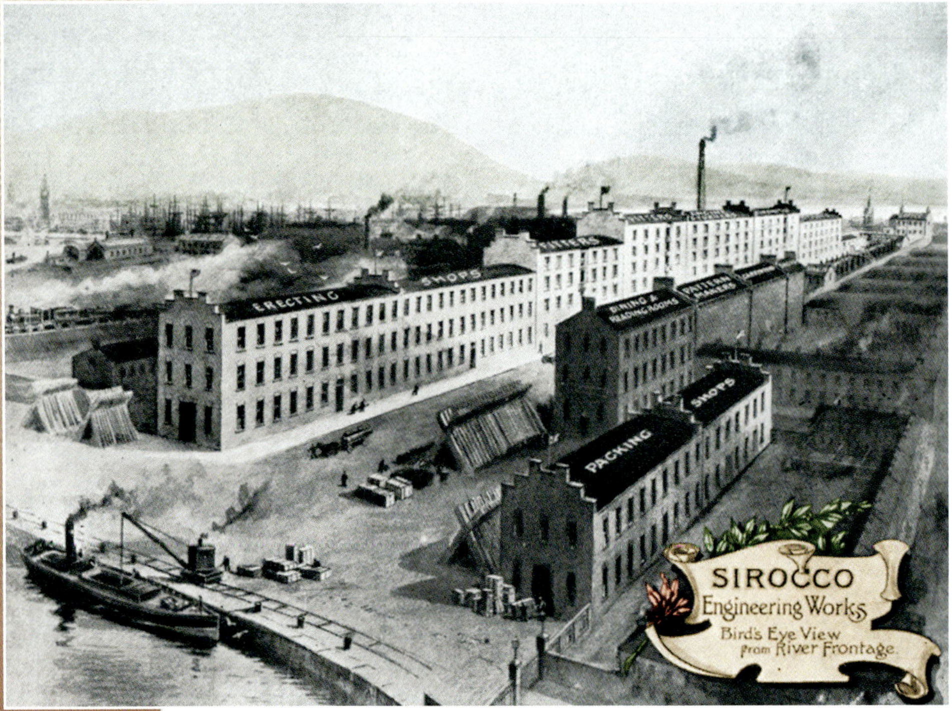

PRONI

Population of Belfast

1800 – 20,000

1831 – 50,000

1861 –120,000

1891 –250,000

1901 –350,000

Sirocco Works

'One of the finest concerns in Belfast. It is as novel as it is extensive.' Samuel Davidson's Sirocco Works was a world leader in ventilation and fan manufacture.

By 1900, the works covered a four-acre site and by 1939 the Sirocco Works supplied around 70% of the world's tea drying machinery. Fans produced by Sirocco were also used for ventilation and dust removal in mines and factories and were supplied to shipbuilding firms including Harland & Wolff.

Textile engineering

James Combe and James Mackie established the largest textile engineering firms in Belfast. They manufactured the entire range of flax processing machinery. At its peak, Mackie's employed around 6,000 people and covered 133 acres.

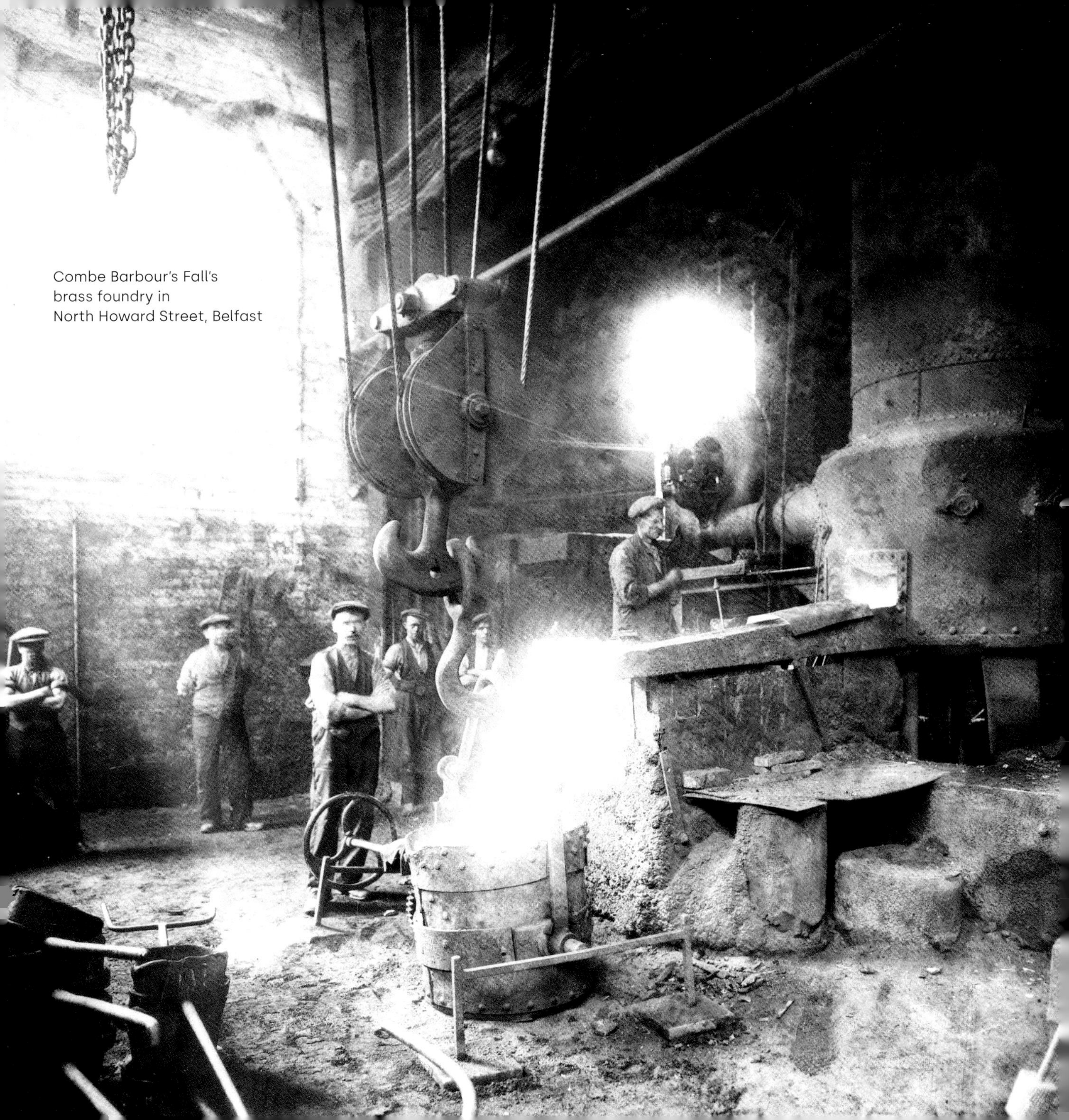

Combe Barbour's Fall's
brass foundry in
North Howard Street, Belfast

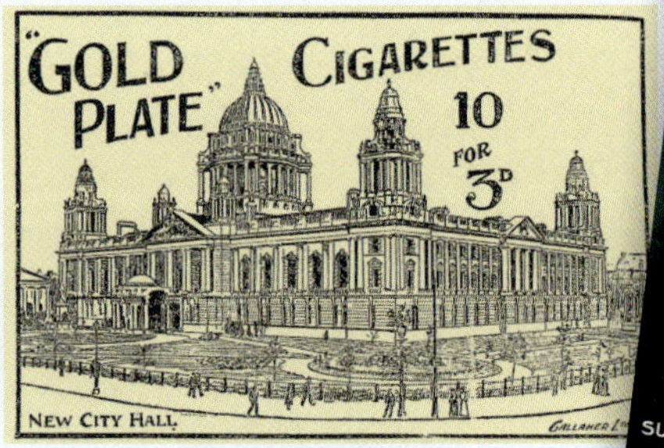

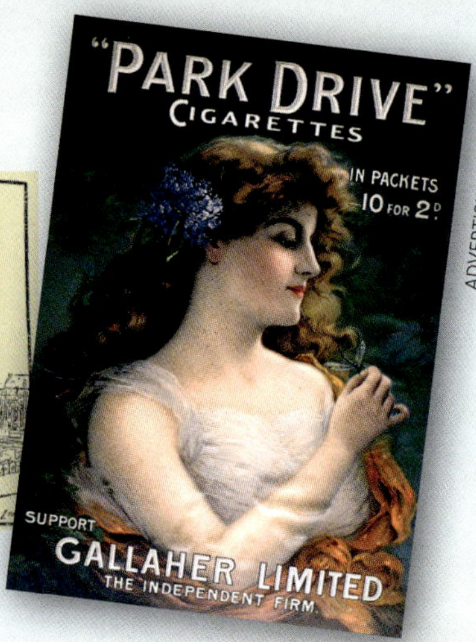

ADVERTISING ARCHIVES

The tobacco industry

manufacturing 'My Lady Nicotine'

'The manufacture of tobacco has become one of the most notable of British industries, contributing a very large sum to the imperial revenue.' There were two large tobacco firms in Belfast – Murray's and Gallaher's. By the early 20th century, Gallaher & Co at York Street was the largest tobacco factory in Ireland and employed over 1,600 people.

Musgrave & Co

supplying luxury stoves to the great and the good

Musgrave's were internationally known for producing high-quality cast-iron work, patent stable fittings and heating equipment. They furnished royal and aristocratic properties across Europe. Belfast's Musgrave Channel is named after Sir James Musgrave, Chairman of the Belfast Harbour Commissioners, and Musgrave Park is named after Sir Henry Musgrave.

NATIONAL MUSEUMS NI

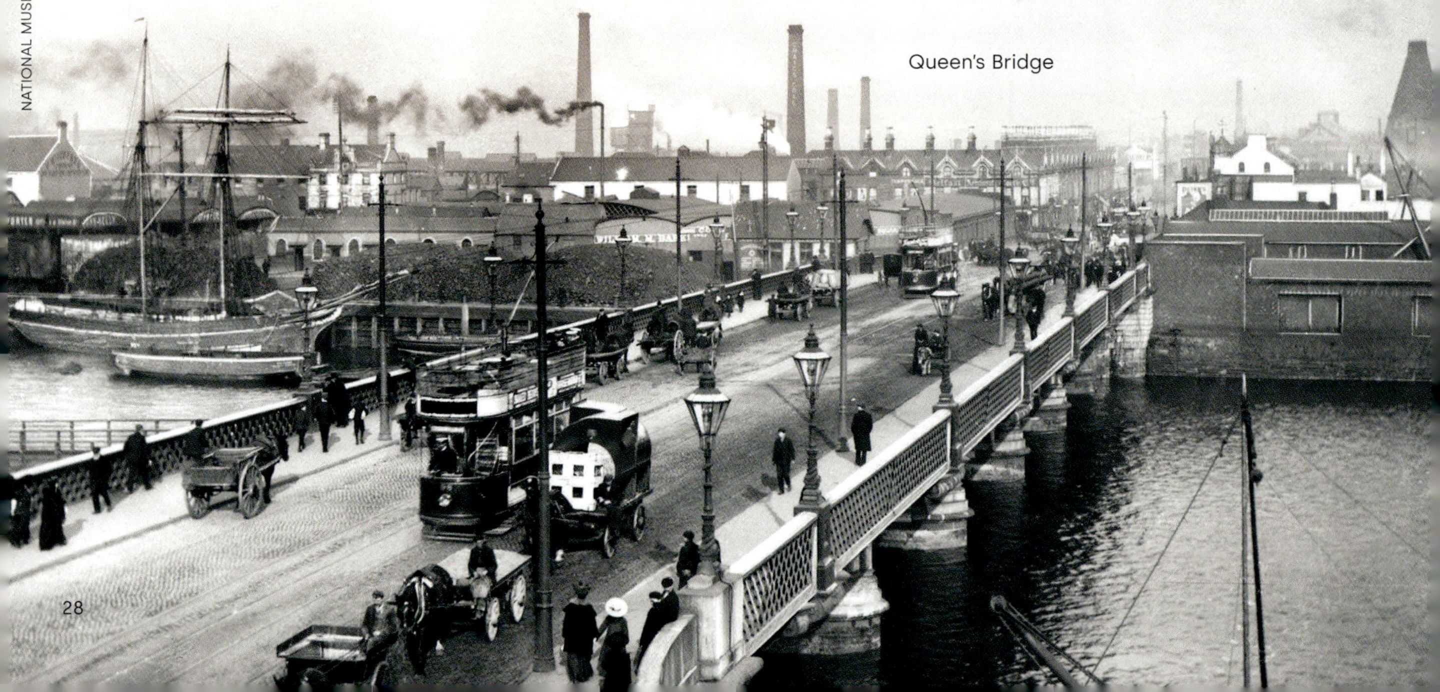

Queen's Bridge

Whiskey

The largest whiskey manufacturing firm in Belfast was Dunville's. Belfast firms were responsible for over half the total whiskey exports from Ireland. The Royal Irish Distillery was a huge modern plant on the Grosvenor Road covering nineteen acres. The working capacity of the distillery was three million gallons (14 million litres) a year. By 1900, Belfast produced 60% of Irish whiskey exports.

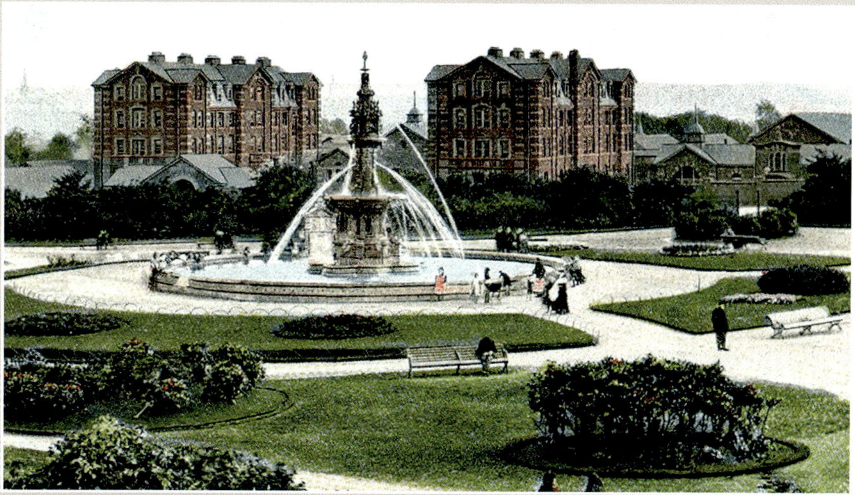

LINEN HALL LIBRARY

Dunville Park, opposite the Royal Victoria Hospital, was given to the city in 1889 by Robert Dunville. At the opening, it was said that 'the provision of such a park in an industrial area was symbolic of a new era when employers would think not only of sanitation and housing for their employees but of their recreation as well.

The soft drinks industry

manufacturing 'Belfast aerated waters'

'It is possible to obtain a bottle of dry ginger ale of Belfast manufacture in the principal cities of the world and even in the most out-of-the-way places.' Established in 1879, Ross's was based at Victoria Square. This establishment included a well of 226 feet (70 metres) that drew water from the Cromac springs, noted for their remarkable purity. Carbonic gas and syrups were added to make the 'aerated water'.

Living in industrial Belfast

As their hours were so long, workers tended to live near their place of work. The two main types of houses for working class families were parlour houses and kitchen houses. Parlour houses had both a parlour and kitchen downstairs, while kitchen houses had a kitchen and bedroom downstairs. The skilled workforce could afford parlour houses with more living space.

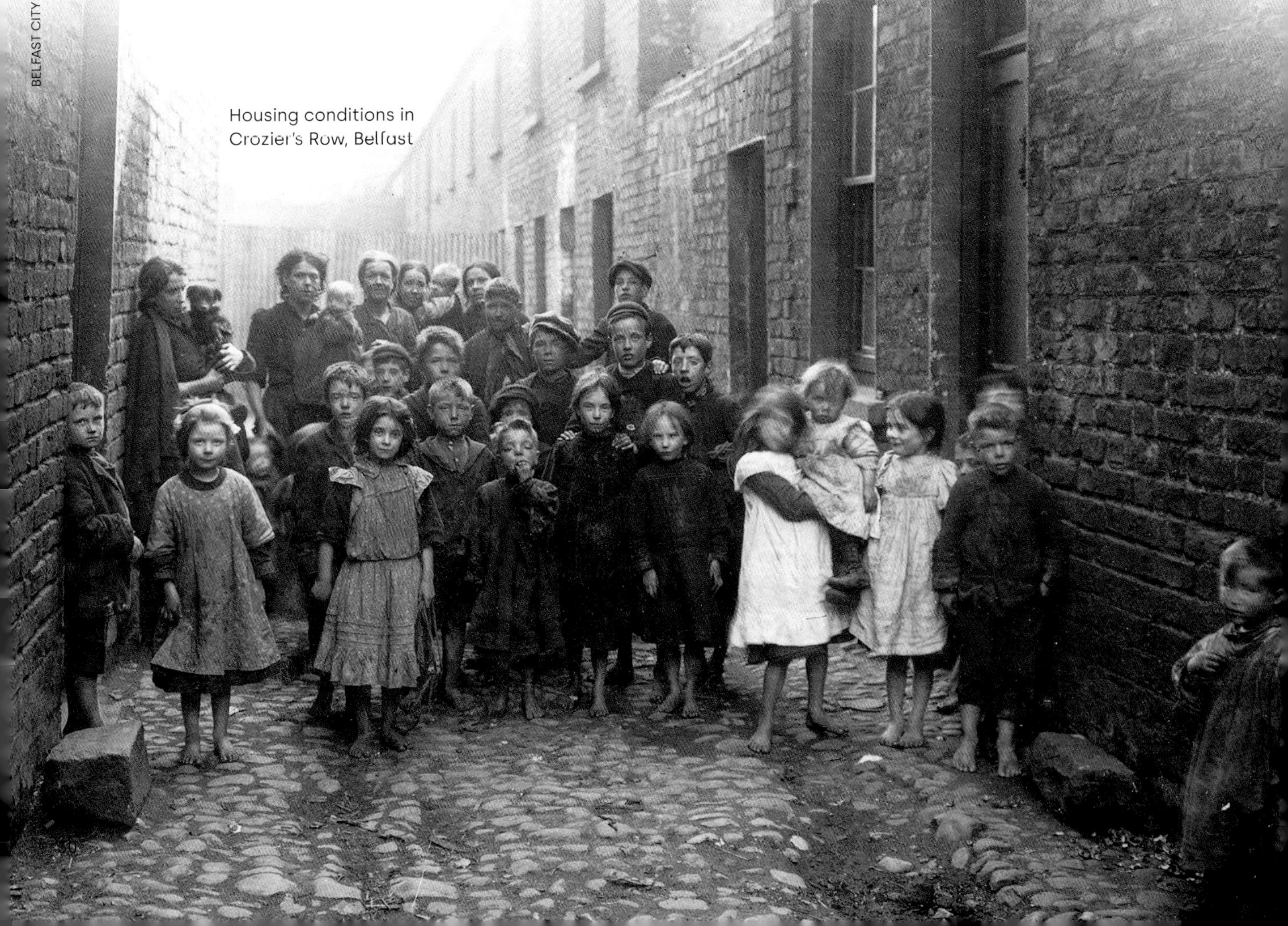

Housing conditions in Crozier's Row, Belfast

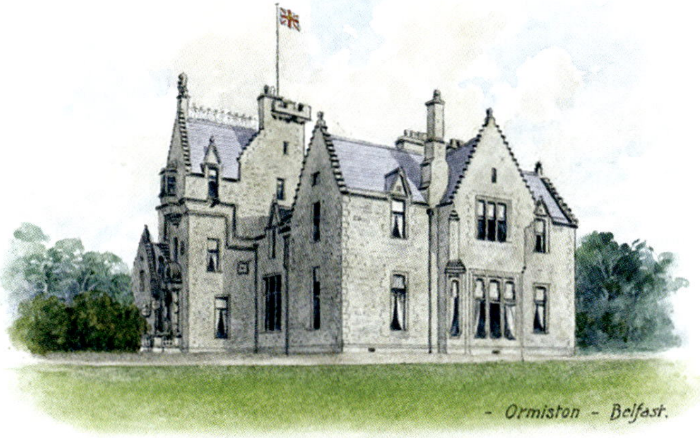

Lord Pirrie, Chairman of Harland & Wolff and the Harbour Commissioners (1893–1906), lived in grand style at Ormiston House, East Belfast. The Pirries also owned a London property in fashionable Belgrave Square and a mansion at Goldalming, Surrey.

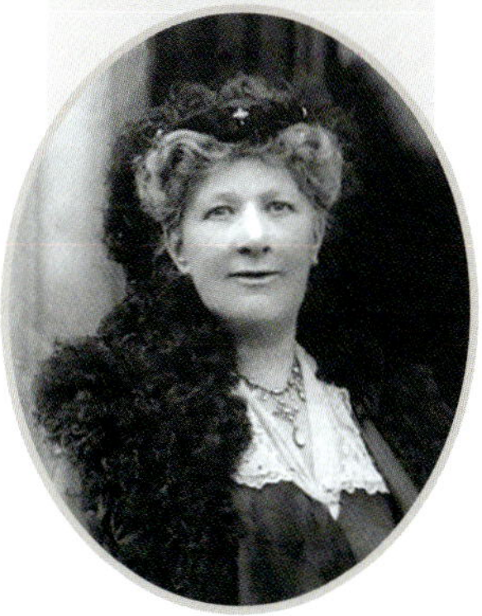

Lady Margaret Pirrie was a tireless fundraiser and benefactor for the Royal Victoria Hospital. She was also President of the hospital from 1914–35.
NATIONAL MUSEUMS NORTHERN IRELAND

A lack of facilities, such as water supply and flush toilets, was common, as was overcrowding. Unhealthy living and working conditions were often accompanied by a poor diet of only tea and bread. Linen mill owners often built housing close to the factories for their workers and schools for the 'half-time' children.

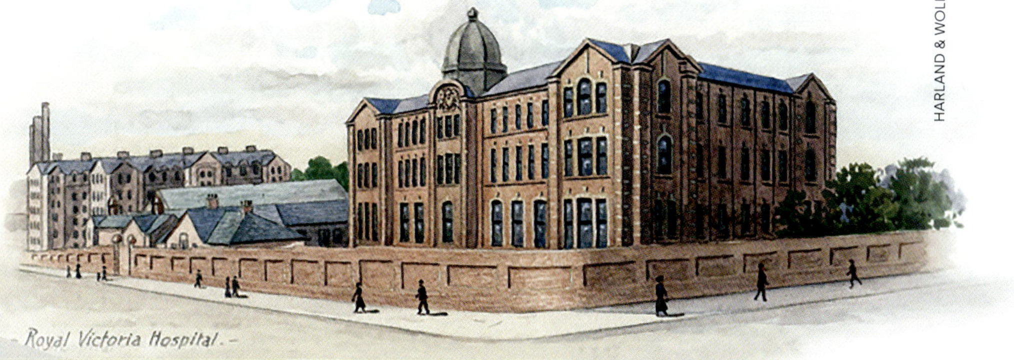

HARLAND & WOLFF

Life as a Belfast dock worker

Working at the docks was low paid, dangerous and physically demanding. In 1907, there were over 6,000 men working as dockers and carters in Belfast's docks. Dockers loaded and unloaded ships both manually and with cranes. Carters used horses and carts to move goods in and out of the docks. Work continued at the docks in all weather conditions.

Accidents, such as falling into the river and being crushed, were common. People worked up to 68 hours a week for low pay. Employment was on a casual basis so, if there was an economic downturn men would quickly find themselves out of work.

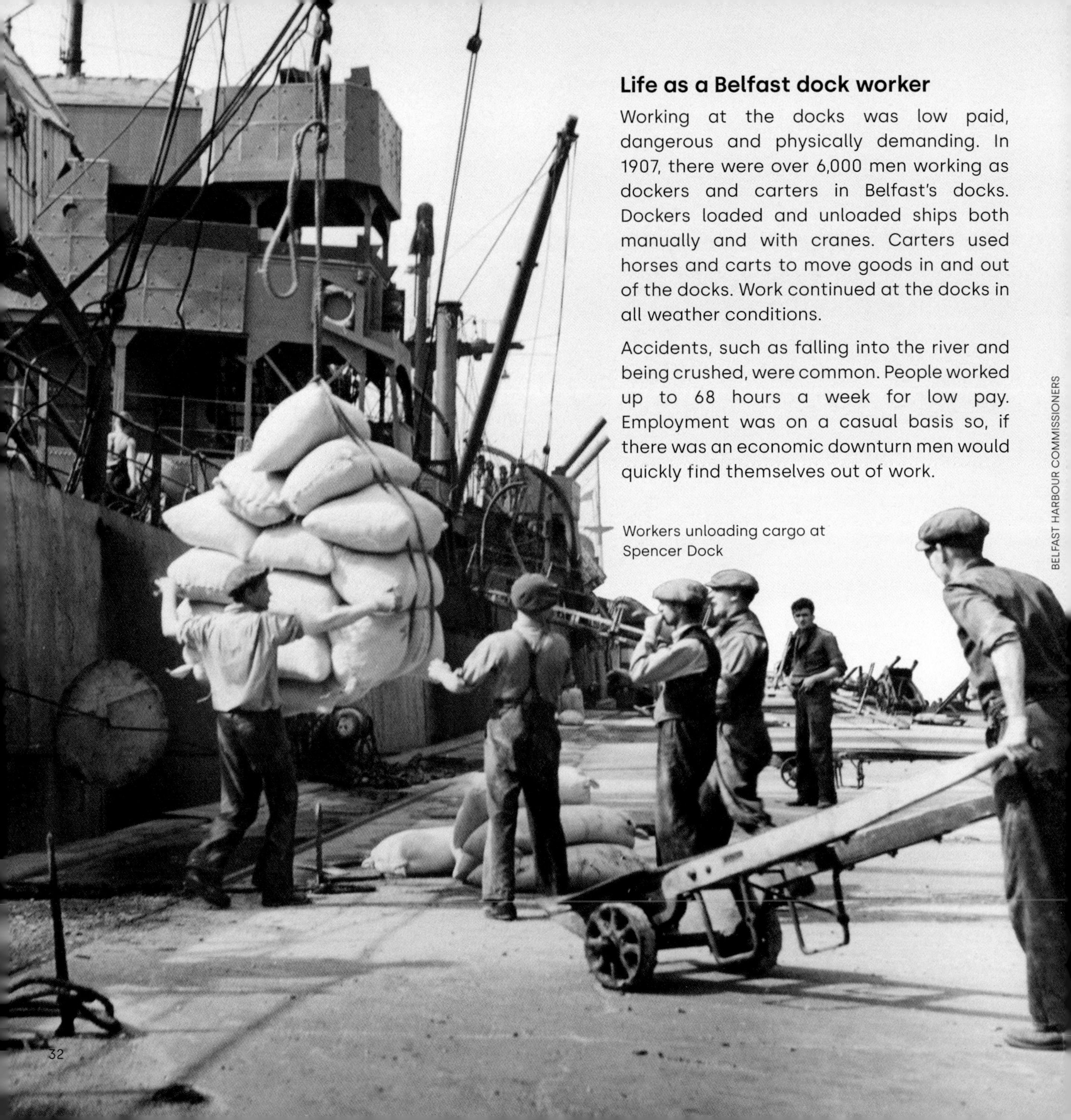

Workers unloading cargo at Spencer Dock

BELFAST HARBOUR COMMISSIONERS

Belfast docks - the largest in Ireland

The docks played an important role in Belfast's economy. They were crucial for the import of raw materials for industry and to export products to the world. Belfast lacked access to local raw materials and energy supplies that were vital for industrialisation.

Coal was imported from Britain. Queen's Quay, on the County Down side of the Lagan, was the coal handling area. This consisted of a mass of cranes, coal yards and coal boats. Likewise, the goods docks at Donegall Quay on the other side of the river were lined with goods sheds and steamers. Ships built in Belfast were used to both import and export goods worldwide.

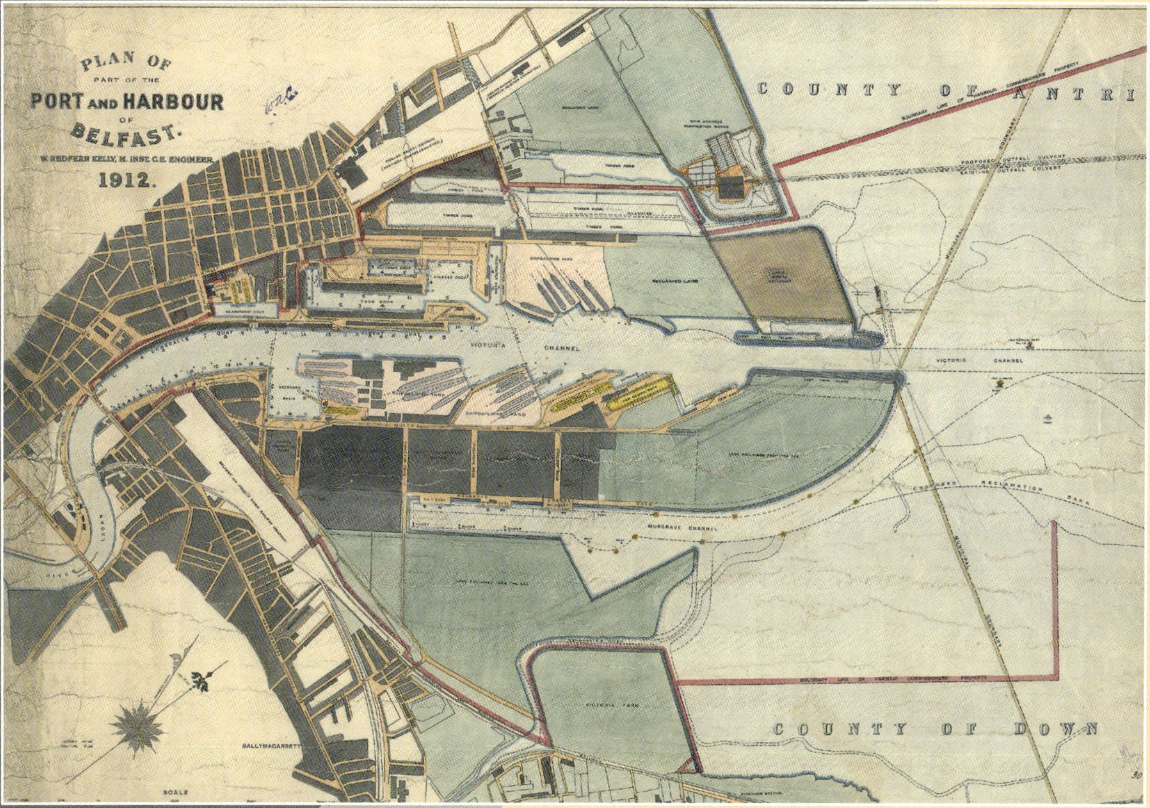

BELFAST HARBOUR COMMISSIONERS

A map of Belfast Port and Harbour in 1912
During the 19th century, the Harbour Commissioners improved the flow of the Lagan and expanded the harbour and shipbuilding facilities. This allowed shipbuilding to flourish on a large scale.

The Belfast Harbour Commissioners

In 1785, the Ballast Board was established to manage and develop the harbour. In 1847, the Harbour Commissioners replaced the Ballast Board. The Harbour Commissioners had much wider powers than the Ballast Board. They developed and improved the port; reclaimed land to make room for new quays and new trades and adapted to accommodate new technology. Much of the success of the shipbuilding industry and trade through the port was due to the farsighted Harbour Commissioners. Today, the Harbour Commissioners remain a powerful force in Belfast.

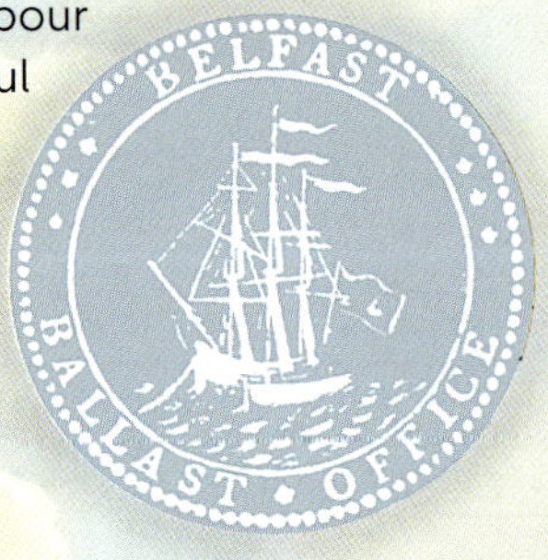

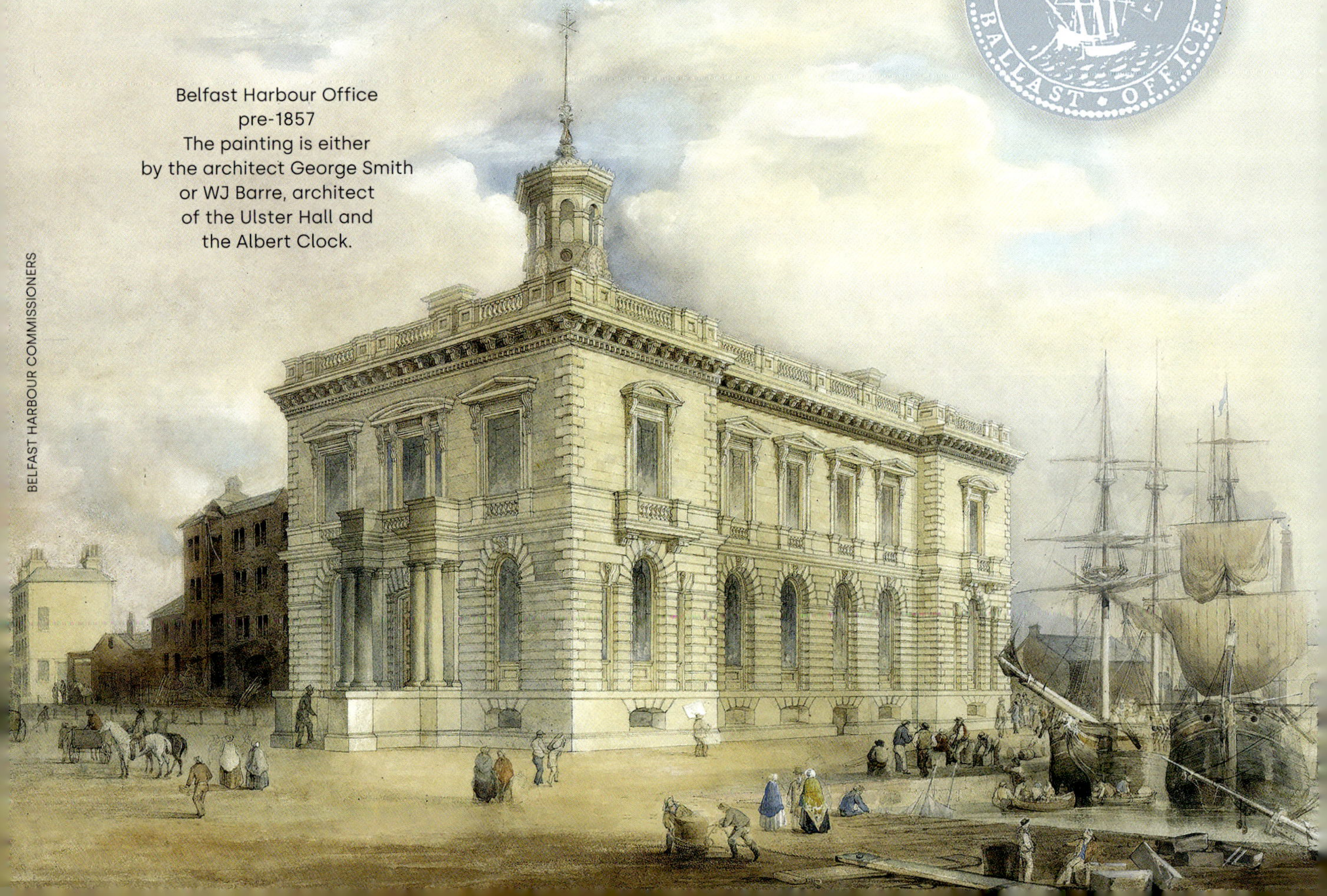

Belfast Harbour Office
pre-1857
The painting is either
by the architect George Smith
or WJ Barre, architect
of the Ulster Hall and
the Albert Clock.

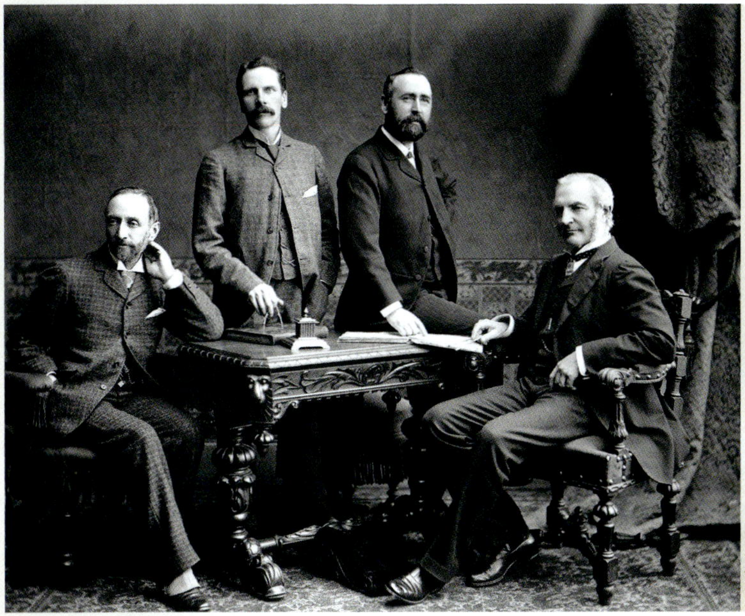

NATIONAL MUSEUMS NI

The four partners of Harland & Wolff 1876–85. From left: GW Wolff, WH Wilson, WJ Pirrie and EJ Harland

Harland & Wolff – the early years

In 1854, Robert Hickson employed Edward Harland as manager of his shipbuilding yard. Three years later, Harland employed Gustav Wolff as his assistant.

Robert Hickson sold his company to Edward Harland and, in 1861, Harland & Wolff agreed their partnership.

Known as Harland & Wolff, the firm quickly gained a reputation for constructing high quality ships. They combined new technologies with innovative naval architecture.

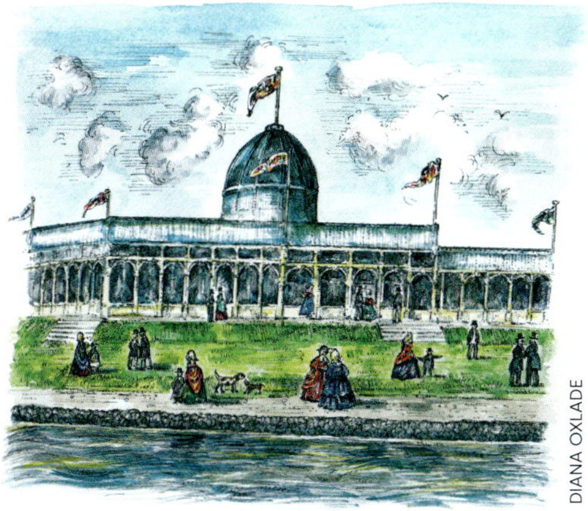

DIANA OXLADE

Queen's Island, a pleasure park

Excavated mud was heaped on the eastern bank of the river to modify its direction. The new land formed was known as Dargan's Island and later Queen's Island, following a visit from Queen Victoria in 1849.

Queen's Island was the main pleasure park in Belfast with dancing, races, Punch and Judy shows and a Crystal Palace. It also became the engineering heartland of Belfast.

While other shipbuilding firms in Britain were often constrained by lack of space, Queen's Island offered Harland & Wolff the opportunity to expand. This led to the closure of the pleasure grounds on Queen's Island.

High levels of European emigration and the growth of American trade resulted in a soaring demand for new ships. Harland & Wolff had the capacity to supply these new ships and to carry out repairs. By 1870, Harland & Wolff began their long and profitable relationship with Thomas Ismay's White Star Line. Until the First World War, they built all but one of White Star's ships.

By 1900, the Harland & Wolff site covered eighty acres and employed 9–10,000 people. Harland & Wolff embraced new technologies to stay at the forefront of maritime engineering. This, coupled with the workings of the forward thinking Harbour Commissioners, meant that Harland & Wolff was equipped to make the largest vessels in Britain.

This iron barque *Aglaia* in full sail, built by Harland & Wolff in 1875, is in sharp contrast with the transatlantic liners built in the early 1900s.

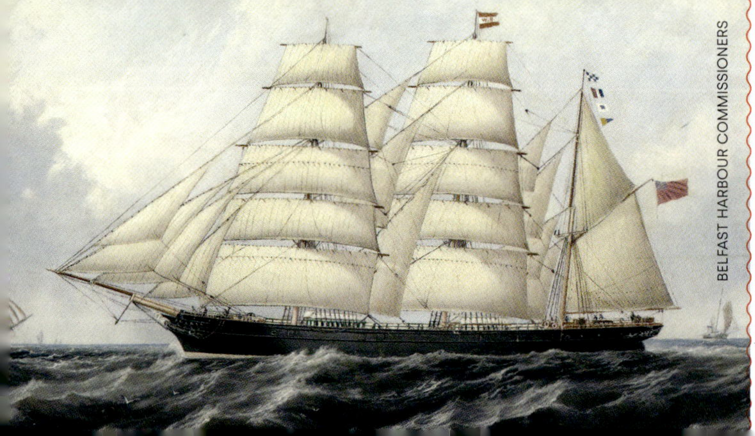

BELFAST HARBOUR COMMISSIONERS

The beginnings of a *Titanic* design

Lord Pirrie and J Bruce Ismay of White Star produced the first concept sketches and design ideas for the Olympic-class ships.

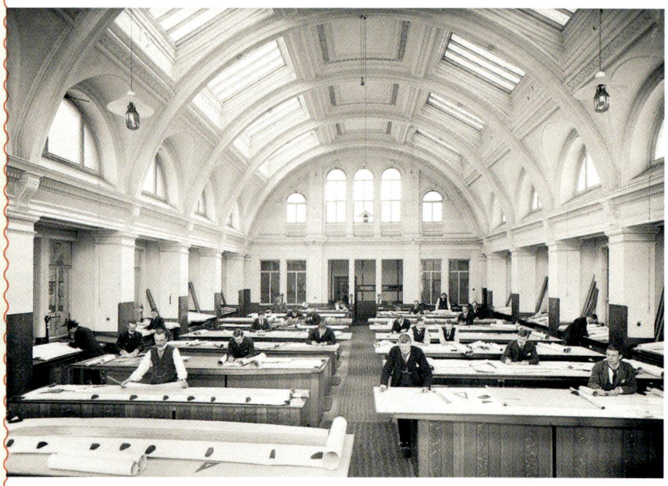

NATIONAL MUSEUMS NI

Harland & Wolff had two large main drawing offices. The staff of the drawing offices were responsible for the design of the ships. Naval architects, marine engineers and draftsmen prepared the necessary plans.

A shipbuilder in Belfast

William James Pirrie was not even thirty years old when he controlled Harland & Wolff, the largest shipbuilding firm in the world at the time. From his days as an apprentice in 1862, he never stopped building new types of vessels, such as the passenger steamers *Majestic*, *Titanic*, *Britannic*, and later diesel liners. An illness probably saved his life: in April 1912, Pirrie was to travel on board *Titanic*, but was too sick to leave home.

He died twelve years later of pneumonia at sea off Cuba, and was brought back home on *Olympic*, one of his ships.

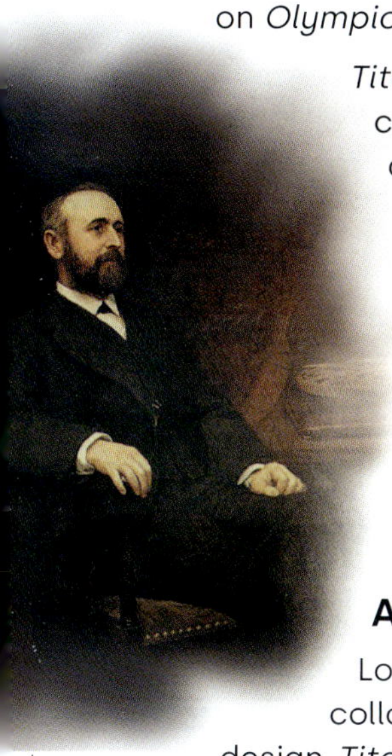

ROYAL VICTORIA HOSPITAL

Titanic and *Olympic* were constructed at the same time as near identical twins. *Olympic* was started first; any change of design for *Titanic* was noted on the plans. If the differences were considerable, a separate drawing was made for *Titanic*.

Around a glass of wine

Lord Pirrie and J Bruce Ismay collaborated over dinner to design *Titanic* and her sister ships. An evening of fine wine and food hosted their intense discussions. Speed would be balanced with Quality of Accommodation. It has been rumoured that when Pirrie enquired as to the length of this new ship, Ismay replied, wine glass in hand: 'Build me a stable ship that will not disturb the sediment in these fine wines.'

And so, a ship of 882 feet, 8 inches (271 metres) was conceived that night: long enough to span three of the tempestuous Atlantic Ocean wave crests and set a new world benchmark of excellence in naval architecture.

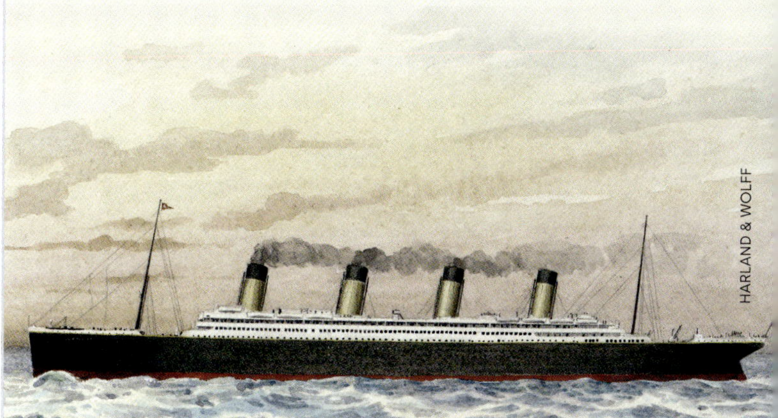

HARLAND & WOLFF

White Star against Cunard

Joseph Bruce Ismay was the Chairman of White Star Line, the company that owned great liners.

He wanted to compete with the Cunard Line, which had already built popular large and fast steamers. Ismay always launched his ships, and *Titanic* was no exception. Ironically, on the night of *Titanic*'s sinking, he was rescued by *Carpathia*, one of Cunard's ships.

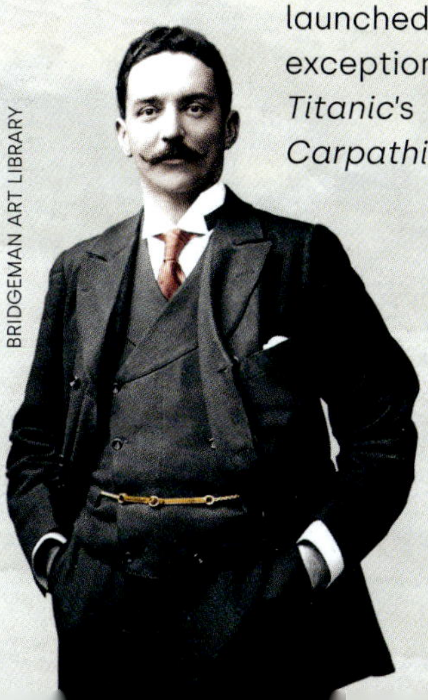

BRIDGEMAN ART LIBRARY

Designing the largest ships in the world

Detailed designs were made at Harland & Wolff before construction of the ships began. This was a complex process involving many stages.

South Yard, Harland & Wolff

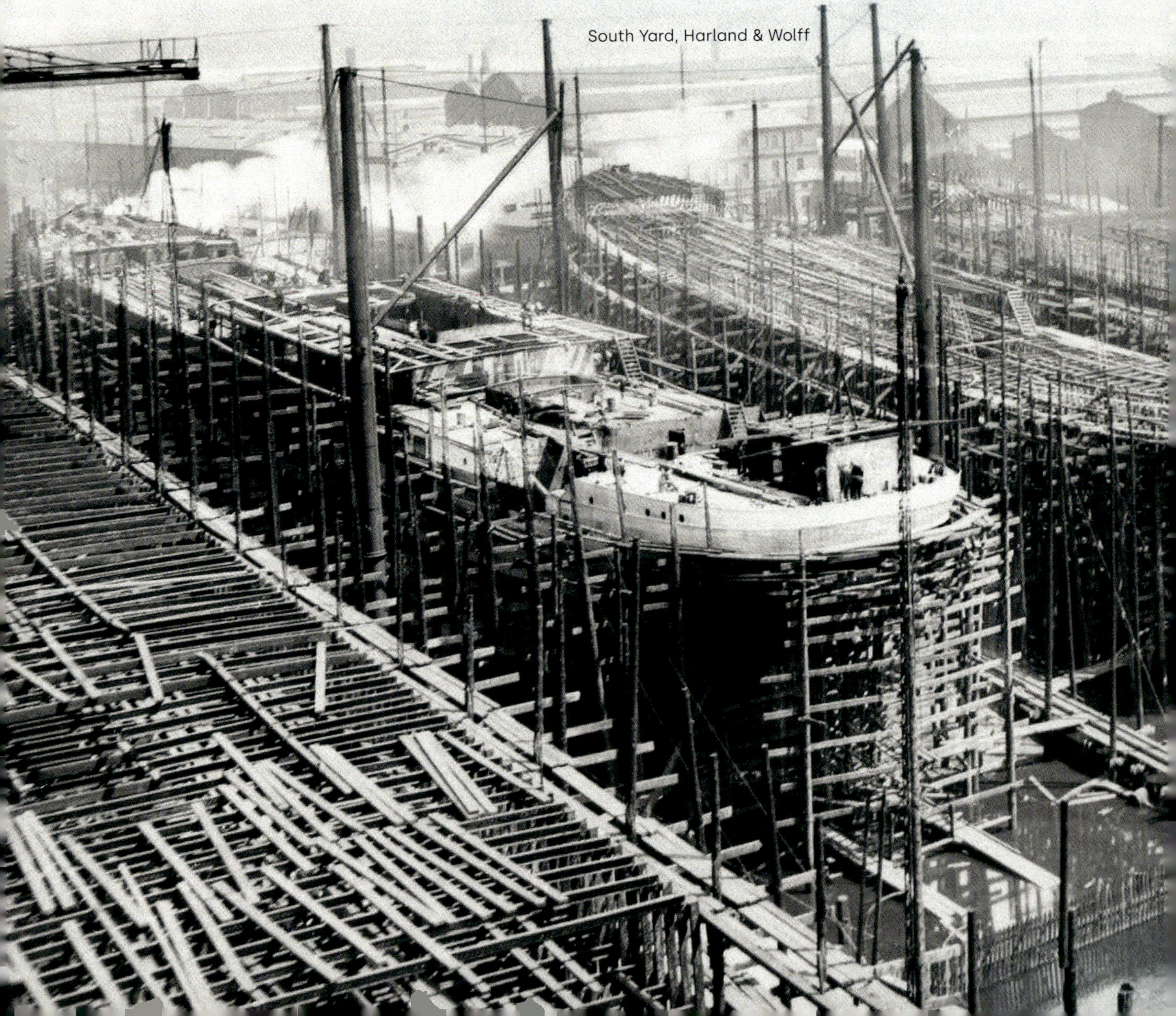

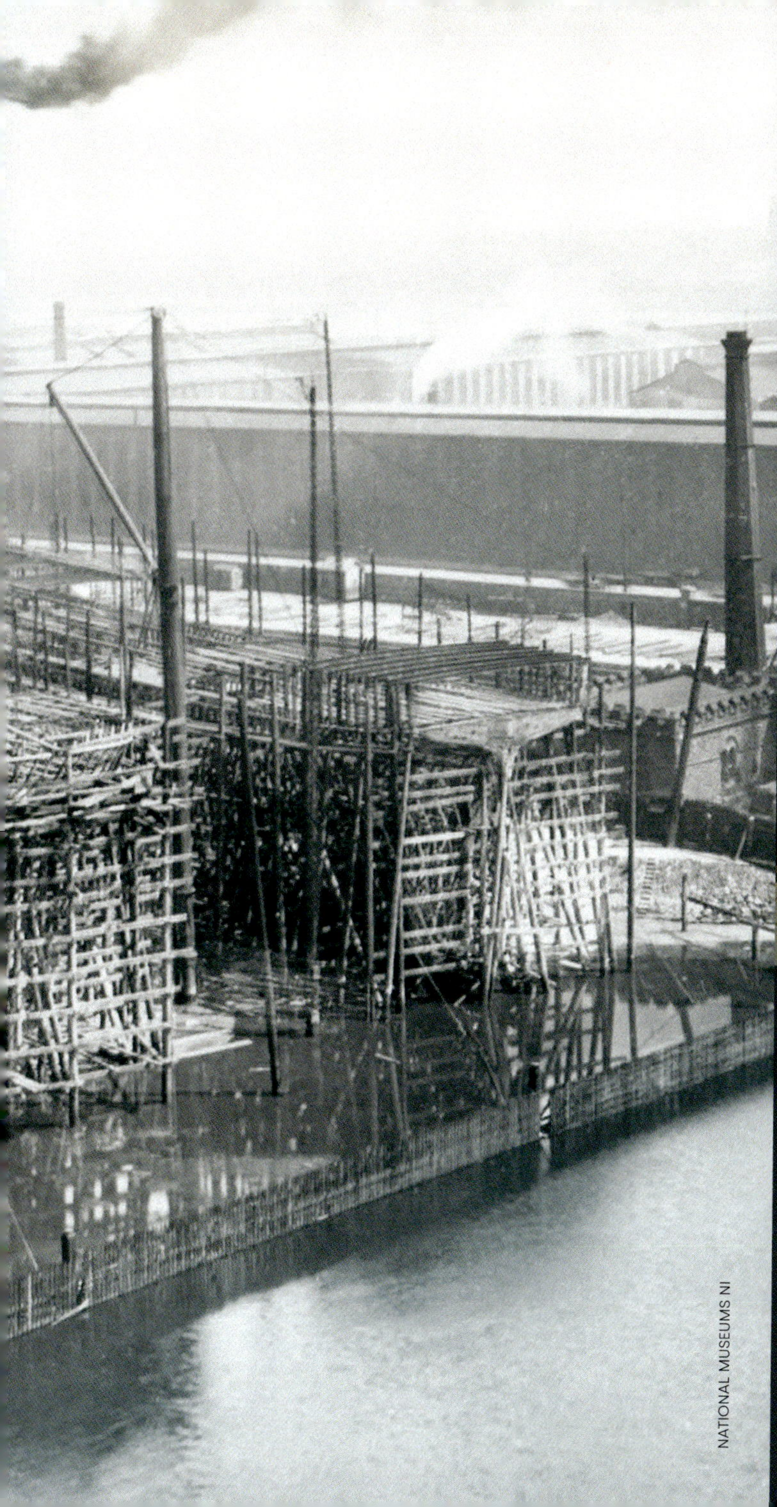

NATIONAL MUSEUMS NI

At 882 feet and 9 inches long (271 metres) the size of the Olympic-class ships was groundbreaking.

The ships were planned with a complex series of 2 dimensional flat plans and 3 dimensional models.

Line plans showed the ship from above, from the side and from the ends. From these plans thousands of more complicated plans were developed. Once completed, the designs were taken to the Mould Loft.

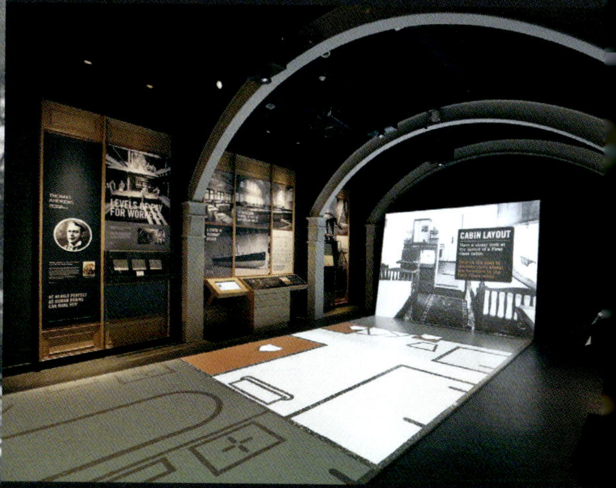

The Map Room & Interactive Floor, Gallery

The Mould Loft was several hundred feet long and a hundred feet (35 metres) wide.

On the floor, the loftsmen would chalk the lines of the cross section of the ship at full size and the length at quarter scale. The loftsmen fixed any mistakes caused by the small scale at which plans were drawn. Once the corrections had been made, the draftsmen in the design department would update the plans. The loftsmen also made templates for all the structural parts of the ship.

Building a gantry of *Titanic* proportions

To build the Olympic-class ships a new gantry was constructed. The steel gantry crane system serviced the slipways where the ships were built.

The gantry was a massive overhead structure that carried a system of cranes and travelling frames. Electric elevators and walkways provided access to the ships and to the gantry itself. The gantry extended across the two slipways where both *Olympic* and *Titanic* would be built.

The gantry was almost 270 feet wide, 840 feet long and 228 feet high and consisted of 3 rows of 11 columns. The 6,000 ton steel structure could be seen from most areas of Belfast.

The contract to build the gantry was awarded to the Glasgow engineering firm of Sir William Arrol & Company and was known by its designer's name – the Arrol Gantry. The Arrol Gantry was completed before construction of the Olympic-class ships and was dismantled in the 1960s.

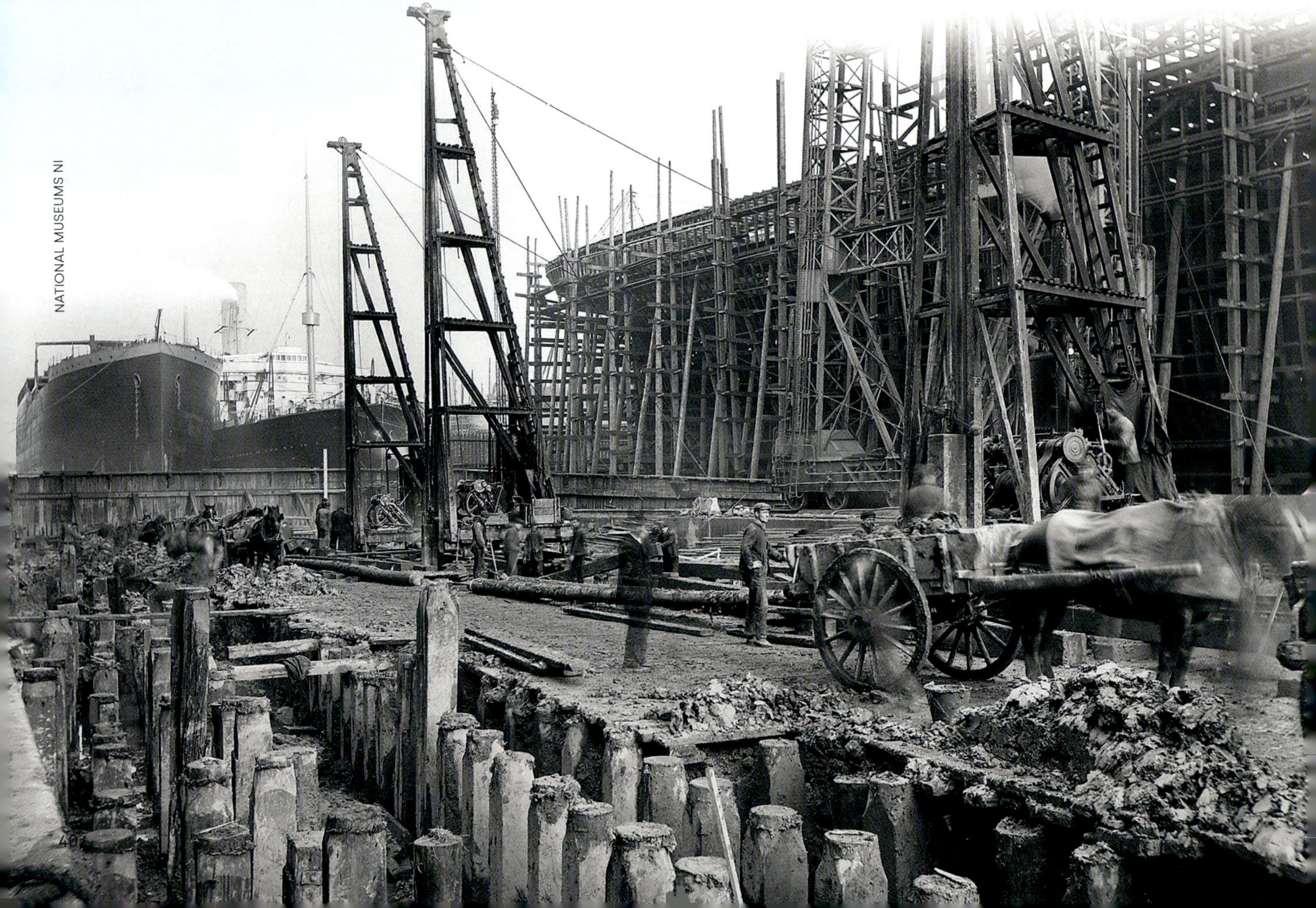

NATIONAL MUSEUMS NI

Preparing Belfast for the Olympic-class ships

In order to build the new Olympic-class ships many improvements were made to the shipbuilding facilities in Belfast.

Harland & Wolff were given orders to proceed with *Olympic* and *Titanic* on 17 September 1908. It took two years to complete all the alterations needed to accommodate the building of these massive new ships.

Four of the existing slips at Harland & Wolff were replaced by two much bigger slips, over which the Arrol Gantry was constructed, and the smaller 'watergantry' slip.

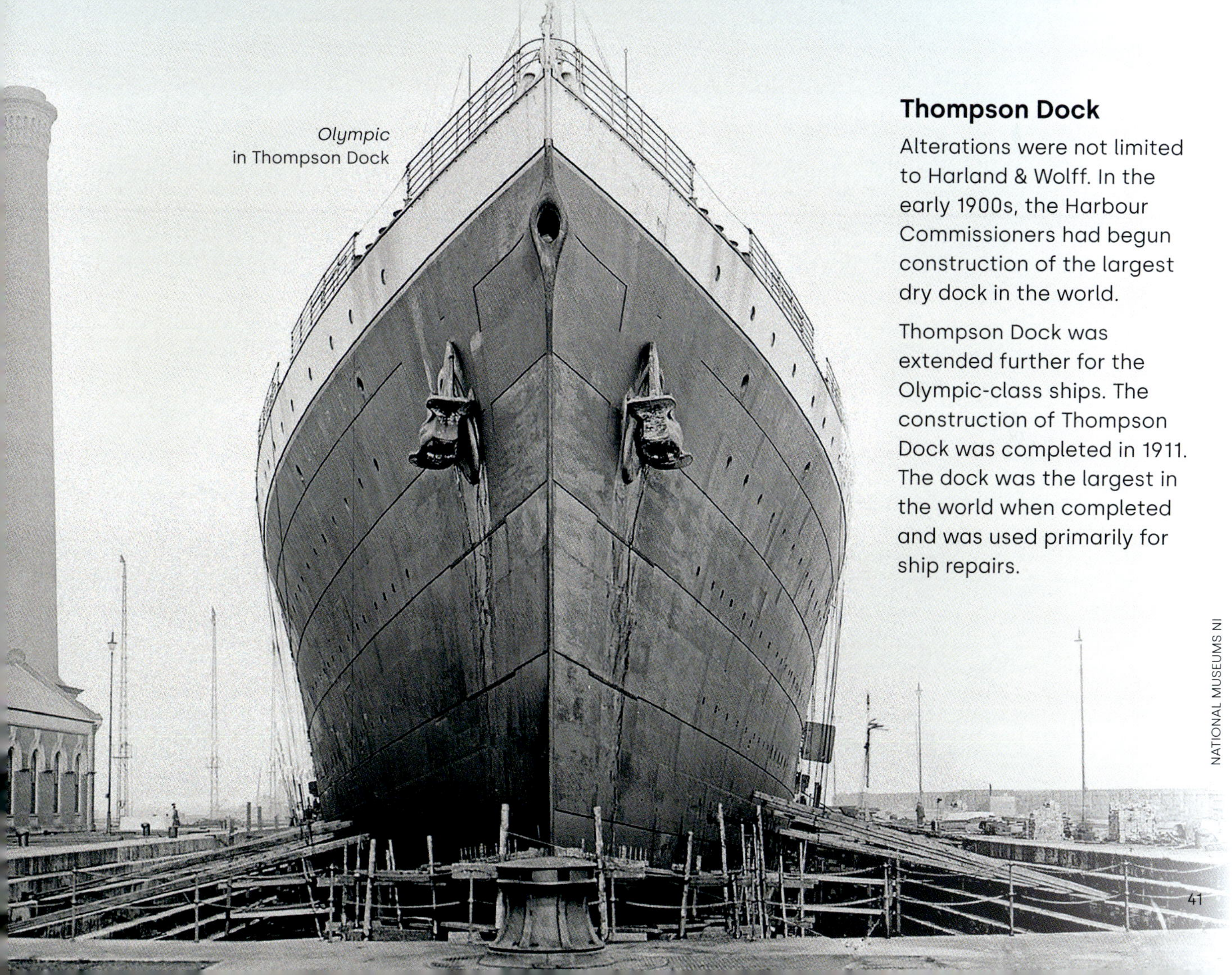

Olympic in Thompson Dock

NATIONAL MUSEUMS NI

Thompson Dock

Alterations were not limited to Harland & Wolff. In the early 1900s, the Harbour Commissioners had begun construction of the largest dry dock in the world.

Thompson Dock was extended further for the Olympic-class ships. The construction of Thompson Dock was completed in 1911. The dock was the largest in the world when completed and was used primarily for ship repairs.

THE SHIPYARD

Building the ship - a complex task

On the slipway, under the massive overhead structure of the Arrol Gantry, the building of *Titanic* began on 31st March 1909. Building the ship started with 'laying the keel', which was her spine. Then rib like steel frames were erected which gave the ship's hull its shape. This was *Titanic*'s skeleton and from this, the structure of the ship was built on the slipway underneath the Arrol Gantry. It took twenty-six months for the structure of *Titanic* to be completed ready for her launch.

The first step, Laying the keel

Titanic's spine

The keel is the backbone of a ship. *Titanic*'s keel was six foot high, ran the length of the ship and carried steel plates that formed the hull. Wooden blocks were laid on the slipway and the keel was built on these. Flat steel keel plates were laid on the blocks.

Titanic was constructed with a double bottom. The outer steel-plating bottom formed the skin of the ship. The vertical keel formed the centre of the double bottom. The inner bottom plating formed a second skin. The double bottom formed a series of tanks used to store water for the boilers and ballast to weight the ship. The double bottom added to safety as the ship had two watertight skins.

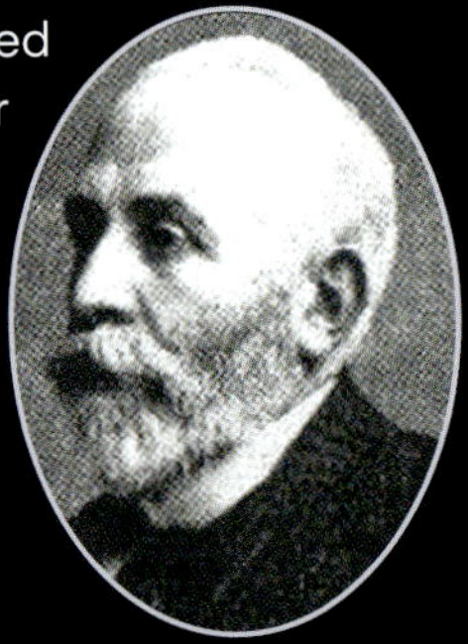

Alexander Carlisle, with Ismay and Pirrie, was the original designer of the three Olympic-class liners.

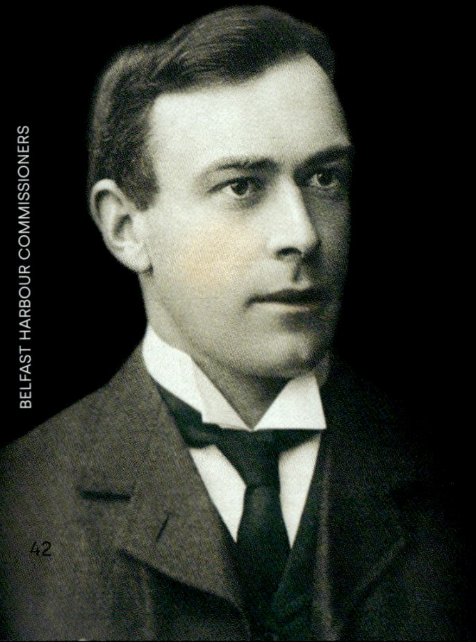

BELFAST HARBOUR COMMISSIONERS

Thomas Andrews

was born in 1873 in Comber, Co Down, Northern Ireland. He left the Royal Belfast Academical Institution aged sixteen to join Harland & Wolff as a fast-track apprentice.
Despite his uncle being Chairman of the yard, Andrews received no special favours on his way up the career ladder. From 1907, he was the Managing Director in charge of design and fifty-three sections of the yard. He tirelessly toured his empire with a 'paint-smeared bowler hat, grease on his boots, and the pockets of his blue jacket stuffed with plans.' He won the respect of ship owners and riveters alike. Among the ships he was responsible for were *Adriatic*, *Oceanic*, *Olympic* and *Titanic*.

Fitting the rudder
providing *Titanic* with direction

The rudder controlled the direction of the ship. It was a wide flat blade fitted on the sternpost. It was made in six pieces and then bolted together. The bolts were covered in cement to protect them from the corroding effects of seawater. The rudder was supported by the stern frame and hung on the sternpost. The sternpost was the hinge that allowed the rudder to pivot, thereby controlling the direction of the ship.

The position of the rudder was immediately behind the central propeller. This made the steering effective as the rudder immediately gave direction to the thrust created by the propeller. The rudder was moved by a steering gear that was powered by two engines. The rudder was fitted shortly before *Titanic*'s launch.

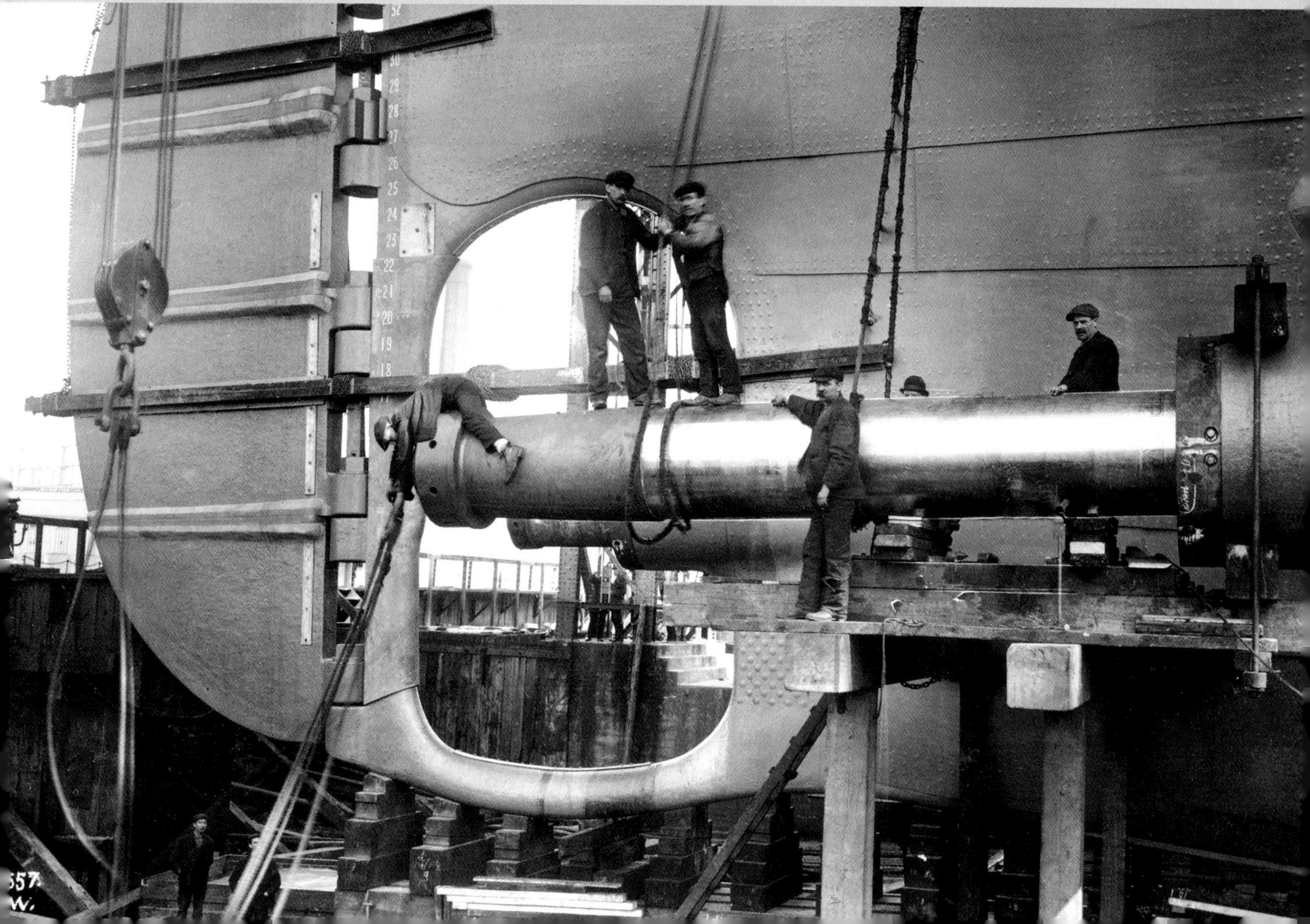

Framing

the skeleton of *Titanic*

Framing was the erection of steel rib like structures that formed the skeleton of the ship. These gave the hull its shape. The keel of the ship was marked with the positions where the frames would go. They were then hoisted into position. Wooden shoring was placed within the framework of the ship to ensure correct spacing of the frames. Deck beams were attached to the frames at each deck level and crossbeams and supporting pillars were also added. This secured the structure and the wooden shoring was then removed. The whole structure was held together by heated iron and steel pins called rivets. The framing, decks and beams reinforced the skeleton and added to the overall strength of the ship. *Titanic* was fully framed by 6 April 1910.

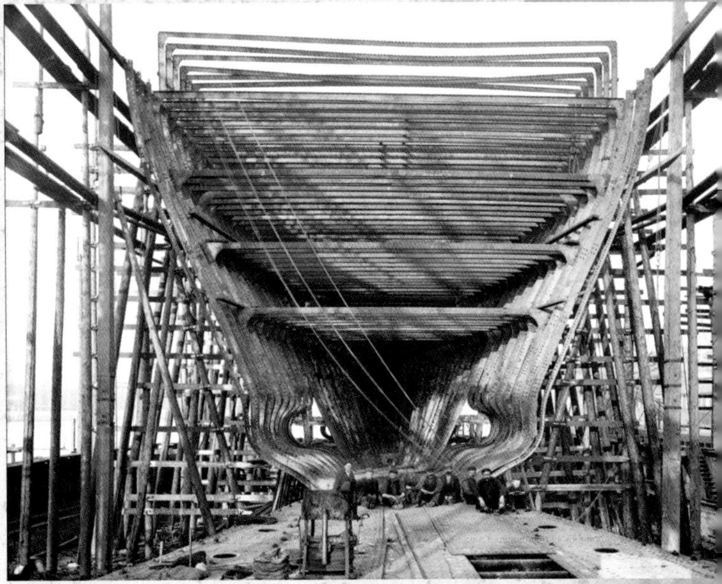

The frame, or skeleton, of the *Oceanic*, built 1897, is clearly shown in this photograph.

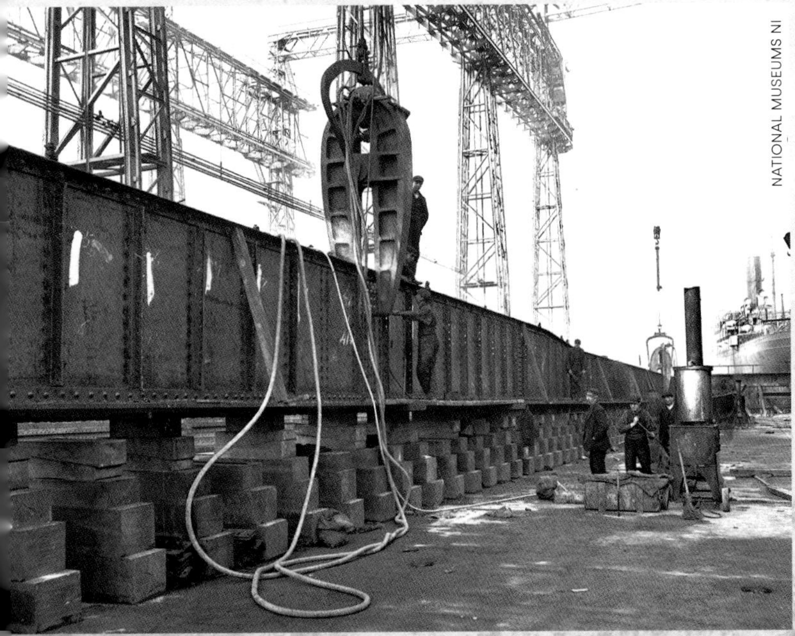

NATIONAL MUSEUMS NI

Plating and riveting

holding *Titanic's* skin in place

Once framing was complete, the ship was fitted with steel plates that formed the watertight skin. These were held in place with iron and steel rivets. The plates that made up *Titanic*'s hull were attached to her frame.

Altogether, over three million rivets were used on *Titanic*. Good quality riveting was essential as it held the structure together.

Hydraulic riveting of *Olympic's* vertical keel plate, the backbone of the ship

Bulkheads and decking
Titanic's internal structure

There were fifteen watertight bulkheads that ran across *Titanic* in the lower decks. These divided the ship's hull into sixteen watertight compartments. The bulkheads were connected to the shell plating. *Titanic* was designed to stay afloat if up to two of her four forward compartments were flooded. The bulkheads were only watertight up to E and D decks depending on their location. This was because crew and passengers needed doors to access parts of the ship. Ordinary doors such as those in most passenger areas were an area of weakness.

Titanic had eight passenger decks and ten decks in total. Steel decks were laid on the deck beams, riveted in place then covered with either wooden decking or other materials such as tiles.

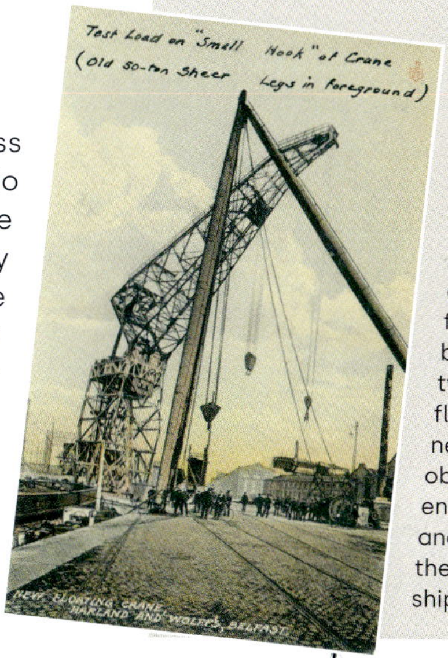

BELFAST HARBOUR COMMISSIONERS

A new harbour crane was ordered for the fitting out berth. This was a two hundred-ton floating crane needed to lift heavy objects such as engines, boilers and funnels onto the Olympic-class ships.

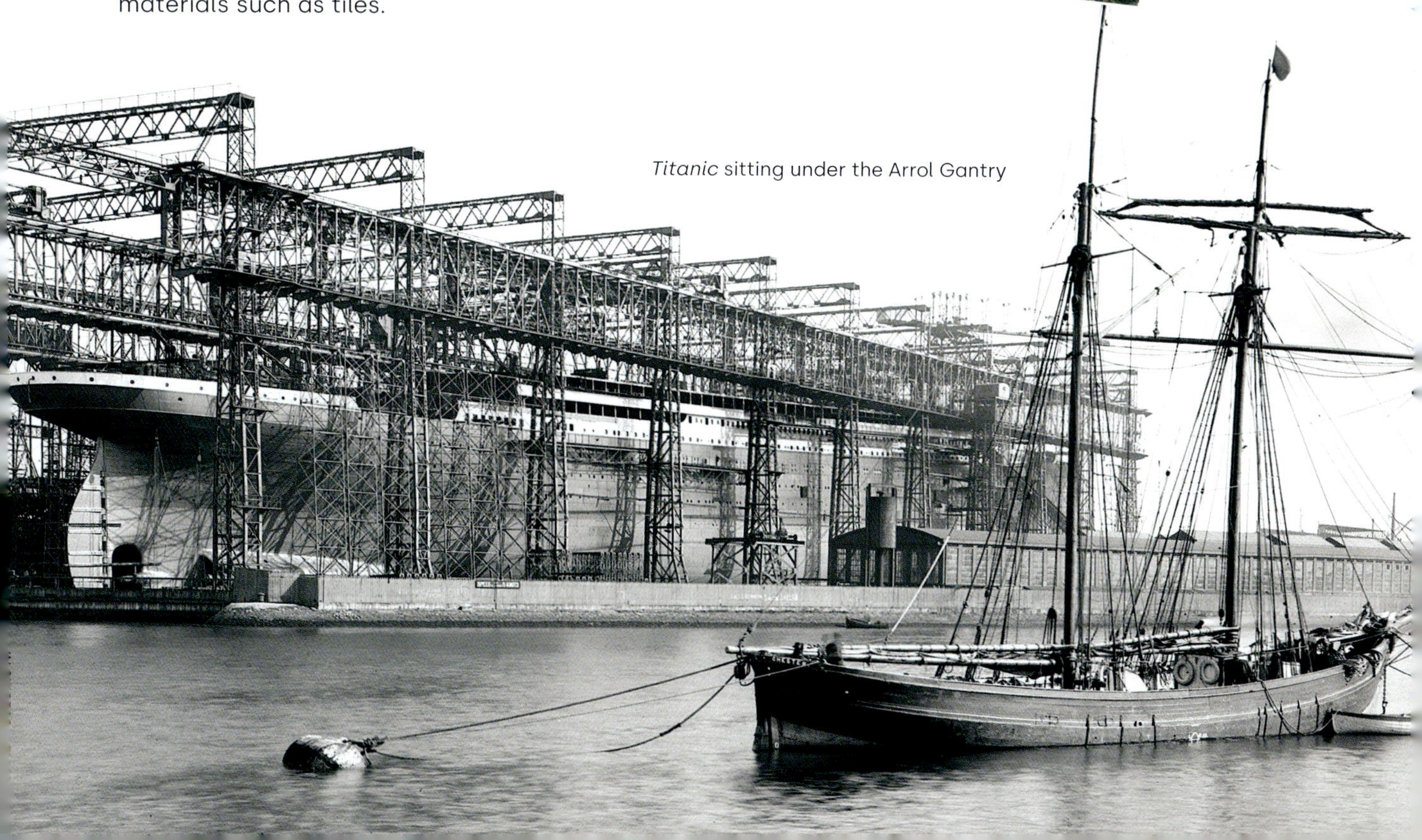

Titanic sitting under the Arrol Gantry

THE LAUNCH

On 31 May 1911, *Titanic* was launched from her slipway into Belfast Lough. This was a prestigious event for Harland & Wolff and White Star. The launch was attended by many important guests and was also witnessed by an estimated 100,000 people gathered on the banks of the Lagan. Journalists had come from as far away as London and America. Huge crowds of shipyard workers and other spectators gathered inside the yard.

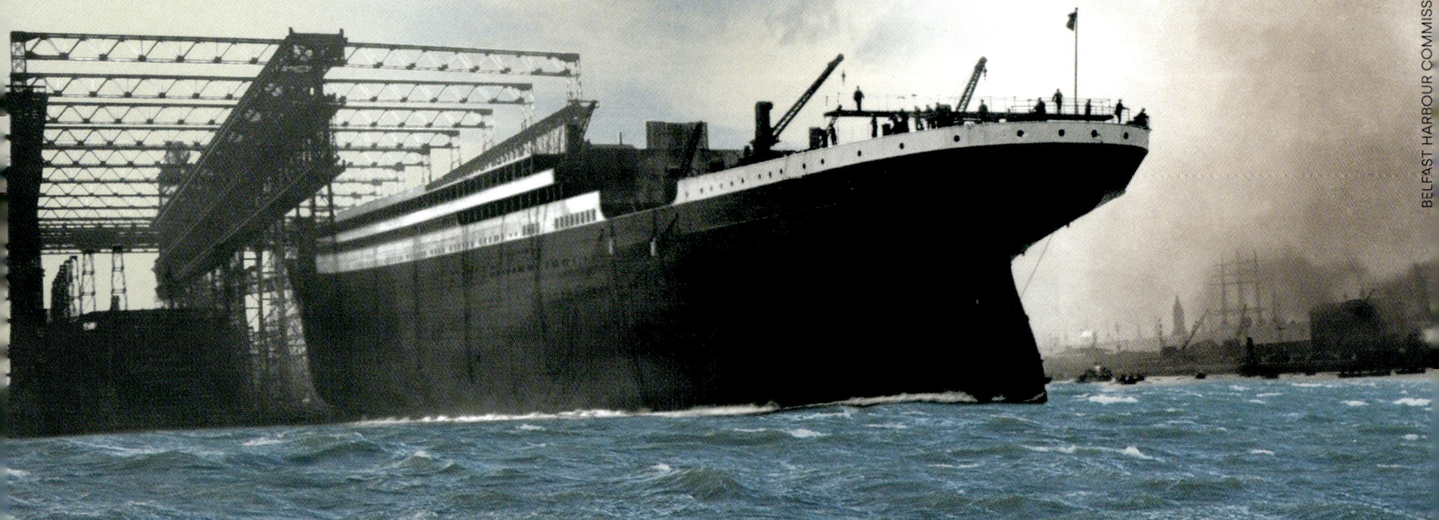

BELFAST HARBOUR COMMISSIONERS

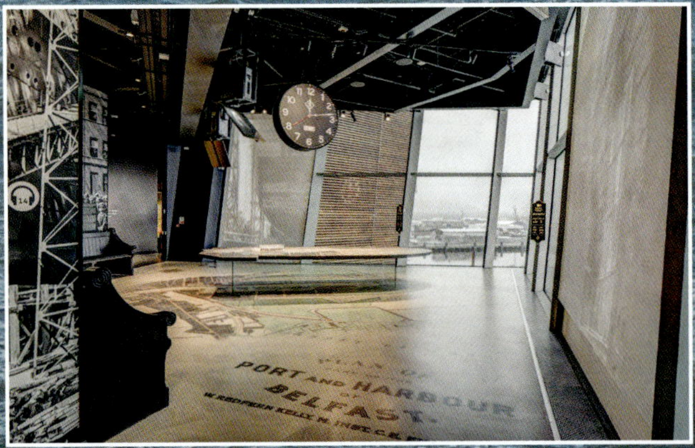

Prior to the launch, the heavy wooden props that held *Titanic* in place were removed. To keep her in place, hydraulic rams were placed on the slips under her bow. The cofferdam was removed to allow water to flood the lower part of the slipway.

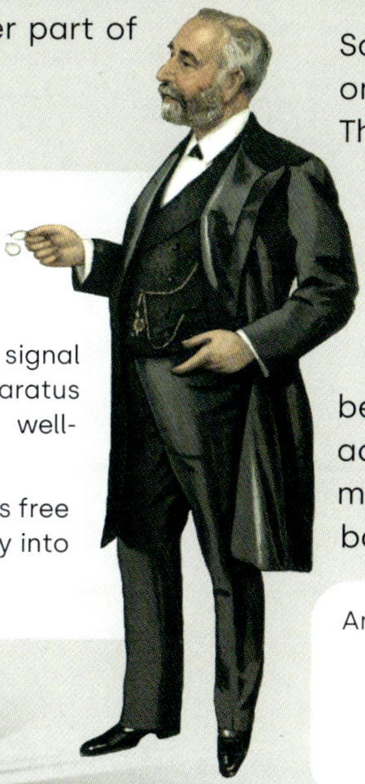

Lord Pirrie and J Bruce Ismay inspected the ship and launching equipment before the launch.

At 12.13pm, Lord Pirrie gave the signal to launch the ship. Hydraulic apparatus started *Titanic* moving down the well-greased slipway.

Within sixty-two seconds, *Titanic* was free of the slips and had glided gracefully into the water.

After the launch, Lord Pirrie treated distinguished guests to lunch in the Harland & Wolff boardroom. Other guests, press and senior Harland & Wolff employees had lunch at the Grand Central Hotel in Royal Avenue.

Some of the distinguished guests sailed to Liverpool on *Olympic*: for its delivery trip later that same day. The tenders, *Nomadic* and *Traffic* also left Belfast on the same day.

Within one hour of the launch, *Titanic* was towed by tugs to the deepwater wharf for fitting out. At this stage *Titanic* was like an empty shell: it had not yet been fitted with passenger accommodation, equipment or machinery including engines, boilers, funnels or propellers.

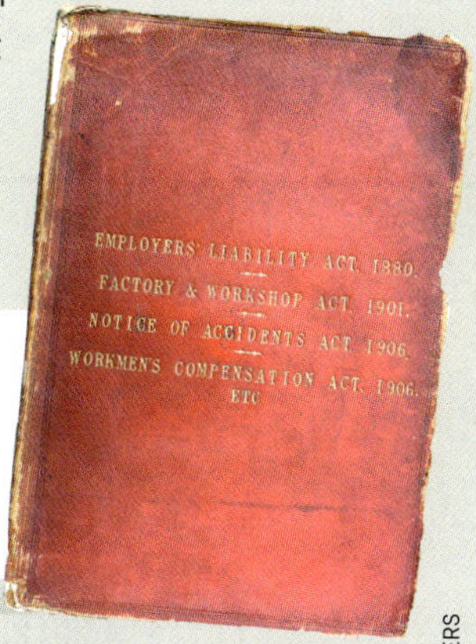

An accident occurred during the launch, when shipyard worker James Dobbin was hit by a falling wooden support. He was rushed to Victoria Hospital but died shortly afterwards.

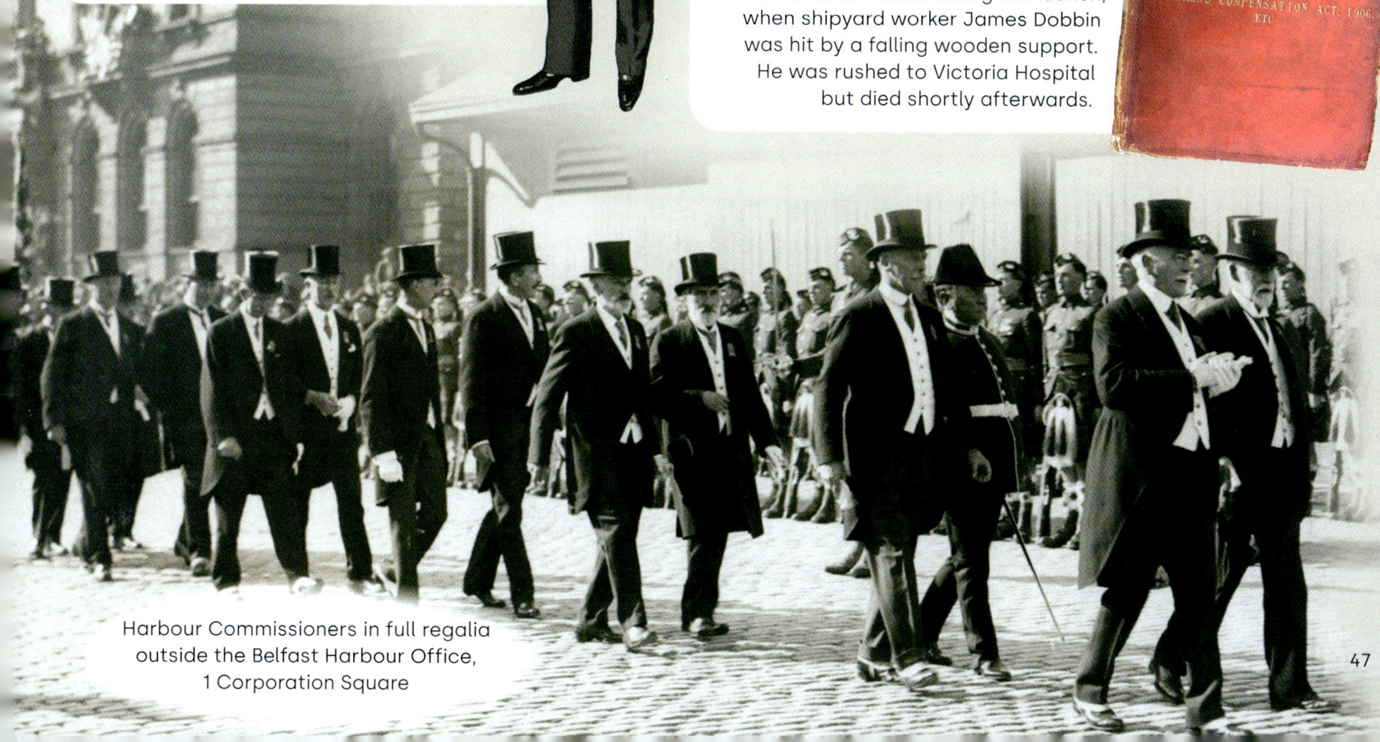

BELFAST HARBOUR COMMISSIONERS

Harbour Commissioners in full regalia outside the Belfast Harbour Office, 1 Corporation Square

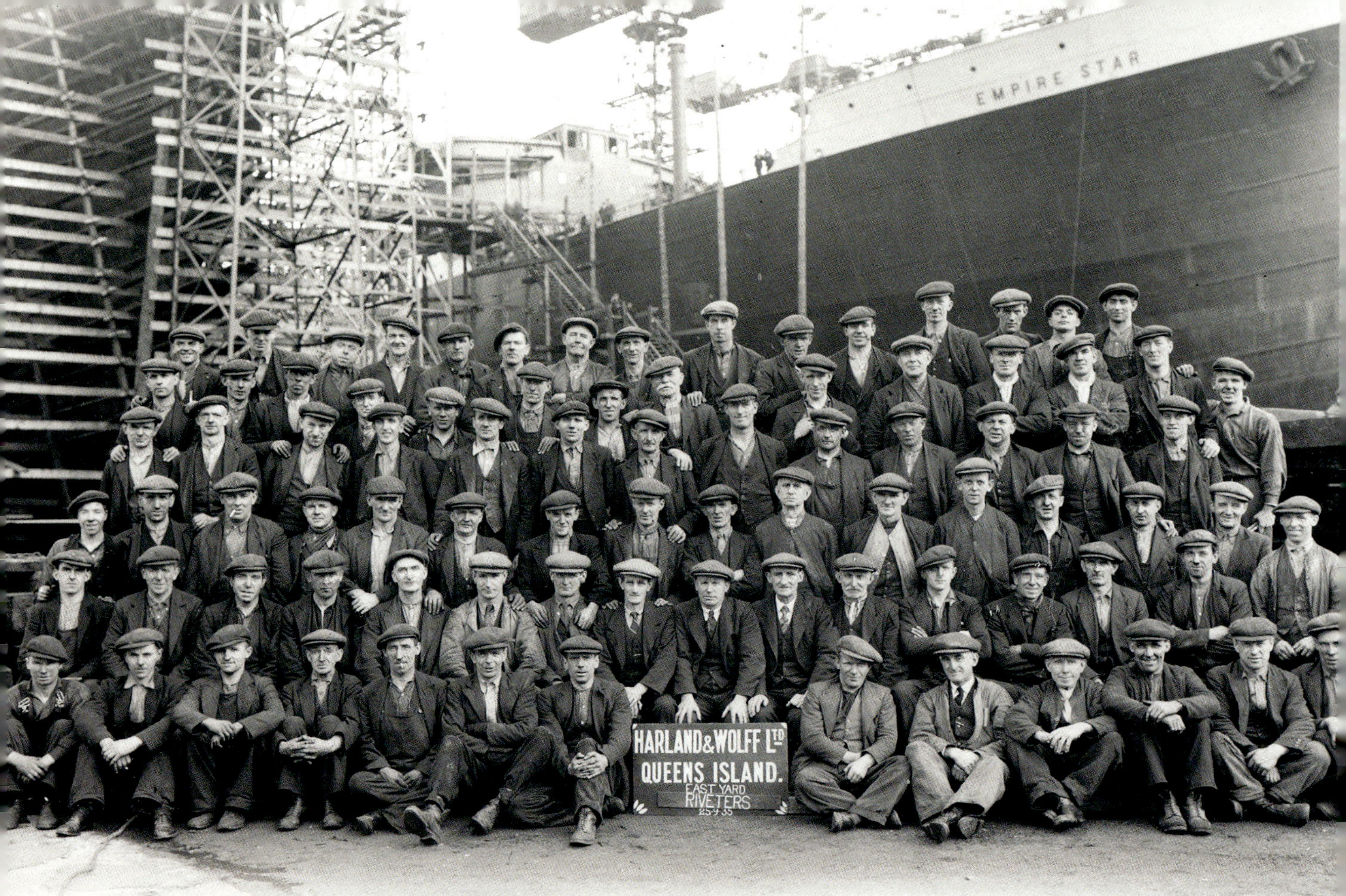

A team of riveters at Harland & Wolff shipyard

THE FIT OUT

Titanic's hull was virtually empty until after she was launched.

None of the permanent machinery needed to power the ship had been installed, although portable boilers were put in to allow *Titanic* to power her own winches so she could pull herself to the dockside. At the fitting out wharf *Titanic* began to take shape internally and to be fitted with equipment. Her fit out took more than 3,000 men ten months to complete.

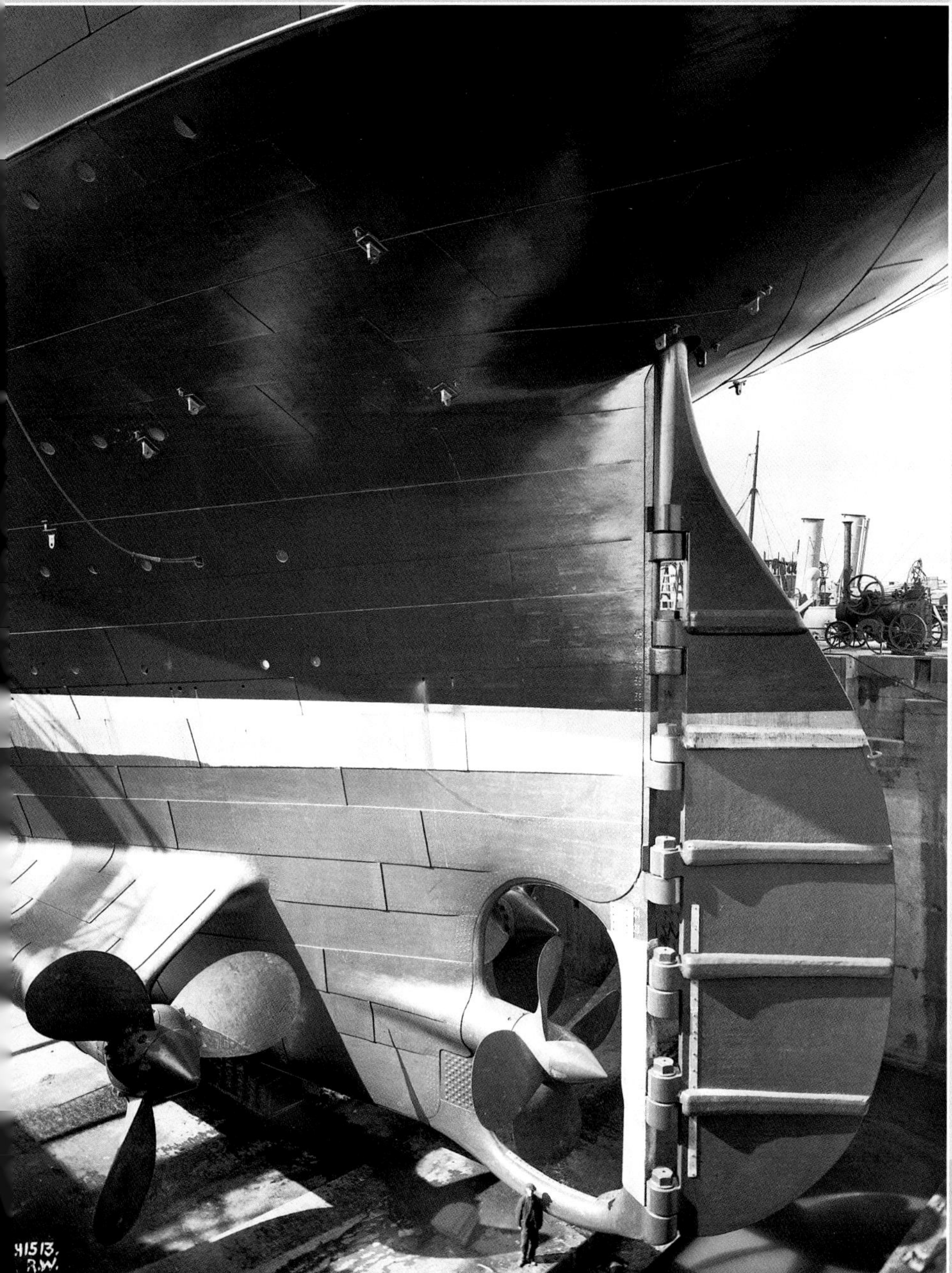

NATIONAL MUSEUMS NI

Titanic had three massive propellers located at the stern of the ship with one at each side and one in the centre. Each propeller was driven by one of the ship's three engines, located on the Orlop deck; they drove the ship ahead or astern. The two wing propellers had a diameter of over twenty-three feet (6.70 metres); the central propeller was over 16ft (5 metres).

Two reciprocating engines drove the wing propellers, and one turbine engine drove the central propeller. The combination of these engines was a recent development in shipbuilding technology, which improved efficiency.

A view of the propellers and rudder on *Olympic* in Thompson Dock. Note the man at the bottom of the picture for scale.

Titanic's funnels were made at Harland & Wolff. Three of the funnels vented combustion gases from the boilers, the fourth was a 'dummy' used for ventilation. They were over twenty-four feet wide (8 metres) and measured seventy feet high above the boat deck (21.3 metres).

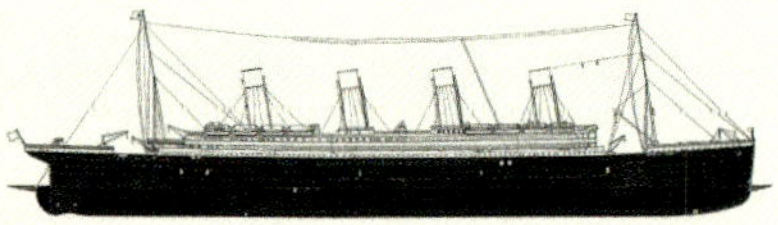

Titanic was fitted with twenty-nine coal boilers in six boiler rooms. These generated steam to power *Titanic*'s engines and electric generating plant and were also located on the Tank Top. They were fed by coal burning furnaces. The boilers drove the ship's engines and electric generating plant.

Titanic had ten decks. The many cabins, public rooms and facilities were located on the higher decks while the propulsion machinery was on the lowest deck.

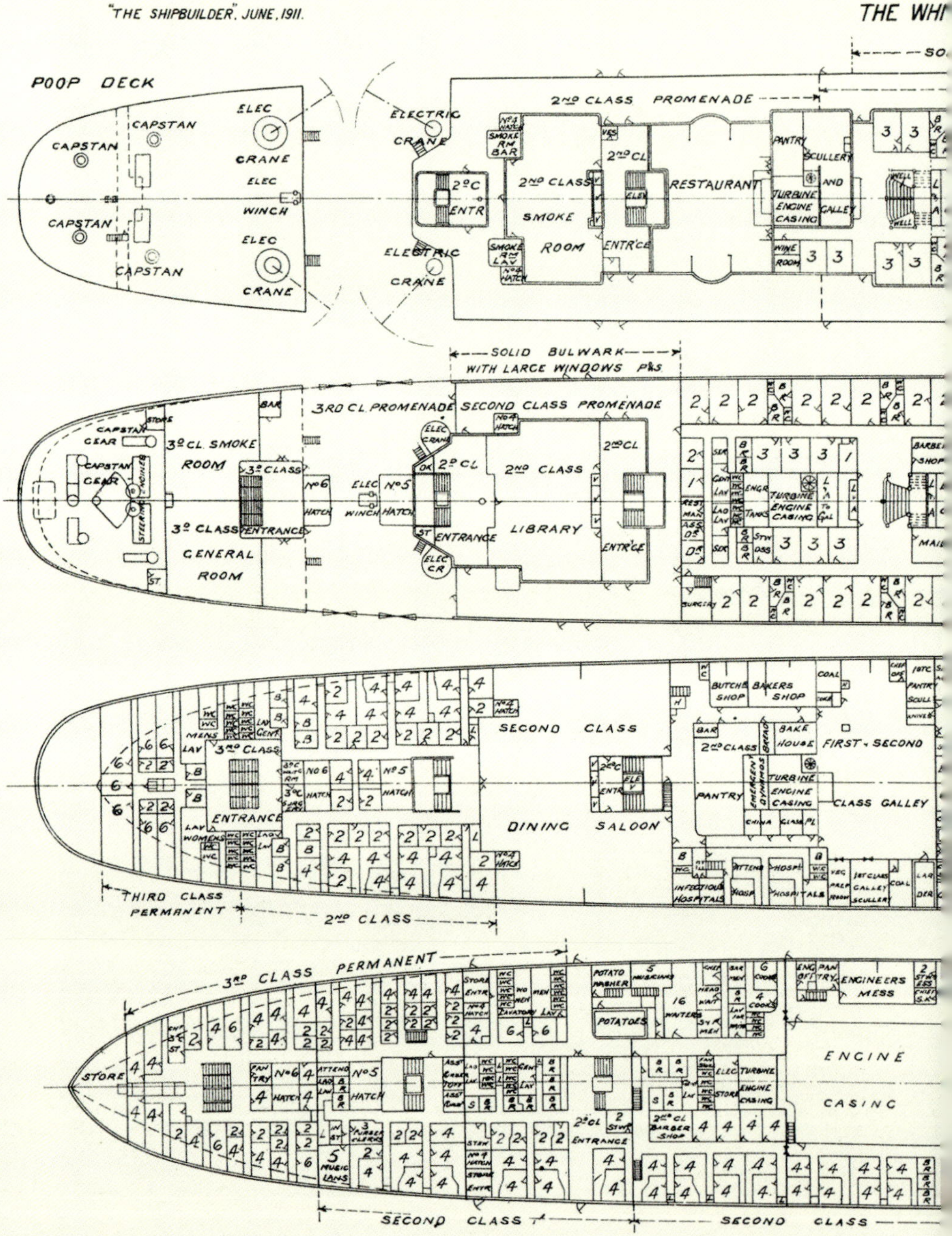

GETTY IMAGES

TRIPLE-SCREW STEAMERS "OLYMPIC" AND "TITANIC."

PLATE IV.

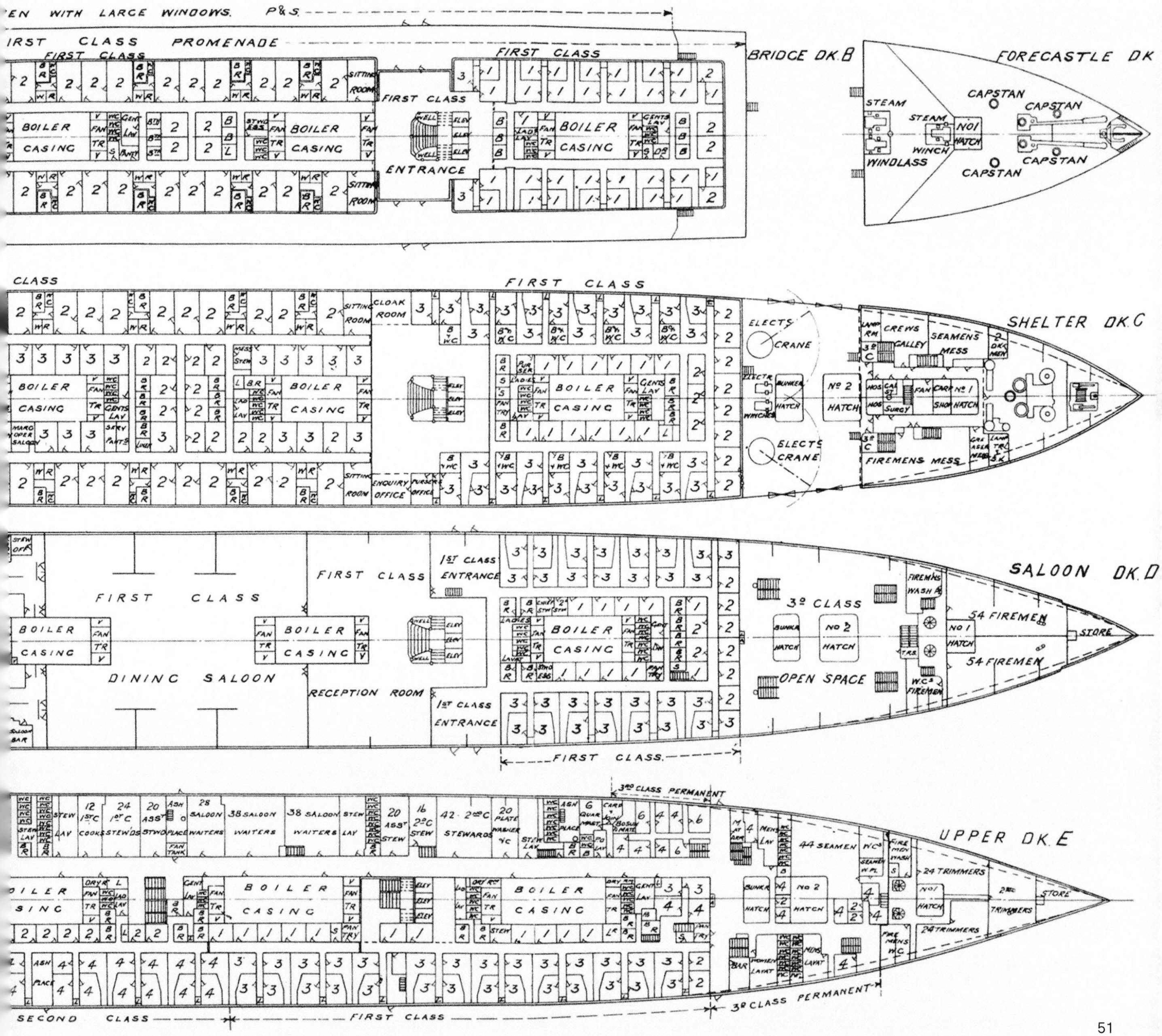

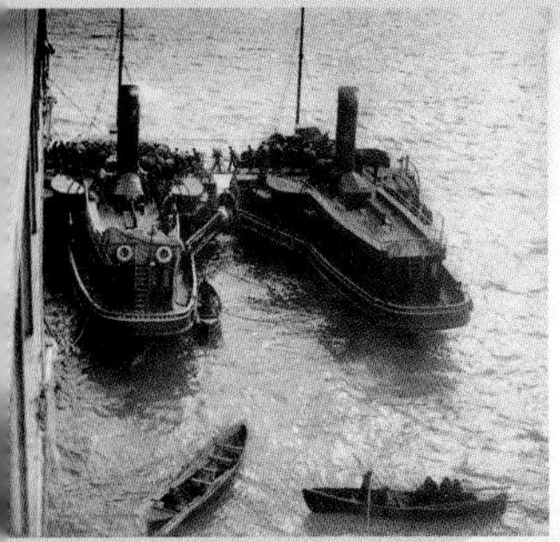

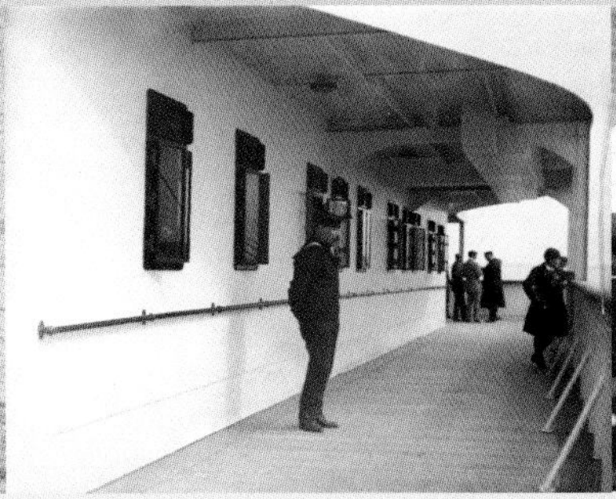

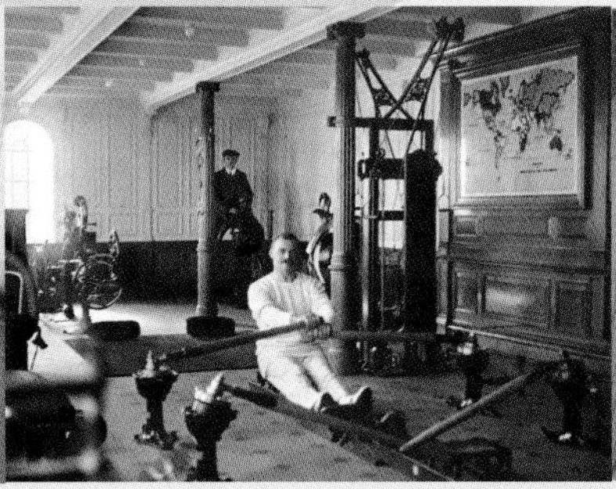

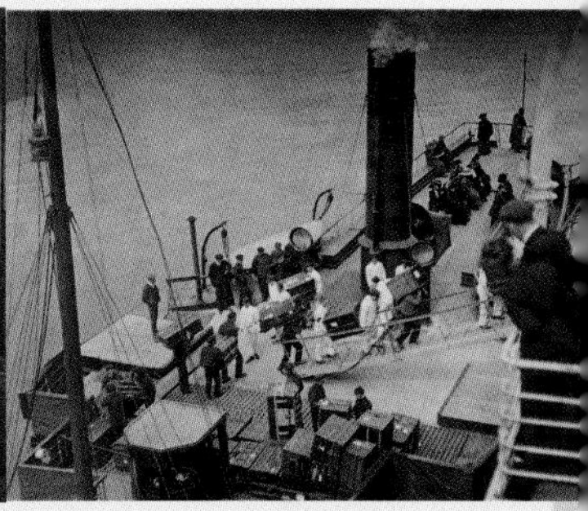

Moving around on *Titanic*

Titanic had a very complicated internal lay out. This was due to the separation of different passenger classes and the need for crew to access all parts of the ship.

The design of the ship made the best possible use of space. The internal fit out included the installation of room divisions, corridors, passageways, staircases and lifts.

Titanic's internal design allowed the crew to work near passenger areas unseen. Meals were prepared for hundreds simultaneously, necessitating moving provisions from stores to kitchens and serving areas. Out of sight, hundreds of crew attended the boilers and coal bunkers twenty-four hours a day. The cargo, baggage and mail storage areas were cleverly located to avoid disruption to on board facilities and services.

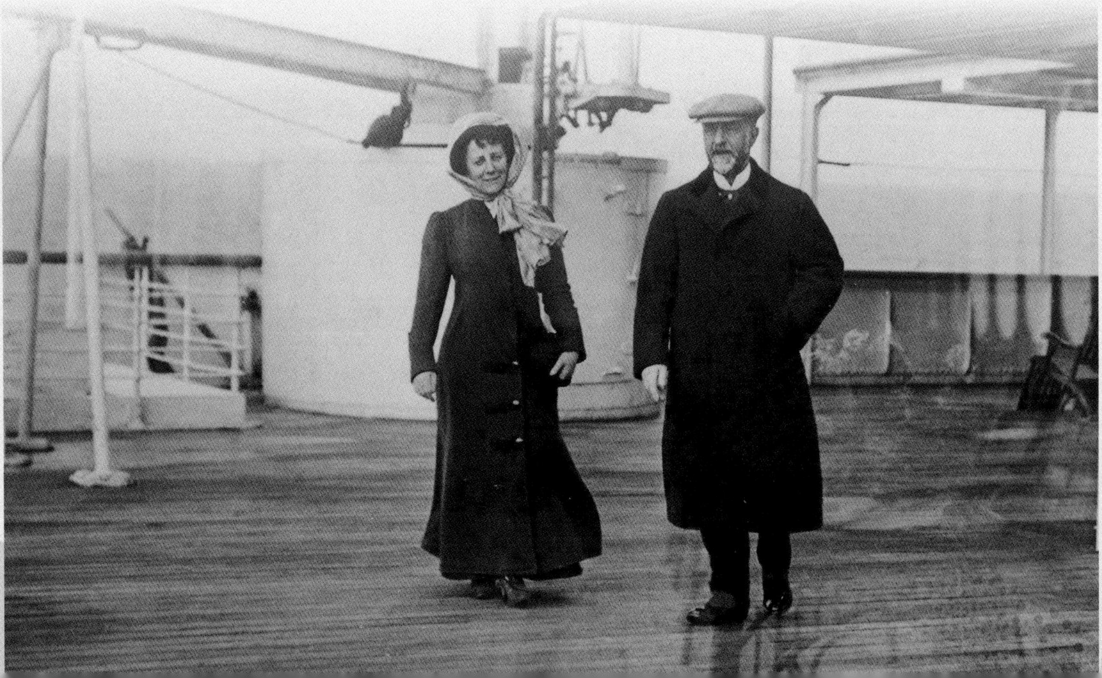

DAVISON PHOTO

Keeping in touch

Titanic's communication equipment

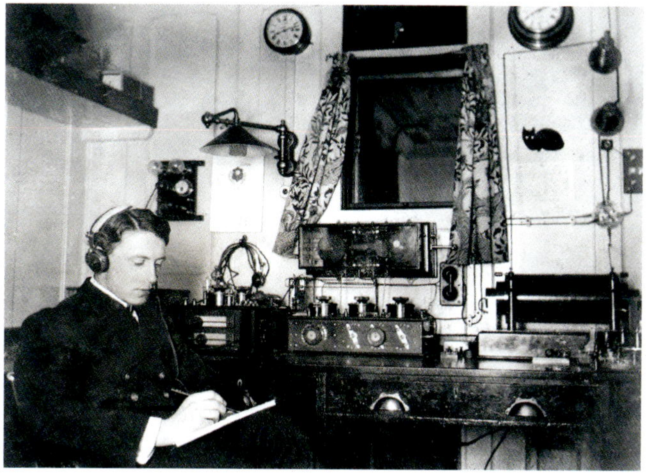

SJ BROWNE

Titanic carried various types of communication equipment. This allowed passengers and crew to communicate on the ship and with the outside world.

Titanic's powerful Marconi wireless equipment allowed her to communicate with stations more than a thousand miles away.

The wireless was manned around the clock and was operated using Morse code. This equipment allowed the ship to both send and receive messages. The Marconi operators communicated shipping messages and personal messages for passengers. News received via the wireless was printed in an on board newspaper.

As a Royal Mail Steamer (RMS), *Titanic* had the capacity to carry 3,635 mailbags with 2,000 letters per mailbag. She also had a Sea Post Office for passenger use. Telephones were in plentiful supply for the crew to communicate on board the ship.

Titanic carried electric lamps that flashed lights in Morse code to signal to other ships at night. A whole range of rockets and flares were also fitted to communicate messages to other ships.

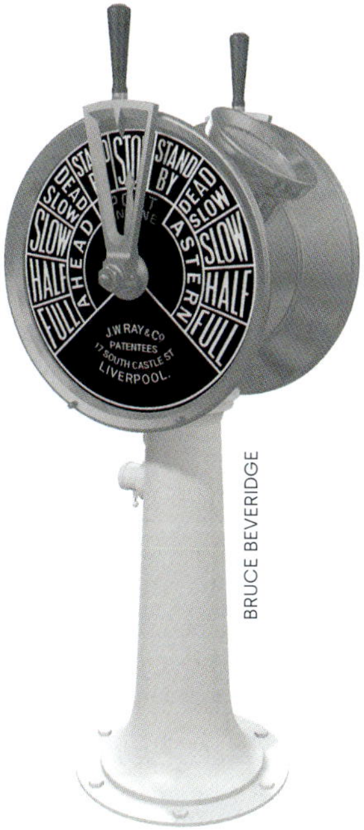

BRUCE BEVERIDGE

Finding her way

Titanic's navigating equipment

Titanic carried a huge amount of navigating equipment to help steer the ship safely in the right direction: four main compasses. A variety of other nautical equipment calculated the position of the ship, distance travelled, speed and depth of water.

Titanic had three wheels for steering. Engine, steering and boiler telegraphs conveyed messages from the navigation bridge. *Titanic* carried barometers and thermometers; its equipment could pick up underwater bell signals sent from lighthouses, buoys and other ships, which warned of dangers such as fog. The ship also had a range of telescopes, megaphones, foghorns, logbooks, diaries, navigational charts and binoculars. Navigational lighting included masthead lamps, sidelights and anchor lights. For communicating with other ships *Titanic* used the Marconi wireless, flags, signal lamps and rockets.

Public rooms and facilities onboard *Titanic*

Titanic had a huge array of rooms and facilities. First, Second and Third Class public areas were separate and were decorated very differently.

First Class areas were very luxurious and were comparable with the best hotels of the time. There was a range of amenities available including a choice of dining, sporting, exercise and leisure facilities. The dining saloon was decorated in early 17th century Jacobean style with detailed ceiling plasterwork, oak furniture and a piano. The walls and ceilings were painted white with decorations in relief. The room was extravagantly lit using 404 light bulbs as well as benefitting from natural light.

A variety of sizes of tables were installed, with chairs upholstered in light green leather.

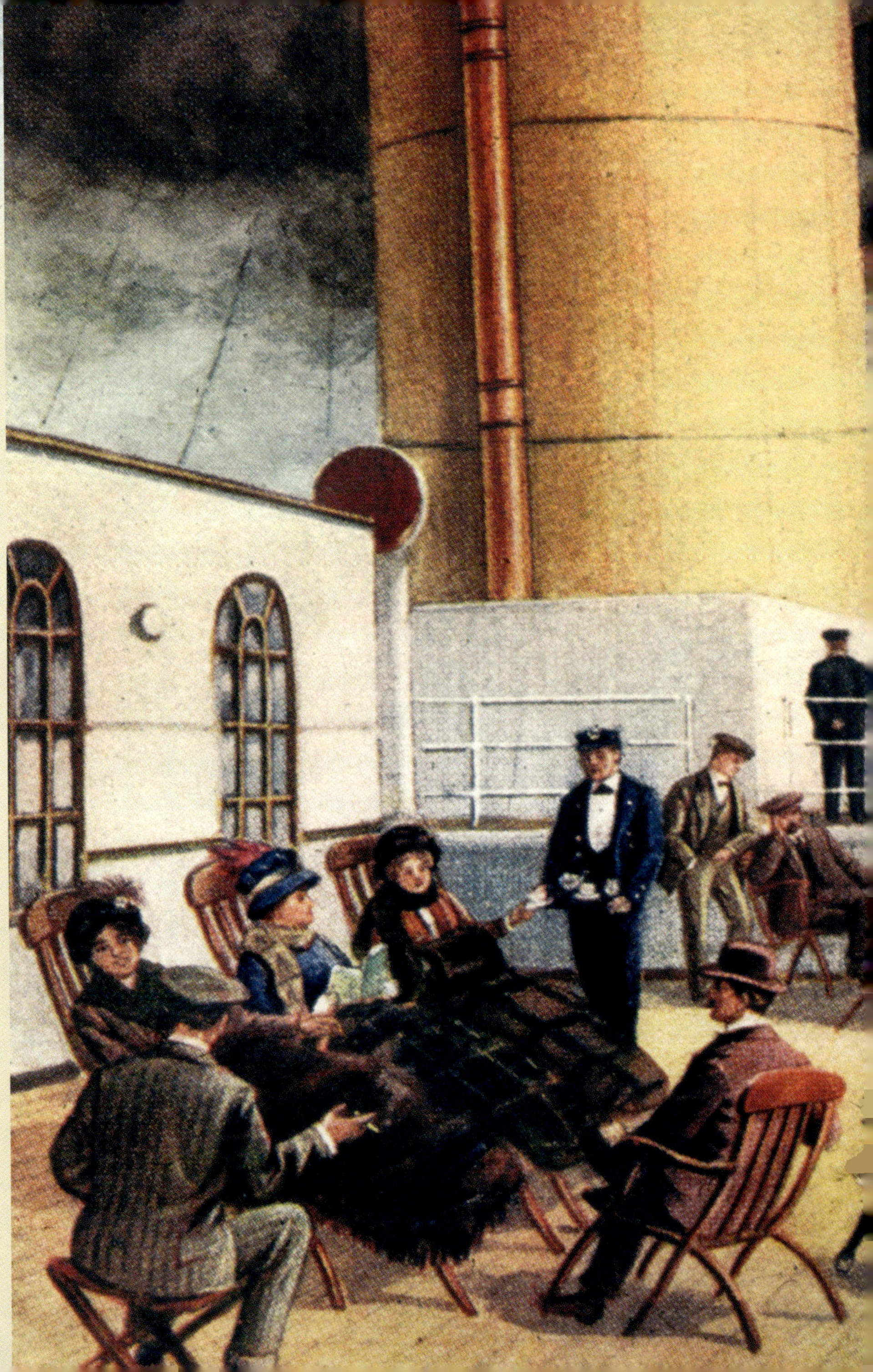

BRIDGEMAN ART LIBRARY

Second Class Promenade on the Boat Deck

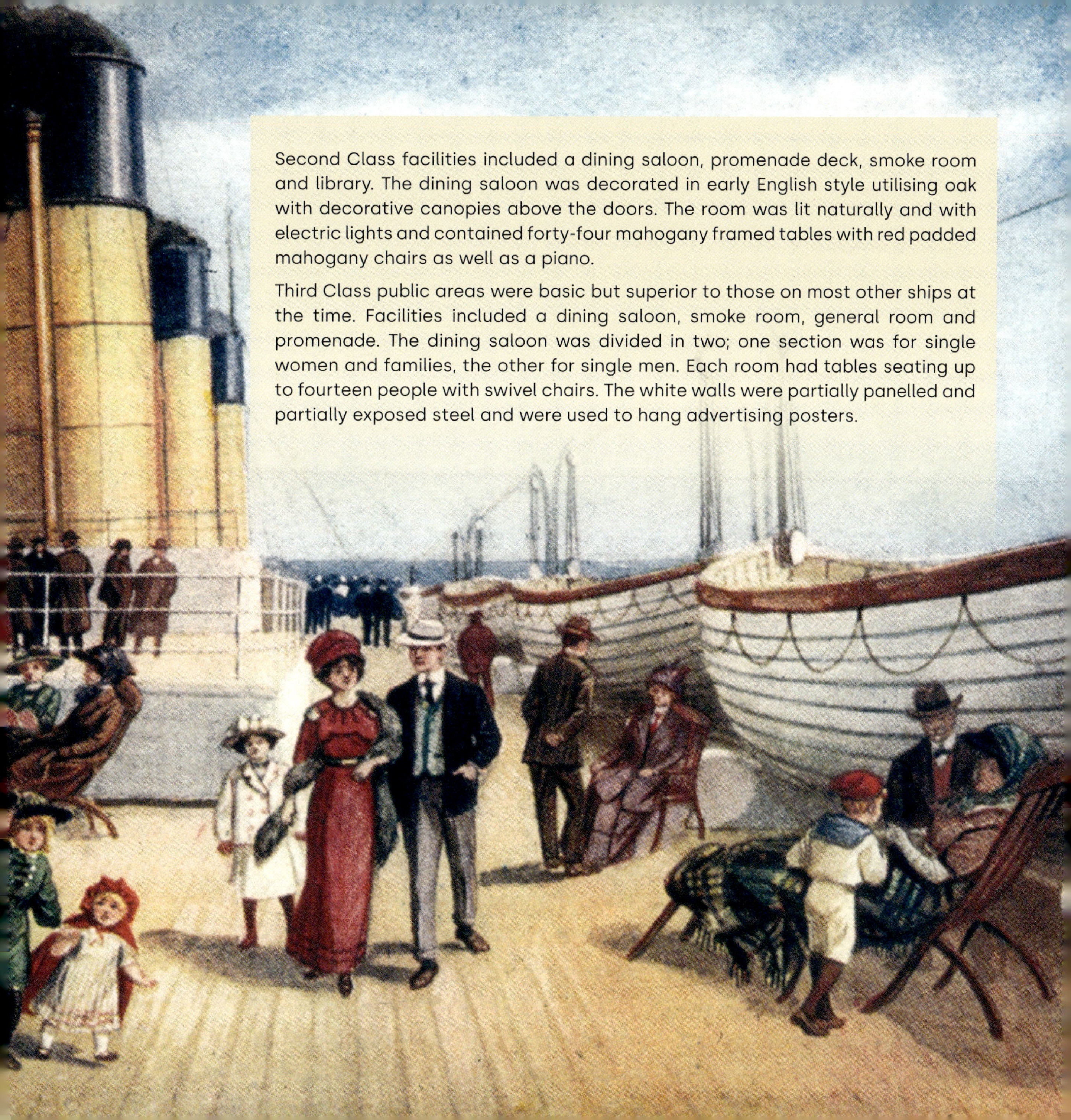

Second Class facilities included a dining saloon, promenade deck, smoke room and library. The dining saloon was decorated in early English style utilising oak with decorative canopies above the doors. The room was lit naturally and with electric lights and contained forty-four mahogany framed tables with red padded mahogany chairs as well as a piano.

Third Class public areas were basic but superior to those on most other ships at the time. Facilities included a dining saloon, smoke room, general room and promenade. The dining saloon was divided in two; one section was for single women and families, the other for single men. Each room had tables seating up to fourteen people with swivel chairs. The white walls were partially panelled and partially exposed steel and were used to hang advertising posters.

First Class cabin in the 'old Dutch style'

The 'special stateroom' was one of the most luxurious and expensive on *Titanic*. This kind of luxury was rarely seen in hotels at this time. The cabin would have been occupied by extremely wealthy people such as members of the aristocracy or very successful business people.

The cabin was fitted with windows letting in natural light and electric lights, including a portable table lamp, wall and ceiling lights. A double washbasin was surrounded by rouge marble with a cabinet below. It also had an oak wardrobe on each side with bevelled mirrors and drawers. A lounge settee, table and chairs ensured that passengers could sit comfortably in their cabin.

Carved oak panelling and heavily embossed coverings decorated the walls. Carved oak beams adorned the white panelled ceiling and both bedsteads were also constructed from carved oak. The cabin had shared private access to a bath and toilet and its own private wardrobe room. The room was also fitted with carpet, a heater, wall tidy, electric fan, notice frame and bell push to call a steward.

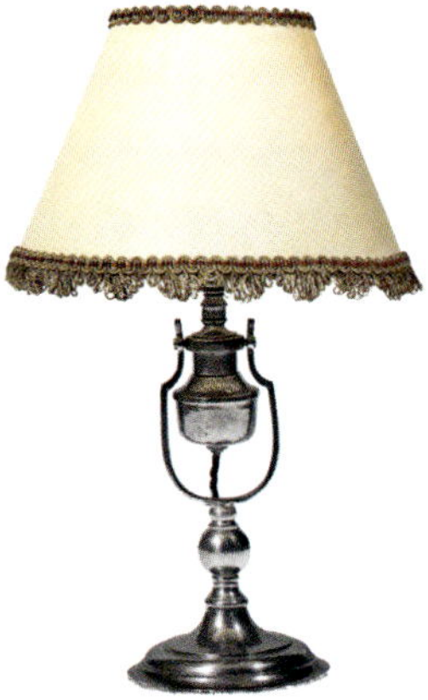

A period Gimbal table lamp in the First Class cabin oscillates with the motion of the ship

A writing cushion

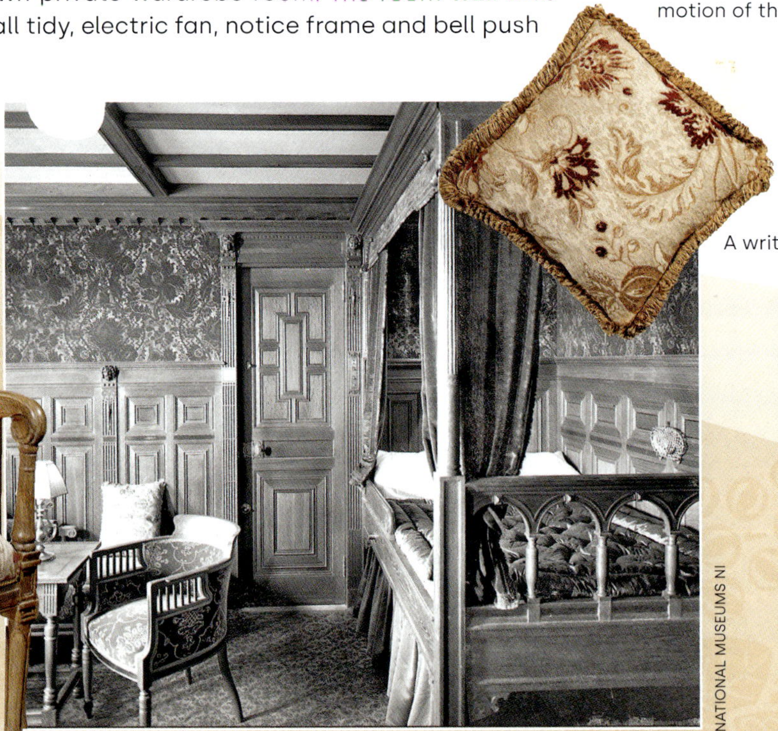

NATIONAL MUSEUMS NI

Dutch style suite

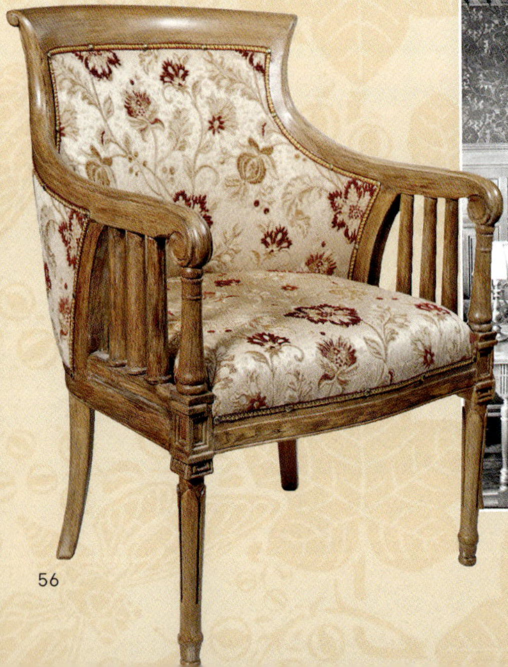

Wooden or brass bedsteads, electric heaters, wardrobes, dressing tables, carpeted bedroom floors and washbasin cabinets with hot and cold running water were standard for First Class cabins.

A number of 'special' staterooms were decorated in period style including Georgian, Italian Renaissance and French styles. These rooms had shared access to private bathrooms and toilets. Large staterooms sometimes had a small single berth room interconnected, which was ideal for a servant.

Parlour suites with their own private promenade were the most expensive. They had a spacious sitting room, two bedrooms, two wardroom rooms, a private bath and toilet, and were fitted out to the highest standard.

First Class cabins

There were almost 330 First Class cabins from which passengers could choose. Prices were wide-ranging and depended on the style and size of the cabin. If travelling in larger groups or families, passengers could hire suites with interconnecting doors.

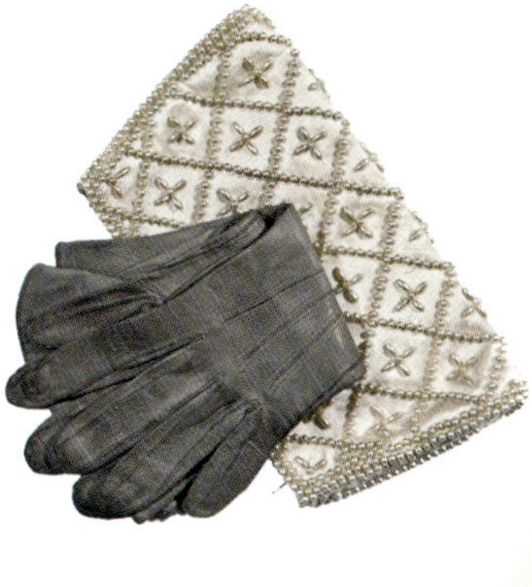

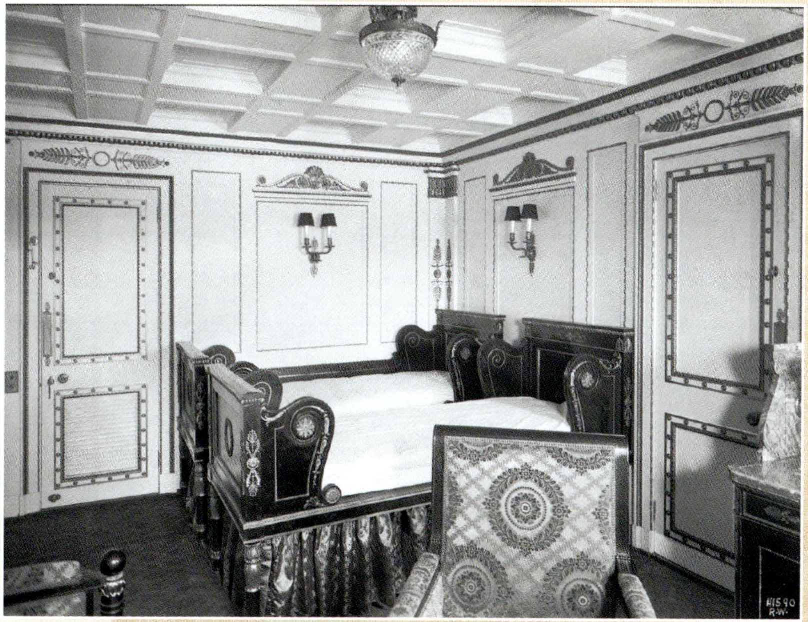

NATIONAL MUSEUMS NI

Empire style bedroom

Second Class cabins

Second Class cabins on *Titanic* were as good as First Class cabins on other ships. A two-berth cabin was designed so that it could also be used for both Second and First Class passengers.

The cabin contained sleeping accommodation of a single tier mahogany bunk that was fitted with an upper Pullman berth above to provide another bed. The wardrobe was made from mahogany and had a mirror on the inside. An upholstered settee provided comfortable seating.

The single washbasin did not have hot and cold running water but had a reservoir filled by the bedroom steward. White panelling decorated the walls. For the comfort of passengers public toilets and baths were situated nearby. As this cabin was also designed to be used by First Class passengers it contained a heater and was fitted with carpet. Other Second Class cabins were fitted with linoleum tiles of either red and white or green and white. Mahogany bunk beds were standard in most Second Class rooms that could be either two or four berth. Four berth rooms generally had one set of bunk beds and a sofa bed that could be converted into two berths.

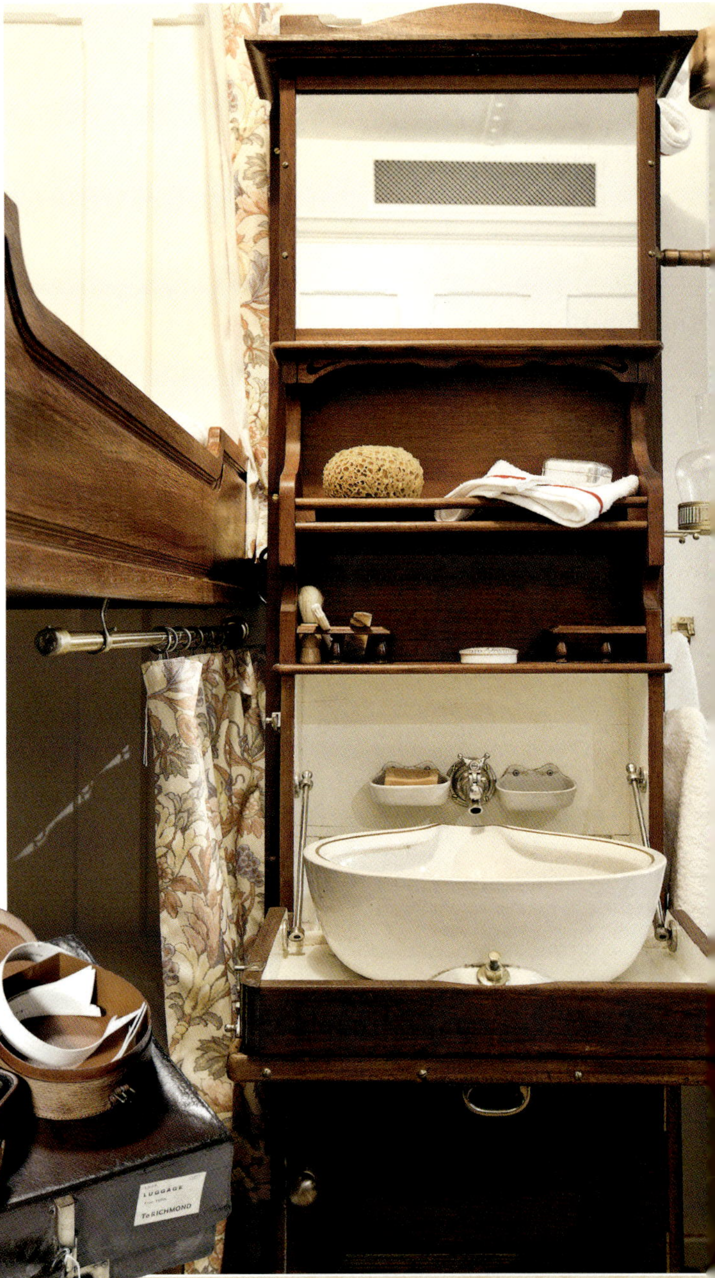

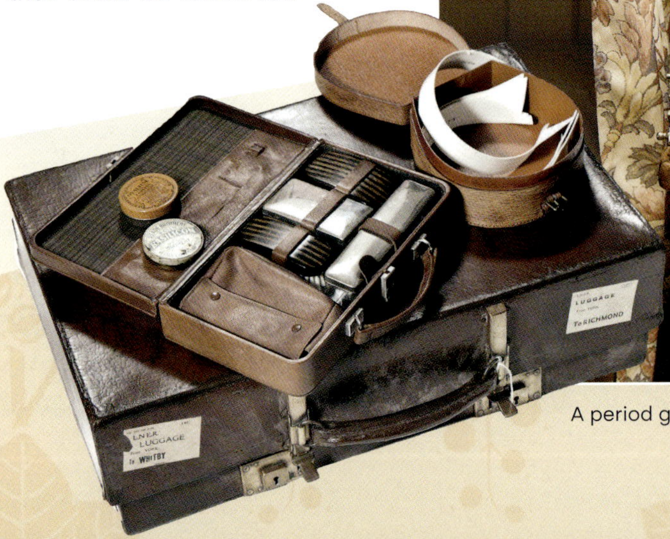

A period grooming case and collar case

Third Class cabins

Third Class cabins on *Titanic* were basic compared to First and Second Class accommodation but were a massive improvement from the large dormitories on other ships.

The majority of Third Class passengers were emigrants heading to America for a better life. They therefore would generally have been going on a one-way ticket. Third Class passenger occupations would have included labourers, servants, unskilled and semi-skilled workers.

Other Third Class accommodation on board included two, three, four, five, six, eight and ten berth cabins.

Cheaper, more basic accommodation was available for single men without washbasins and with lower quality mattresses and no pillows. Other cabins were designed with families or single women in mind. No single berth accommodation was available for Third Class passengers.

The cabin contained a double bunk made from mahogany with pillows and sheets provided. The room had a washbasin with a mirror above and a wall seat. Hard Litosilo covered the floor and the walls were covered in white panelling. Passengers would have had to go up two decks to reach the public toilets from their cabin.

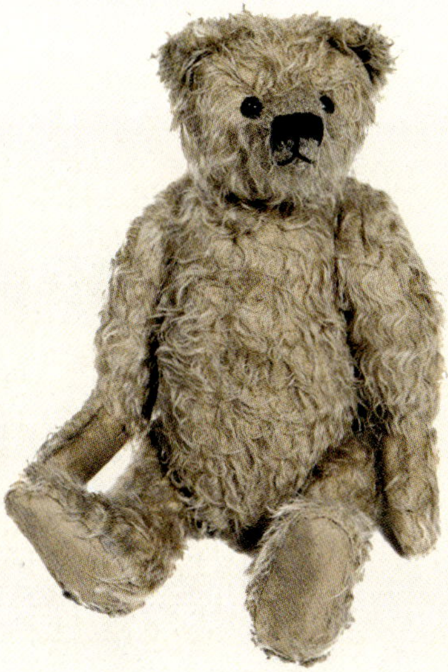

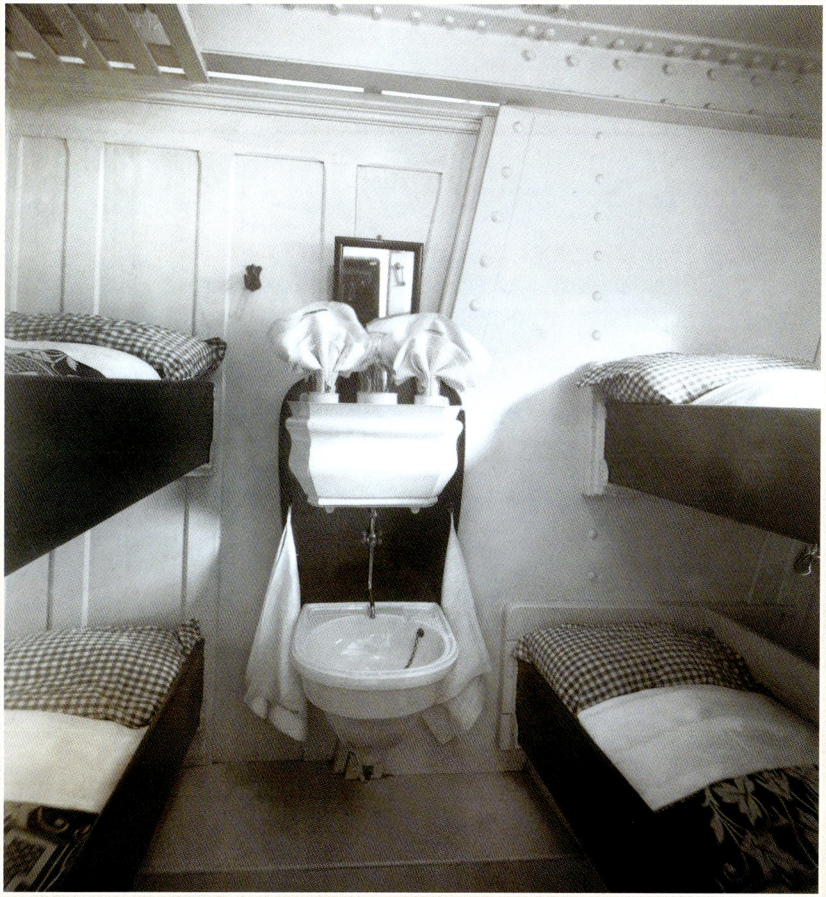

NEW YORK MUSEUM

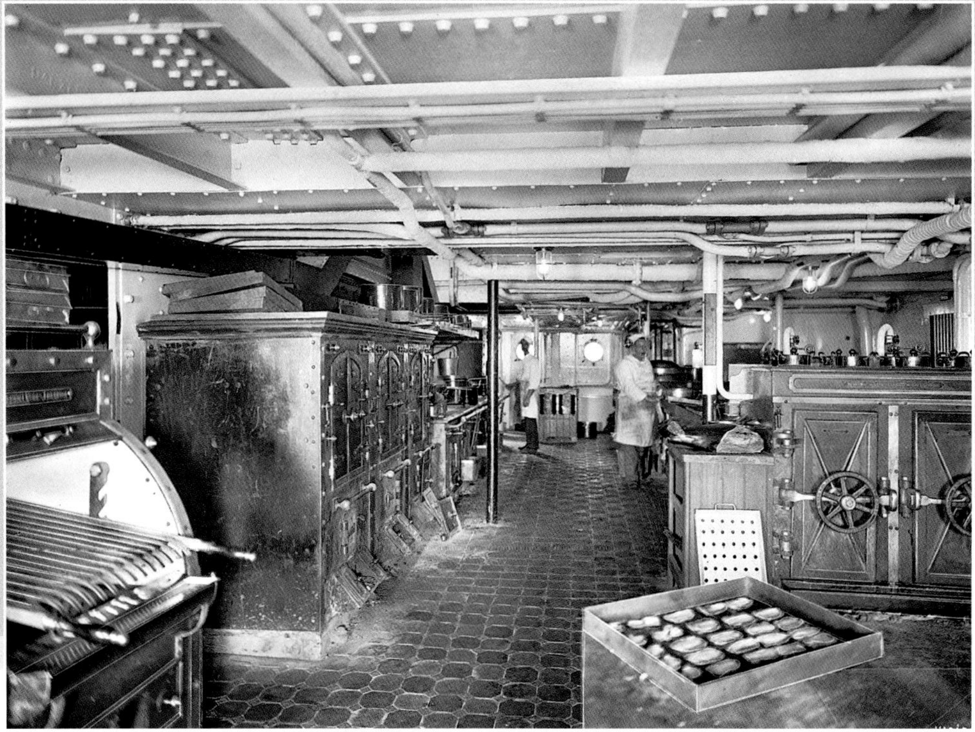

NATIONAL MUSEUMS NI

Galley on the *Amazon*, 1909

Back of house

behind the scenes on *Titanic*

Titanic could accommodate 945 crewmembers. There were many different working areas and crew accommodation areas on board.

The Victualling Department provided all the passenger services ranging from food, housekeeping, laundry and room service. With thousands of mouths to feed, food storage, preparation and serving was a major responsibility of the Victualling Department. *Titanic* had several kitchens to feed all the passengers and crew. The kitchens were equipped with the latest kitchen gadgets available.

Soft drinks and hard liquor

a *Titanic* drinks cabinet

With the capacity to carry over 3,500 passengers and crew, *Titanic* was stocked with literally tons of food and drink. First Class passengers were requested to sign a card when they ordered a drink and to settle their bill at the end of the journey. Third Class passengers also had access to alcoholic drinks; the bar was accessible from the Third Class smoking room.

A breath of fresh air

Titanic's air conditioning and ventilation equipment

Titanic was fitted with seventy-five fans supplied by Belfast's Sirocco Works. The fans were needed to supply a draught for fires in the boiler room and to ventilate certain areas of the ship.

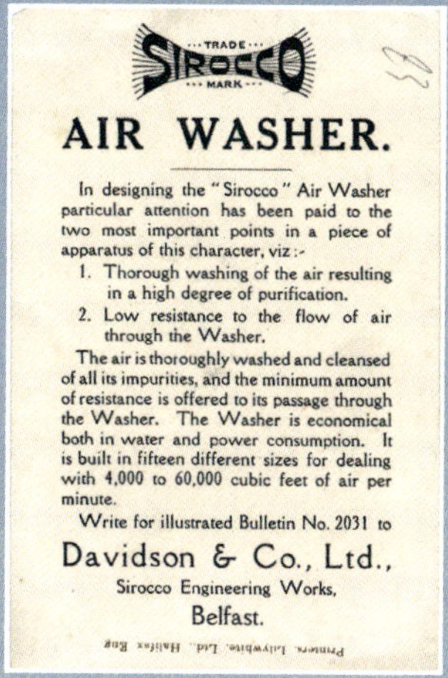

TRADE SIROCCO MARK

AIR WASHER.

In designing the "Sirocco" Air Washer particular attention has been paid to the two most important points in a piece of apparatus of this character, viz:-

1. Thorough washing of the air resulting in a high degree of purification.
2. Low resistance to the flow of air through the Washer.

The air is thoroughly washed and cleansed of all its impurities, and the minimum amount of resistance is offered to its passage through the Washer. The Washer is economical both in water and power consumption. It is built in fifteen different sizes for dealing with 4,000 to 60,000 cubic feet of air per minute.

Write for illustrated Bulletin No. 2031 to

Davidson & Co., Ltd.,
Sirocco Engineering Works,
Belfast.

Printers, Lilywhite, Ltd., Halifax, Eng

OAMFP NATIONAL MUSEUMS NI

A magnificent linen cupboard

Titanic's Linens

Titanic needed huge quantities of linen for her journey. Her table and bed linens were made by Wm. Liddell & Co Ltd in Belfast and Co Down.

Titanic's special linens, such as First Class tablecloths and napkins, were damask linens patterned with the White Star emblem. *Titanic* carried thousands of aprons and tablecloths and over 10,000 cloths for use in the food preparation areas. She also stocked 18,000 bed sheets and 45,000 table napkins. As there were no facilities on board ship to wash linen, *Titanic* needed to carry all the linen for the voyage with her.

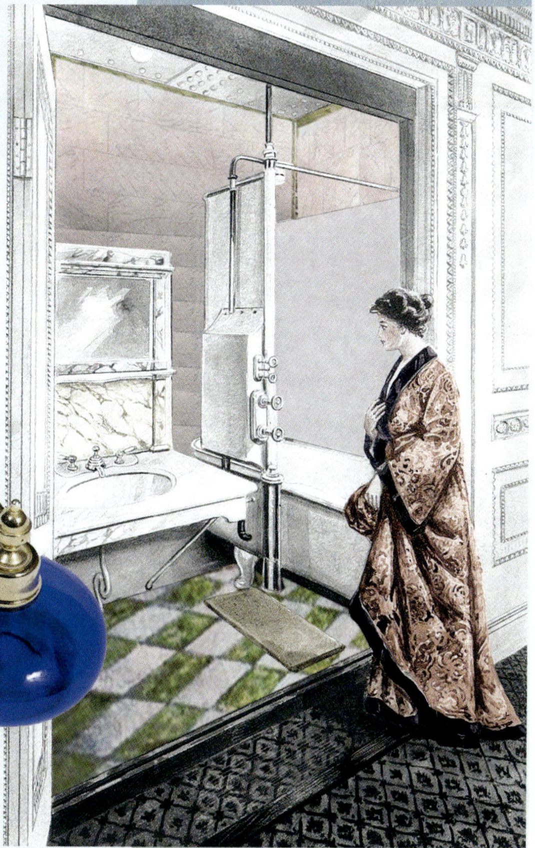

Keeping clean on board

Titanic's sanitary fittings

Titanic had bathing and toilets facilities that rivalled contemporary hotels. A limited number of private bathrooms were provided within First Class staterooms. Within Second and Third Class, all bathrooms were public, with only two bathrooms provided for all the Third Class passengers. Public baths used hot and cold salt water. Fresh water shower sprays were provided only with First Class private baths and in the Captain's quarters. Most cabins had washbasins fitted, with the exception of Third Class single male accommodation. Some First and Second Class washbasins could be folded away within a wash cabinet.

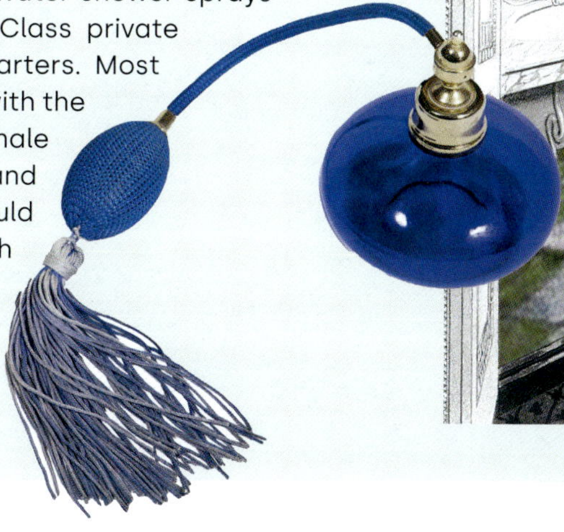

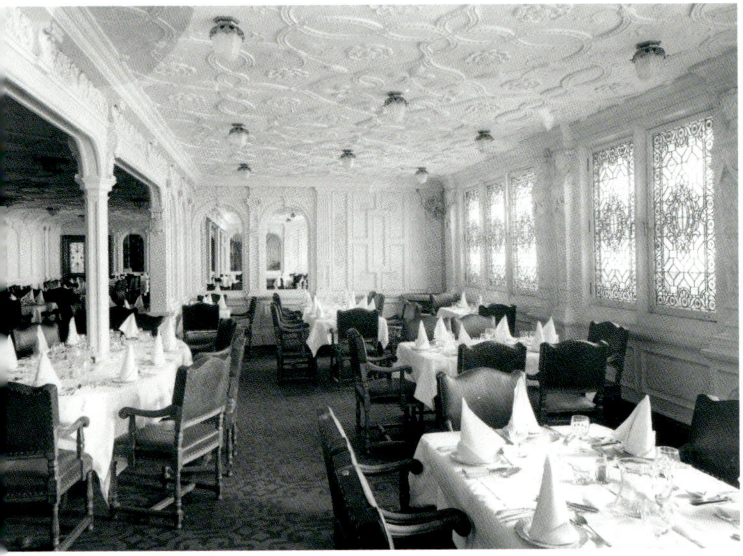

A First Class dining room on board the *Olympic*.

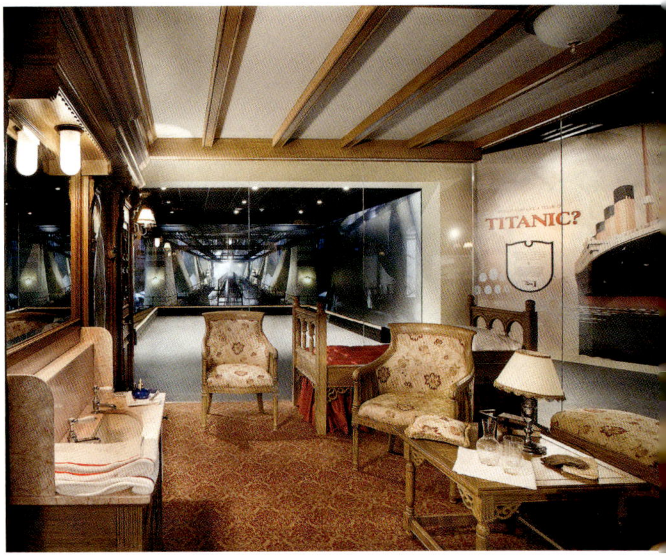

BRUCE BEVERIDGE

Service with a smile

Titanic's china

Titanic carried a huge amount of tableware for passengers and crew. Different types of china and tableware were supplied for each class of passenger. First Class passengers were provided with fine bone china. Second Class passengers dined from blue and white delft china bearing the White Star logo. This type of china was popular at the time and was used in many restaurants. Third Class tableware was white with the White Star red logo.

For Jewish emigrants, tableware was supplied for kosher dietary requirements.

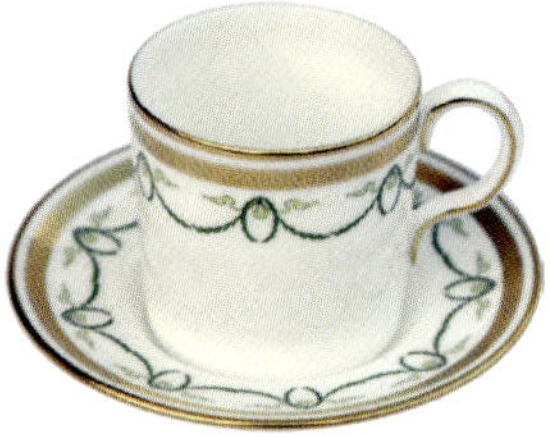

Replica *Titanic* coffee cup and saucer reproduced by Royal Doulton

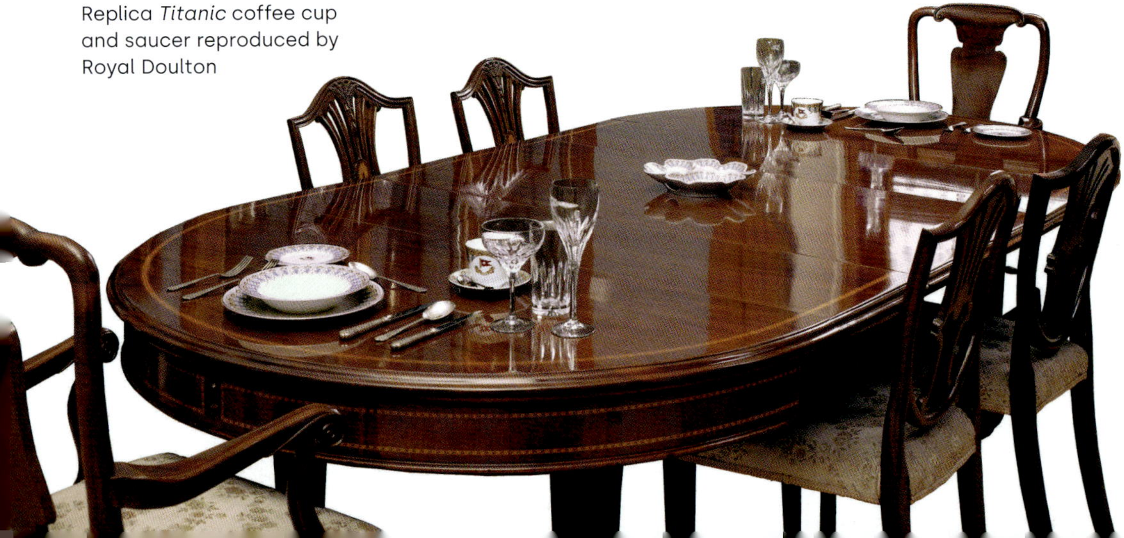

Titanic Table

This table was unfinished at the time of *Titanic*'s fitting out. It has been preserved and along with the table settings is on display at the Harbour Commissioner's Office in Belfast.

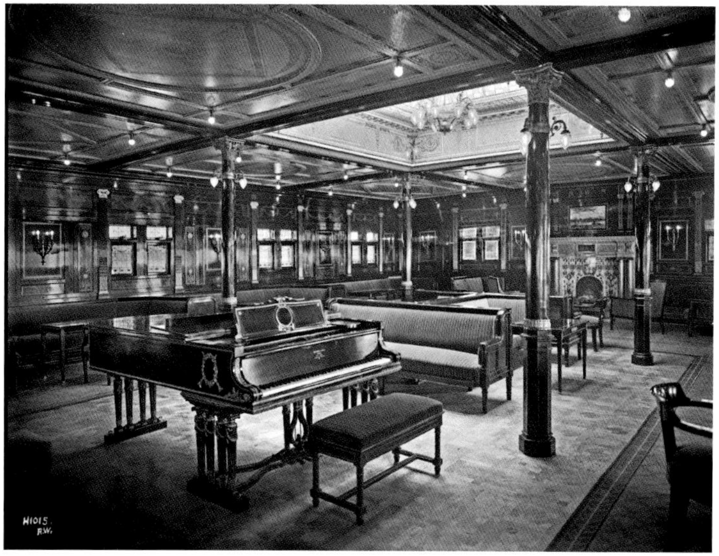

NATIONAL MUSEUMS NI

A First Class smoking lounge with piano on the *Nieuw Amsterdam*, 1906

Tunes for everyone
Titanic's pianos

Titanic carried six pianos: three in First Class, two in Second Class and one in Third Class. The First Class pianos, very ornate, were situated in the reception room, entrance hall and dining saloon. The Second Class pianos were located in the entrance hall and dining saloon. The Third Class piano was in the general room.

A Third Class smoke room with piano on the *Pericles*, 1908

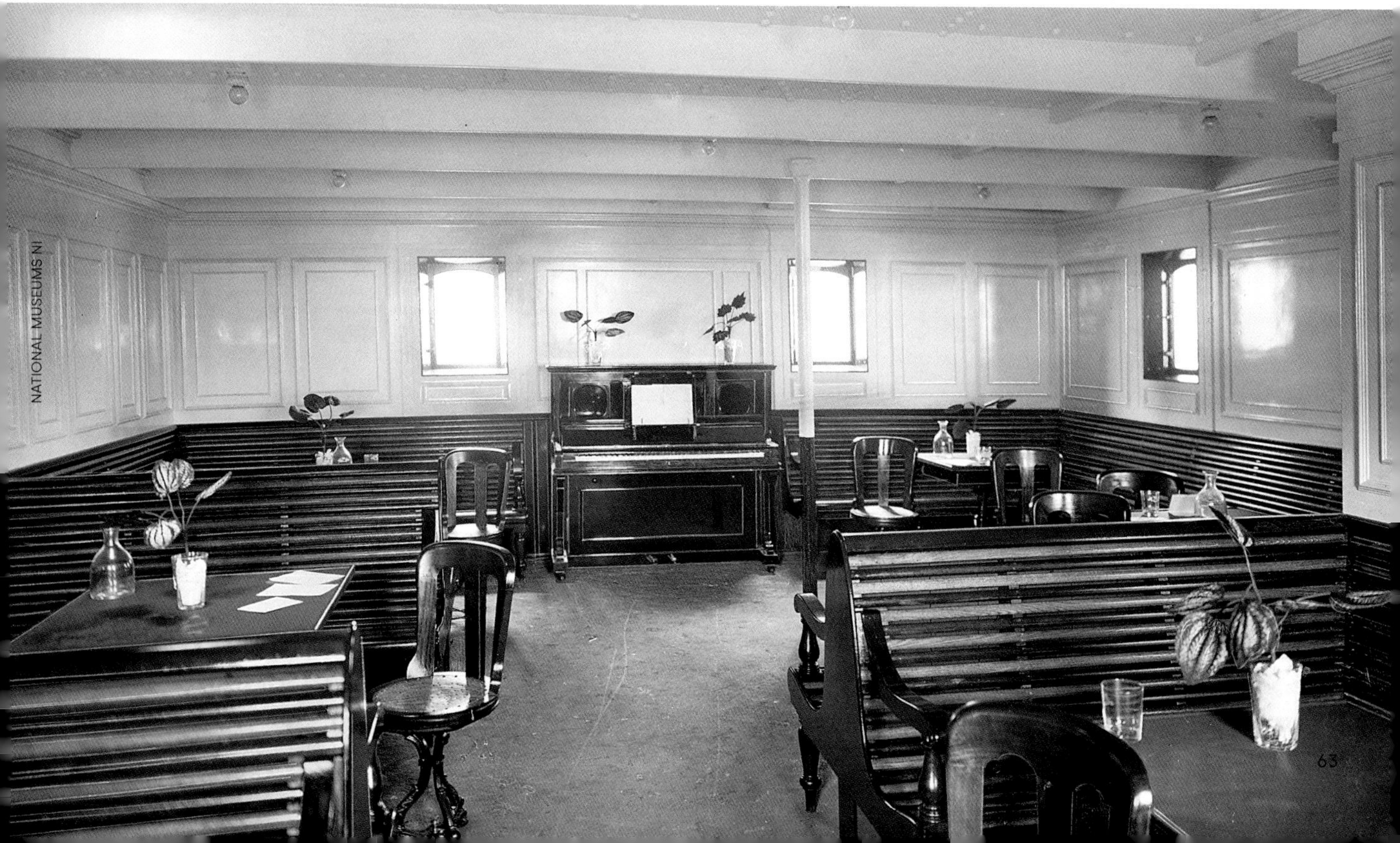

NATIONAL MUSEUMS NI

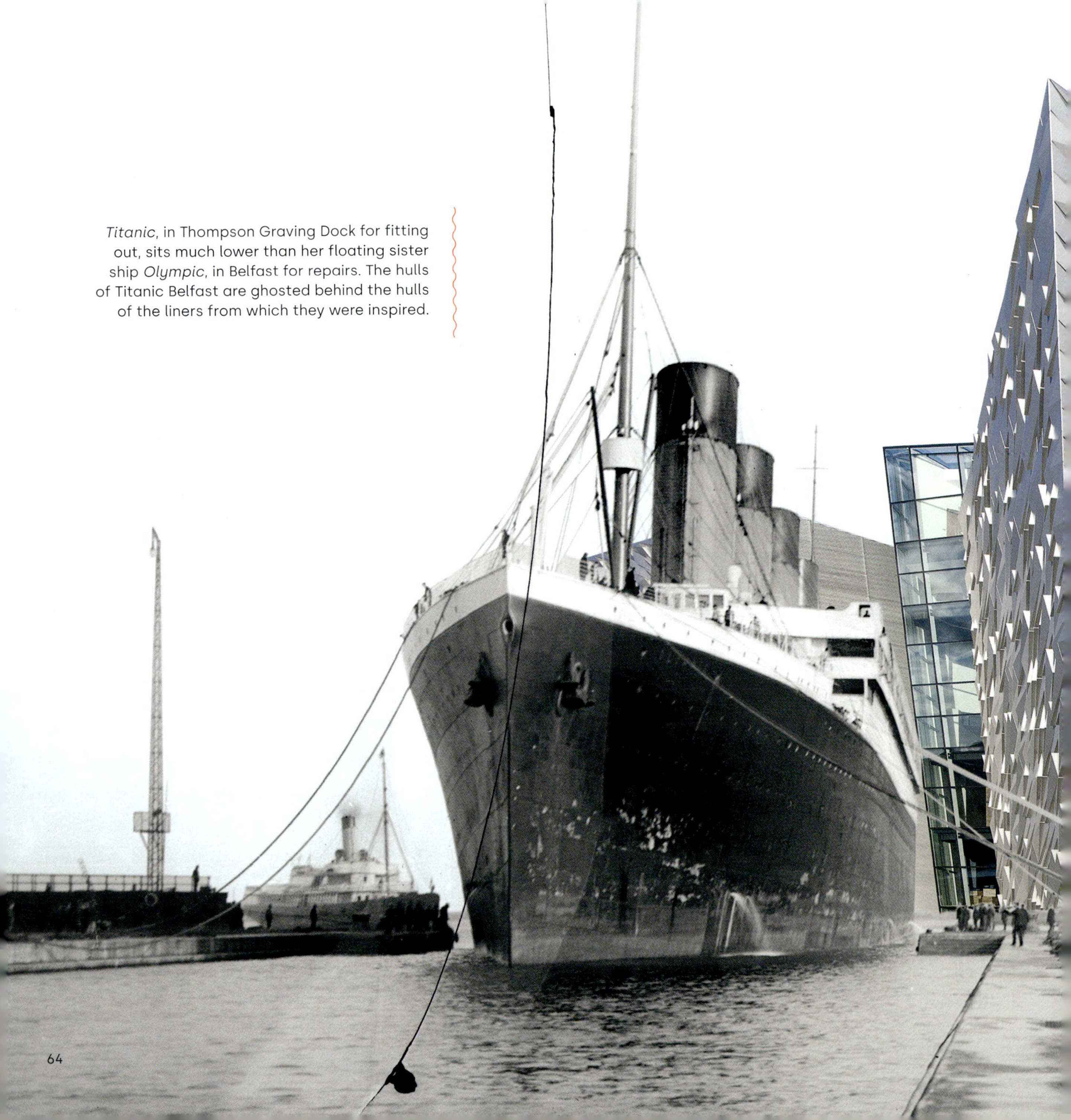

Titanic, in Thompson Graving Dock for fitting out, sits much lower than her floating sister ship *Olympic*, in Belfast for repairs. The hulls of Titanic Belfast are ghosted behind the hulls of the liners from which they were inspired.

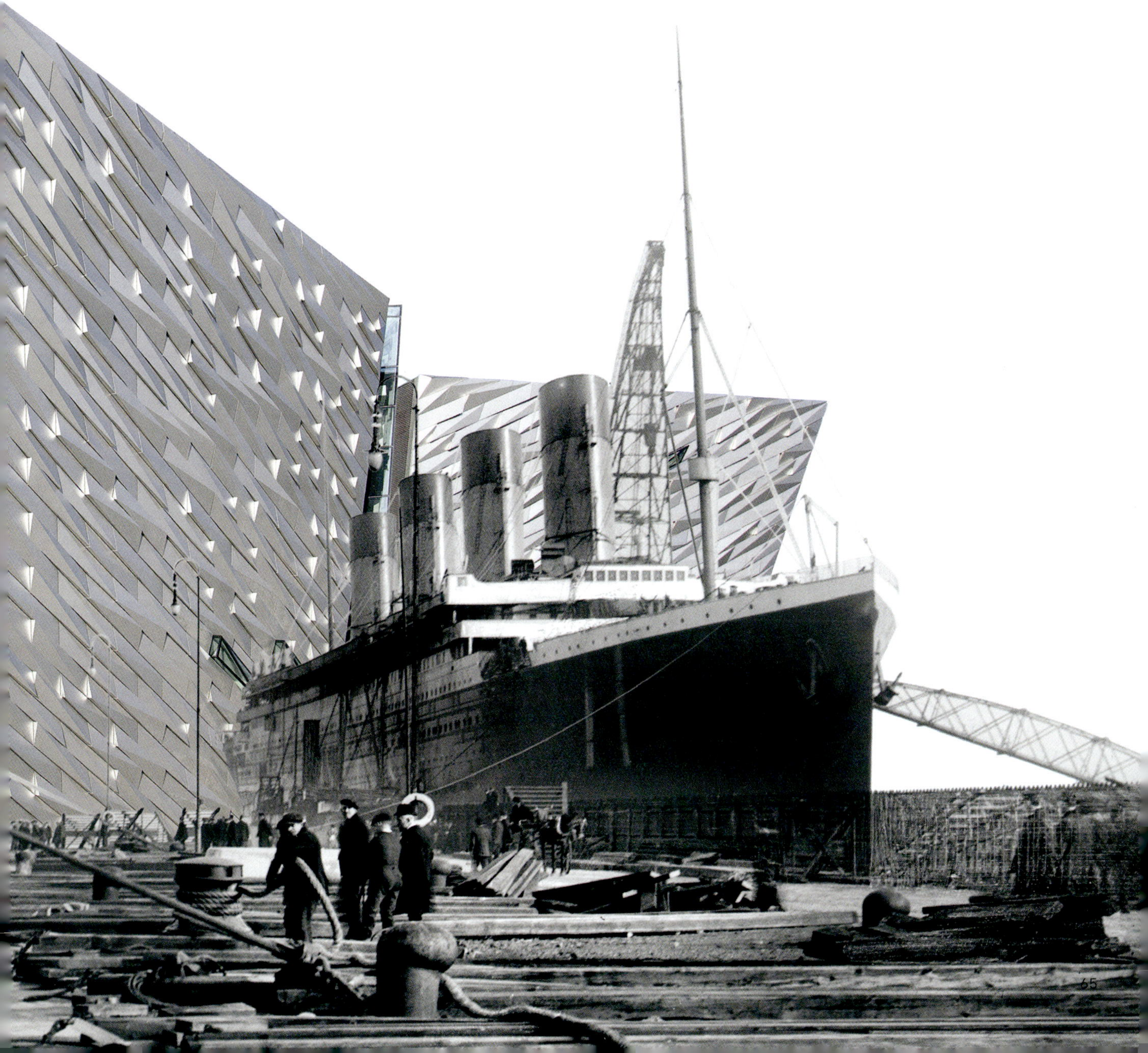

THE MAIDEN VOYAGE

On 2 April 1912, *Titanic* left Belfast for the last time after completing her sea trials. She headed to Southampton to prepare for her maiden voyage. The paperwork was complete. On 25 March 1912, the Board of Trade had certified *Titanic*'s port of registry as Liverpool and her displacement (weight), a mighty 52,310 tons. After successful sea trials to test her engines and equipment, Harland & Wolff formally handed *Titanic* over to White Star. The Board of Trade surveyor signed her certificate of seaworthiness as 'good for one year from today'. On the evening of 2 April, four Liverpool tugs guided *Titanic* down Belfast Lough. On board were 280 seamen and engine room crew, stewards and workmen putting the final touches to her interiors. *Titanic* steamed down the Irish Sea.

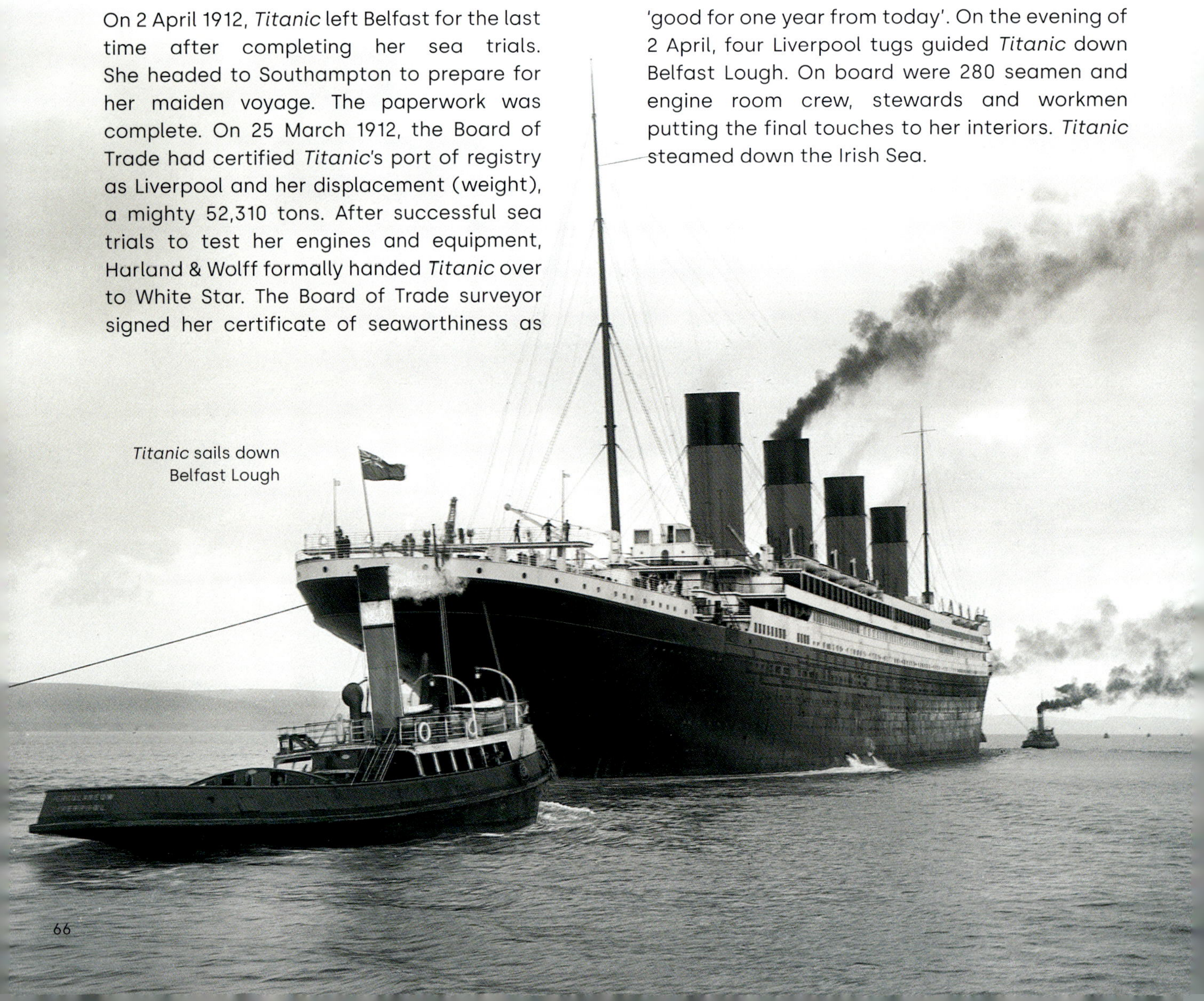

Titanic sails down Belfast Lough

Titanic's maiden voyage timetable

1 April
High winds delay *Titanic*'s sea trials. Captain John Edward Smith takes charge of the ship.

2 April 6am
Tugs escort *Titanic* down Belfast Lough for her sea trials.

2 April 8pm
Titanic leaves Belfast.

4 April early morning
Titanic arrives at Southampton and is dressed in signal flags and pennants to celebrate her maiden voyage.

4-10 April
Provisions, coal and cargo are loaded and her crew come aboard.

10 April noon
After all the Southampton passengers have boarded, *Titanic* leaves on her maiden voyage.

10 April 6.30pm
Titanic arrives at Cherbourg to pick up passengers and mail.

10 April 810pm
Titanic leaves Cherbourg for Queenstown (Cobh), Ireland

11 April 11.30am
Titanic anchors briefly off Queenstown (Cobh) to pick up more passengers and mail.

11 April 1.30pm
Titanic heads into the Atlantic. Her next port of call is New York.

The Guarantee Group

The Guarantee Group was a collection of Harland & Wolff employees selected to travel on the maiden voyage to record the ship's performance and rectify any minor problems that might arise.

The possibility of being part of the Guarantee Group for *Titanic* was motivation for staff to work hard and prove their abilities to the company.

On *Titanic*, the nine-man Guarantee Group ranged from an apprentice plumber to one of the ship's chief designers – Thomas Andrews. None of them survived the sinking.

40,000 eggs and 15,000 bottles of ale

Titanic spent nearly a week in Southampton, taking on cargo, supplies, crew and passengers. Southampton had overtaken Liverpool as Britain's leading trans-Atlantic port. Passengers wanted to be closer to London and mainland Europe. Southampton Water provided room to manoeuvre super-liners. White Star moved its express service there in 1907 and Cunard followed in 1909.

Titanic tied up in Berth 44, White Star Dock, which had been extended for the Olympic-class ships. Quayside cranes travelling on rails loaded stores and cargo. Additional crew especially stewards, waiters and kitchen staff, signed on. Over 600 of *Titanic*'s 885 crew were local to the Southampton area. On the morning of 10 April boat trains from London's Waterloo Station steamed into Southampton. Around 930 travellers crossed the gangway from the new passenger terminal.

At midday, *Titanic* cast off.

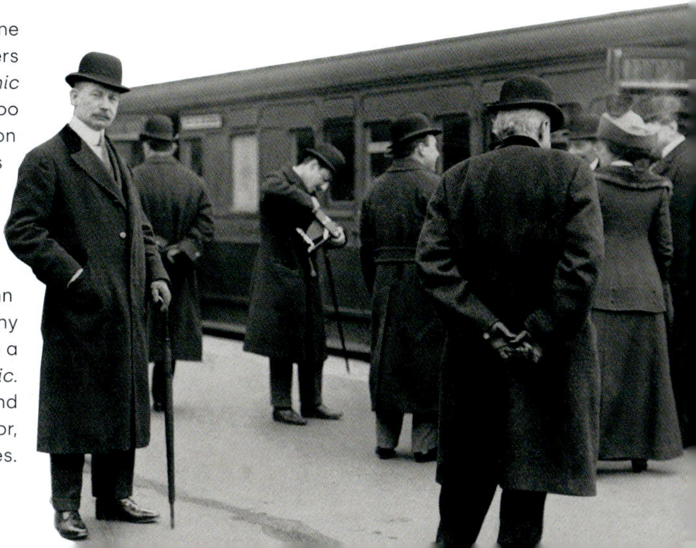

Father Browne photographed passengers boarding the *Titanic* Special train at Waterloo Station to Southampton to join the ship for its maiden voyage to New York. The man in the background is believed to be William Waldorf Astor whose cousin John Jacob Astor IV, a wealthy American industrialist, was a passenger on the *Titanic*. Over 1,500 passengers and crew, including Mr Astor, lost their lives.

Au revoir ... Bon voyage

After crossing the English Channel, *Titanic* arrived in the French port of Cherbourg. She was an hour late due to a near collision in Southampton. *Titanic* had an eventful start to her maiden voyage.

As she left her berth, her wake was so strong that the liner New York broke from her moorings. As New York was sucked towards *Titanic*, a tug crew's fast action prevented a collision.

Cherbourg was the gateway for the growing number of wealthy Americans 'doing Europe'. First Class stewards were busy welcoming 274 passengers. Thirty Second Class and 102 Third Class passengers also joined the ship. Twenty-two passengers disembarked at Cherbourg. Some may have crossed the Channel simply to say that they had sailed on the world's largest ship.

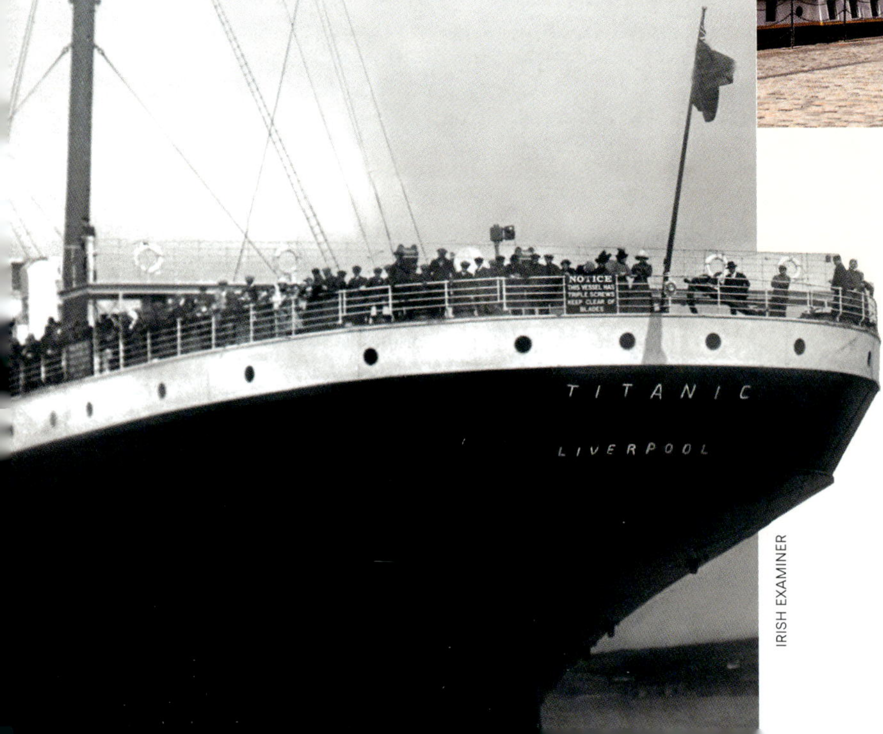

IRISH EXAMINER

Nomadic

White Star's tenders *Nomadic* and *Traffic* – boats for ferrying passengers and luggage – moved between the Cherbourg quayside and *Titanic*, anchored in the outer harbour. Thomas Andrews wrote to his wife: 'The two little tenders look very fine. You will remember we built them last year.'

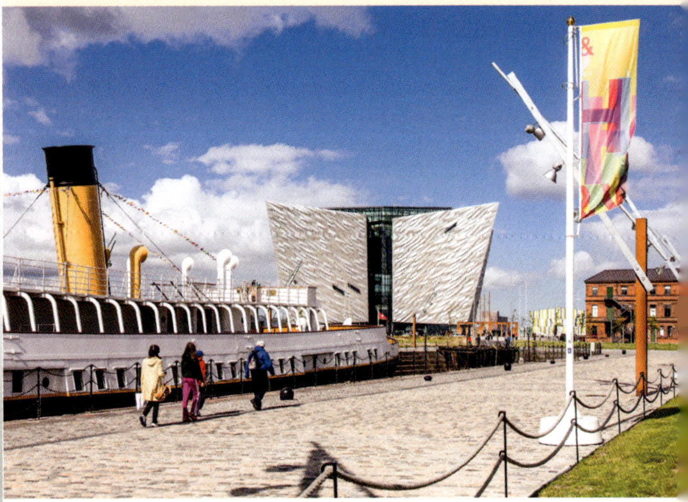

Following a colourful lifetime that included war work *Nomadic* was retired from seafaring duties in 1968 to become a floating restaurant on the River Seine, Paris. In 2006 enthusiasts persuaded the government of Northern Ireland to purchase and restore the vessel to its former glory. The boat can be seen in Hamilton Dock outside Titanic Belfast and admission is included in the Titanic Experience ticket.

Queenstown (Cobh) on the south coast of County Cork was Ireland's main emigration port. *Titanic* called briefly to pick up mail and passengers. Its natural harbour made Cobh an important naval base from the 1800s. The name Cobh was changed to Queenstown in honour of Queen Victoria's visit in 1849.

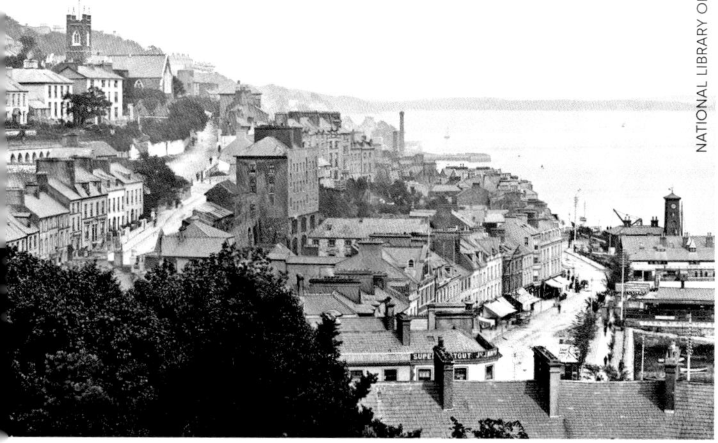

NATIONAL LIBRARY OF IRELAND

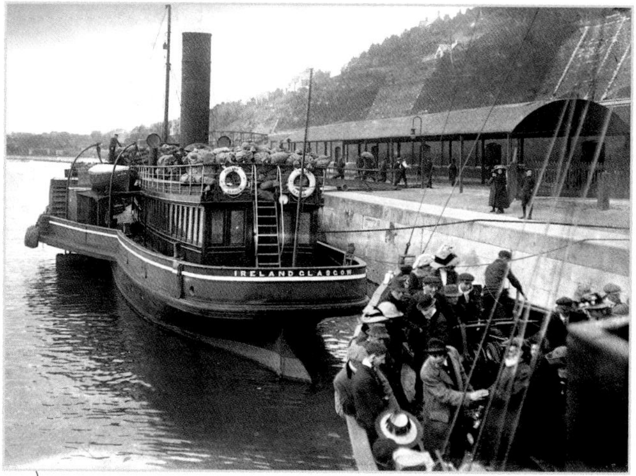

IRISH EXAMINER

A total of 123 passengers embarked at Queenstown. The photograph shows two tenders about to leave Queenstown, carrying cargo and passengers to the liner.

Farewell Europe

Many of the two million emigrants who left Ireland for North America between 1851 and 1921 made their last farewells to family and home on the quayside. Queenstown became known as the 'saddest place in Ireland'.

Titanic anchored offshore as Queenstown's harbour facilities could not handle so large a vessel. Three First, seven Second, and 113 Third Class passengers, 100 of whom were Irish emigrants, joined the ship. *Titanic*'s onboard sorting office received 194 sacks of mail, Queenstown being the last pick-up point for North America.

At 1.30pm, *Titanic* left Queenstown. Second Class passenger Lawrence Beesley recalled, 'The last we saw of Europe was the Irish mountains.'

'Get off that ship'

Frank Browne, a passenger sailing from Southampton to Queenstown, was a keen photographer. He made a unique record of the start of *Titanic*'s maiden voyage.

Born into a wealthy Cork family in 1880, Frank Browne took up photography as a young man on a tour of Europe. His uncle, the Bishop of Cloyne had gifted him the camera. Later he gave him a more unusual present – a ticket for *Titanic*'s maiden voyage from Southampton to Queenstown. At the time Frank was training to become a Jesuit priest.

An American couple so enjoyed Frank's company that they offered to pay his fare to New York. On learning of this, Frank's Superior cabled: 'GET OFF THAT SHIP – PROVINCIAL.' Frank obeyed and his Superior's strict orders almost certainly saved his life.

After the disaster Frank's photographs appeared in newspapers round the world.

It is thanks to Father Browne that we have a unique visual record of *Titanic*'s maiden voyage. The series starts at London's Waterloo Station with passengers boarding the '*Titanic* Special'. It ends with *Titanic* steaming into the open Atlantic. By the time *Titanic* sank, Frank was back at his studies in Dublin.

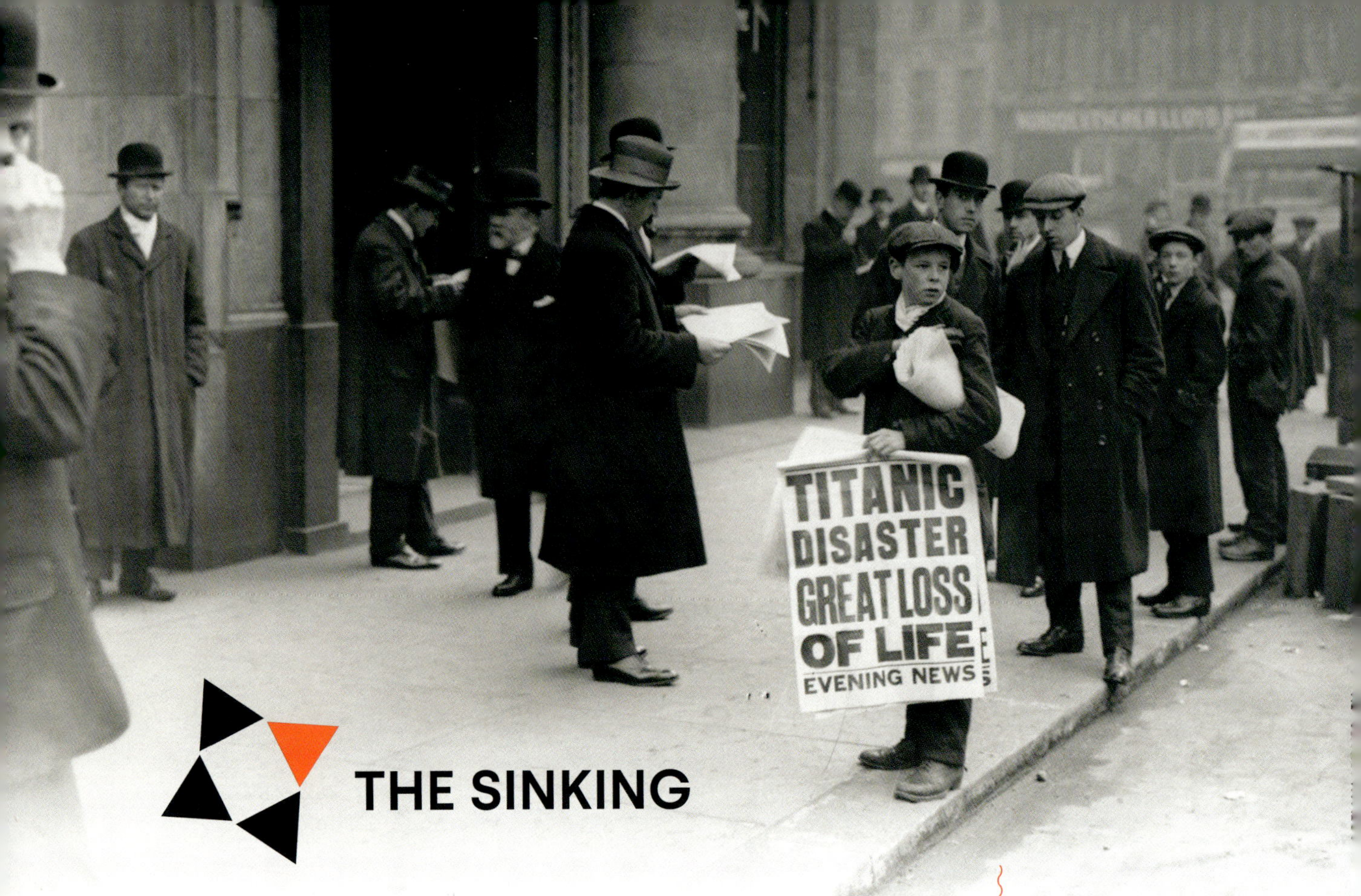

Newsboy Ned Parfett announcing the sinking of the *Titanic* outside the offices of the White Star Line, Oceanic House, London on 16 April 1912.

THE SINKING

Titanic sailed for New York on 10 April 1912 with 2,225 passengers and crew. On the night of 14 April, disaster struck as she hit an iceberg on her right side at high speed. Five of her sixteen compartments were flooded, but the ship was not designed to stay afloat with more than four damaged compartments. In barely two and a half hours, *Titanic* had disappeared into the ocean causing the death of 1,517 people. She was carrying lifeboats for only 1,178 people. These small boats were not even full when they left.

Titanic broke in two as she sank with hundreds of people on board. Among the travellers who fell or jumped into the water, many died from hypothermia.

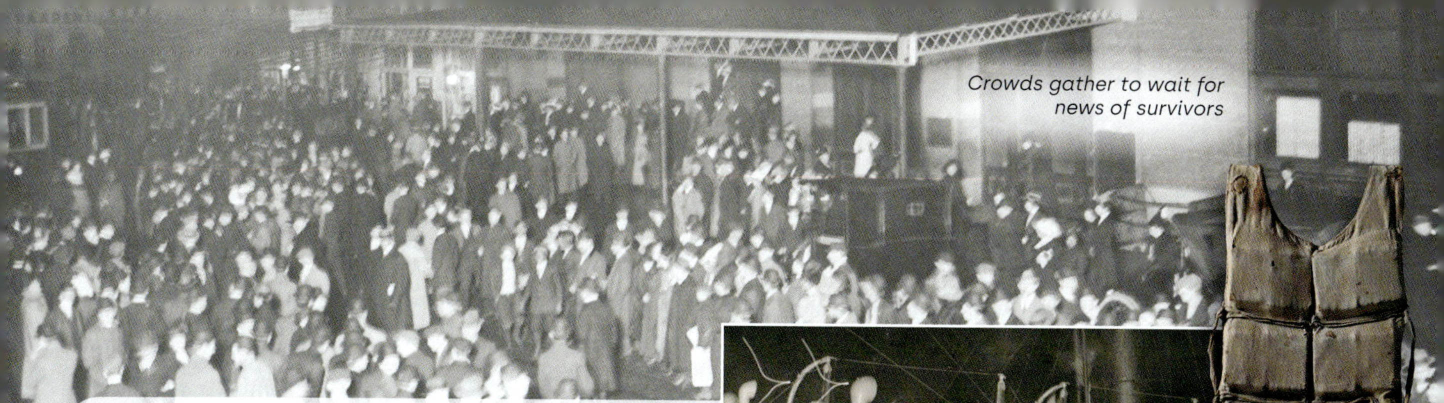

Crowds gather to wait for news of survivors

UNDERWOOD PHOTO ARCHIVE

Belfast in mourning

Belfast mourned its dead and the loss of the ship on which so many workers had left their mark. Anxious relatives queued outside the office of Whiting & Tedford, the White Star Line agents in Victoria Street.

The Belfast Newsletter described the mood of the city: 'Wherever one went – in the train, the tram or in the street – one heard the disaster discussed, and in the hearts of all there appeared to be a feeling of sorrow too deep to express itself in words.'

On Saturday 20 April, Belfast was silent when Harland & Wolff closed as a mark of respect. None of the bodies of the Guarantee Group from the yard were ever recovered.

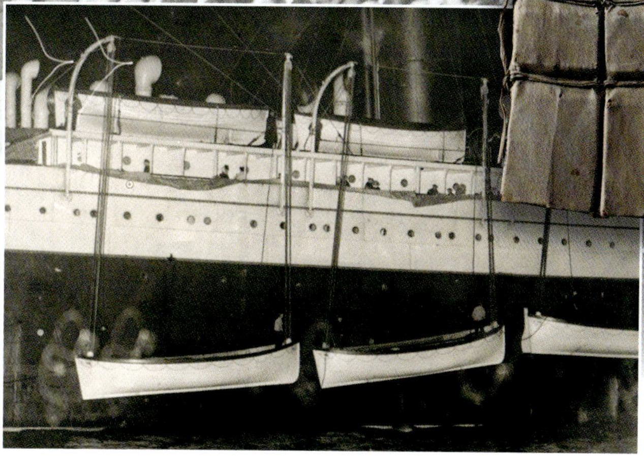

CORBIS UK LTD

Titanic's lifeboats on the side of Carpathia

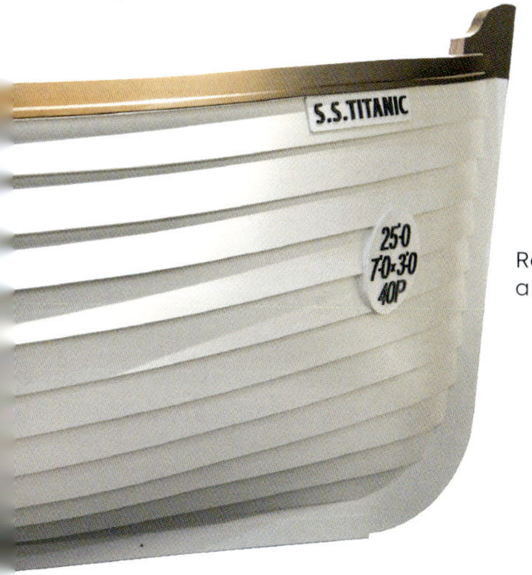

Replica of a *Titanic* lifeboat

Carpathia

Carpathia was the first ship to reach the scene of the disaster. She picked up 713 passengers and crew from the lifeboats and made for New York. Captain Arthur Rostron, commander of Cunard's liner *Carpathia*, was heading from New York to the Mediterranean. He had turned in for the night when his wireless operator burst into his cabin with the news of *Titanic*'s distress signals. He ordered *Carpathia* to turn around under full steam. At 4.10am, *Carpathia* sighted a lifeboat. The first passenger rescued, Elizabeth Allen, informed *Carpathia*'s purser that *Titanic* had sunk. Four hours later, *Carpathia* had found the twenty boats and rescued 713 passengers and crew, and Rostron decided to go back to New York.

Conflicting rumours

Lack of information led to conflicting rumours about *Titanic*'s fate. Harold Cottam, *Carpathia*'s only wireless operator worked round the clock forwarding the names of survivors and sending messages to relatives. He ignored press enquiries.

No language can describe the pity and horror

The news spread around the world. As the days passed, local newspapers started to feature stories of interest to their readers. For days, newspaper reports remained inaccurate. The time difference between the US and Europe did not help. The latest news did not reach London in time for the next day's first editions.

Enthusiastic reporters used their imagination to fill in gaps in information. Survivors added to the confusion as individuals remembered the details of those dreadful hours very differently. Newspaper coverage was strongest in cities associated with *Titanic* – Belfast, Liverpool, Southampton, New York and Halifax.

On 17 April, the first death notices appeared in local papers. On 19 April, the American press started to ask who was to blame.

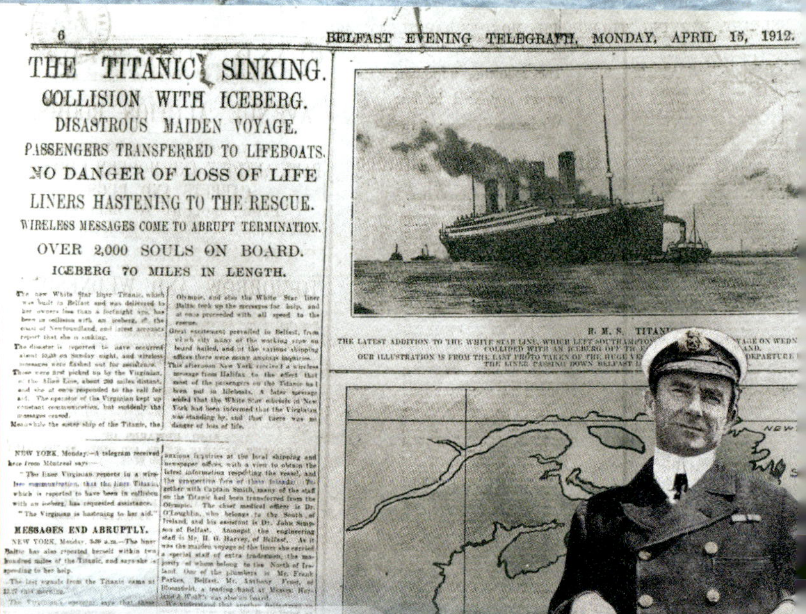

6 BELFAST EVENING TELEGRAPH, MONDAY, APRIL 15, 1912.

THE TITANIC SINKING.

COLLISION WITH ICEBERG.

DISASTROUS MAIDEN VOYAGE.

PASSENGERS TRANSFERRED TO LIFEBOATS.

NO DANGER OF LOSS OF LIFE

LINERS HASTENING TO THE RESCUE.

WIRELESS MESSAGES COME TO ABRUPT TERMINATION.

OVER 2,000 SOULS ON BOARD.

ICEBERG 70 MILES IN LENGTH.

MESSAGES END ABRUPTLY.

R. M. S. TITANIC

First reports in the 15 April edition of the *Belfast Telegraph* erroneously said there was no loss of life

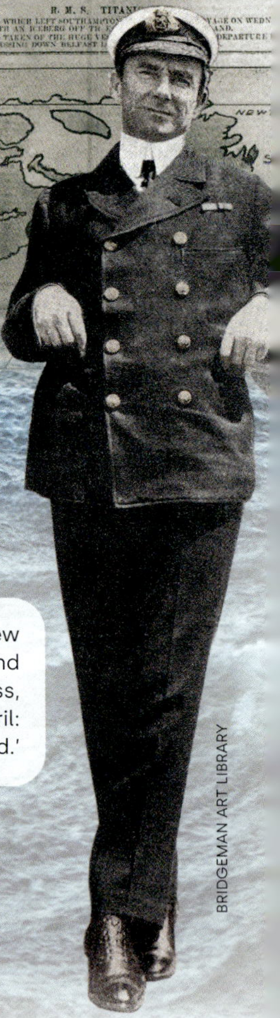

The man whom everyone wanted to interview was Captain Rostron. Exhausted and under orders not to talk to the press, he issued a short statement on 19 April: 'I am all done up and cannot say a word.'

BRIDGEMAN ART LIBRARY

'Funeral Ship *Carpathia* Brings First Story.'

The full horror of the *Titanic* disaster was revealed when *Carpathia* docked in New York late on 18 April. Watched by a crowd of 30,000, *Carpathia* arrived at Pier 54 at 9.30pm. Many survivors were too exhausted, injured or shocked to appreciate the sensation that their arrival caused. Some Irish women were so frightened by the crowd that they refused to leave *Carpathia*. Some passengers like Mrs Turrell Cavendish were happy to talk to the press about their experience: 'The time we spent in that small boat after those noble, heroic men went down were hours of torture.' Some claimed that everyone could have been saved had there been enough lifeboats.

'The terrible cry'

One celebrity survivor was film actress Dorothy Gibson who, only weeks later, starred in the first film about the disaster. She was returning from a holiday in Europe with her mother. She told *Moving Picture World*: 'I will never forget the terrible cry that rang out from people who were thrown into the sea and others who were afraid for their loved ones.'

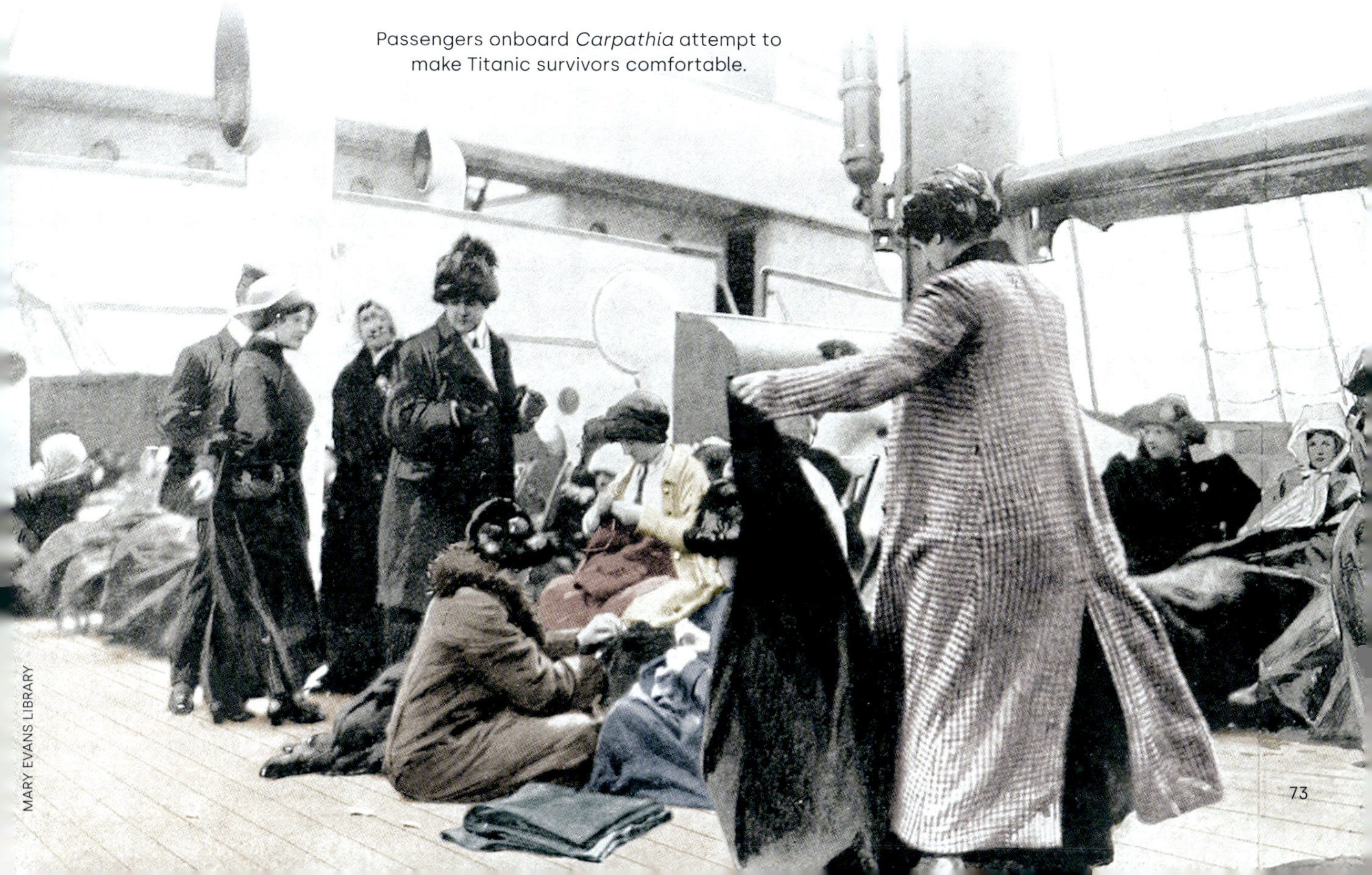

Passengers onboard *Carpathia* attempt to make Titanic survivors comfortable.

The baby in a postbag!

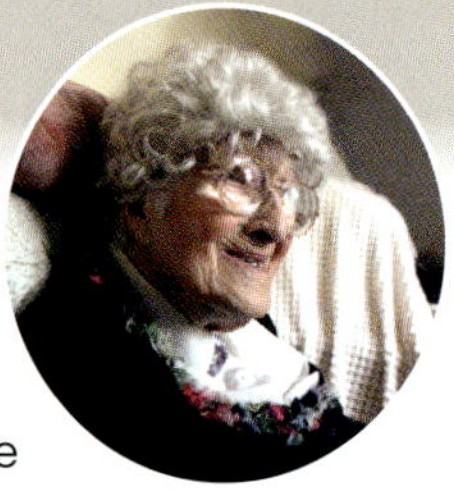

Miss Millvina Dean was one of the children rescued with her brother from *Titanic*; she was only nine weeks old at the time. Millvena was handed out to a lifeboat in a postbag and ferried to safety. Five days before her death, an interviewer jokingly asked her if she could remember the sinking. She replied, 'No, I could not see out of the bag!' Miss Dean was the last survivor from *Titanic*: she died on her 98th birthday, 31 May 2009, which is also the anniversary of *Titanic*'s launch...

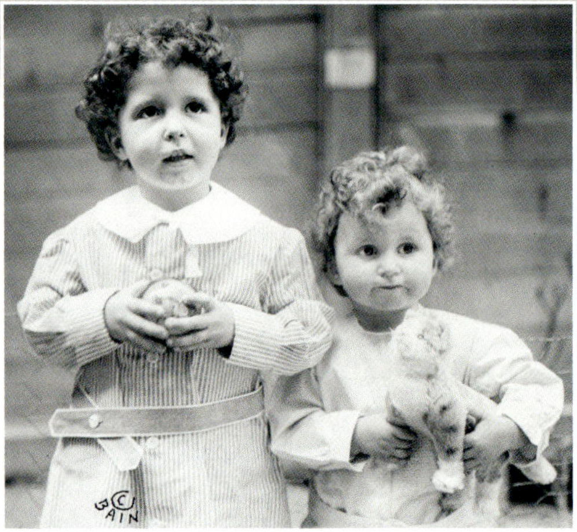

BAIN COLLECTION LIBRARY OF CONGRESS

The *Titanic* 'orphans'

Marcelle Navratil, from France, did not know that her two young sons, Michel and Edmond, were on *Titanic*. She was separated from her husband, who kidnapped the boys and took them with him on his way to the United States. He had told passengers that their mother was dead.

The father died when *Titanic* sank, but Michel and Edmond survived: Marcelle recognised them from a photograph in a French newspaper telling the story about the two rescued 'orphaned' boys, who were soon reunited with their mother.

'His last act was to save a child's life.'

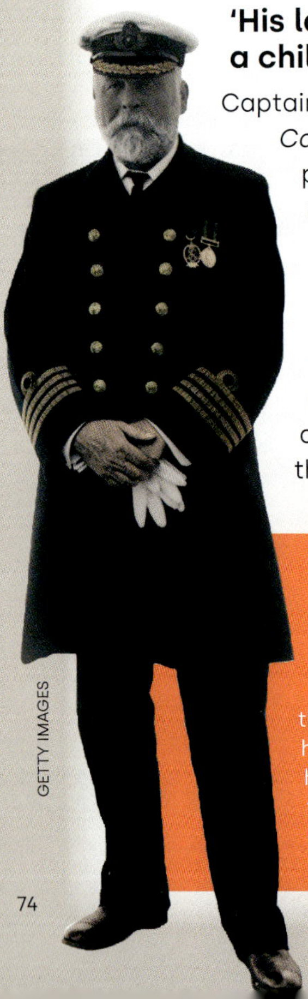

GETTY IMAGES

Captain Rostron and the crews of *Titanic* and *Carpathia* were forbidden to talk. The press had to rely on other survivors to make heroes of the crew.

Captain Rostron and *Carpathia*'s officers were instant heroes. First Class passenger Adolphe Saalfeld told the press, 'They did all that was possible to make us comfortable, and to those that were sick or injured, they gave their most tender care.'

Survivors wanted Captain Smith to have died like a hero. 'The water on the bridge was to Captain Smith's waist. I saw him no more. He died a hero.' Accounts of the captain's fate differed wildly – he shot himself on the bridge; he dived overboard; he rescued a child but refused a place in the lifeboat. 'The ice-caked sea closed over his head forever.'

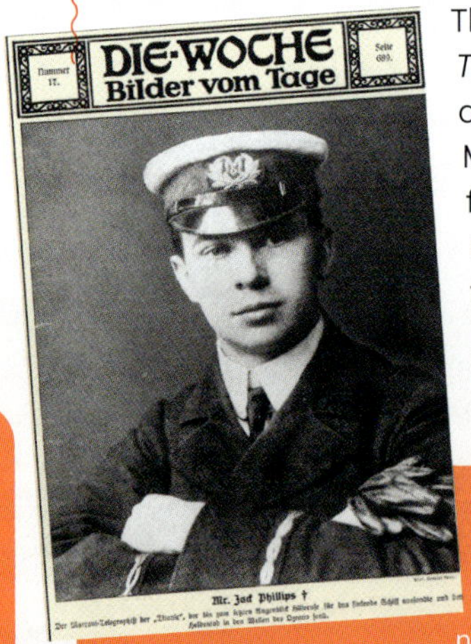

DIE·WOCHE
Bilder vom Tage

Mr. Jack Phillips †

As a Marconi employee, Harold Bride was free to sell his story to the newspapers.
He spoke of his fellow operator Jack Phillips. 'I suddenly felt for him a great reverence to see him standing there sticking to his work while everybody else was raging about.'

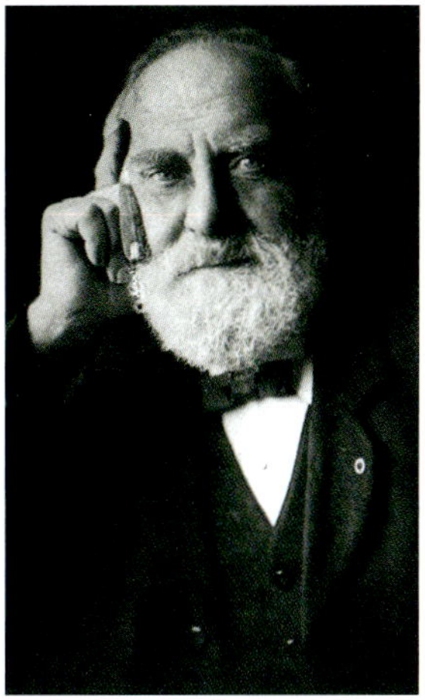

'I'll die either from lynching or drowning'

This was claimed by William Stead, a famous British journalist, who, in 1886, wrote an article *How The Mail Steamer Went Down In Mid-Atlantic, By a Survivor*, in which many people die because of a lack of lifeboats. Six years later, in 1892, he published a story titled *From The Old World To The New:* featuring a White Star Line vessel, *Majestic*, that rescues survivors from a vessel that has collided with an iceberg. In the book, Edward John Smith was the captain of that liner! Ten years later, William Stead sailed on *Titanic's* maiden voyage; a psychic friend urged him not to. He drowned: Captain Smith could not rescue him, he was now *Titanic*'s captain.

'Comb, razor, purse, tobacco pouch'

The Halifax authorities devised a very efficient system to record the bodies and prepare them for burial.

Laden with coffins, *Mackay-Bennett* arrived in Halifax on 30 April. Church bells tolled and flags flew at half-mast. Around a hundred relatives gathered to claim their dead.

White Star and government officials were ready to receive the bodies. They converted the Mayflower Curling Rink into a temporary morgue and recruited undertakers. The police guarded the bodies round the clock, burning clothing to deter souvenir hunters. White Star set up a centre for distressed relatives.

Its identifying number followed each corpse to the mortuary, the coroner's office and the grave. The coroner's report and list of possessions reduced an individual's life into a few lines.

'All floating face upwards'

The search for bodies was harrowing. Only a fifth of the victims were ever found. Ships brought 209 bodies to Halifax and buried over 100 at sea.

On 20 April, *Mackay-Bennett*, a cable-repair ship chartered by White Star, arrived at the wreck site. On board were 125 coffins, ice, materials to preserve the bodies, an undertaker and his assistant, a clergyman and crew.

The captain compared the first sight of the bodies to 'a flock of sea gulls resting upon the water'. Small boats were lowered to pick up corpses. On *Mackay-Bennett* crew noted features like the sex and hair colour of each body. They attached a number to each corpse and the same number to a canvas bag containing any personal belongings. Insufficient coffins had been provided. As there were not enough coffins, many bodies were simply wrapped in canvas and lowered into the sea.

White Star contracted other ships to continue the *Mackay-Bennett*'s work. The search was called off around 25 May when the last ship found only one body. Wind and ocean currents had scattered the rest.

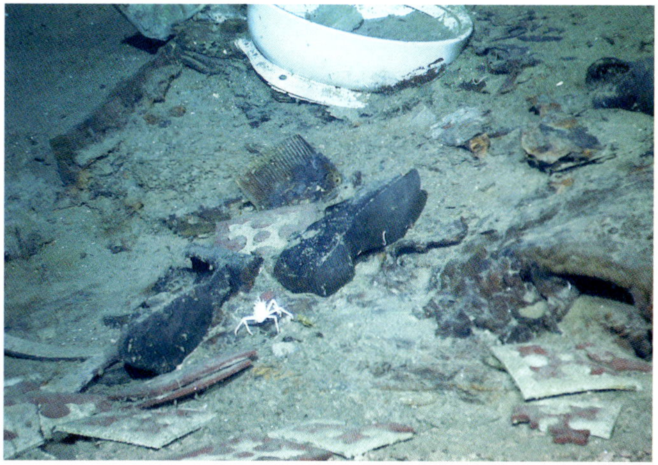

Personal belongings remain on the seabed of the Atlantic

Frederick Wormald

White Star paid for the wife and six children of saloon steward Frederick Wormald to travel on *Olympic* to claim his body. They were refused entry at New York as having 'no visible means of support'. They returned to Southampton to discover that they had lost their home. Although an Anglican, Wormald was buried in the Jewish cemetery by mistake.

No 4 – Male – Estimated Age, 2

The cemeteries have their own, poignant stories to tell.

Mackay-Bennett's crew found body No 4 floating on its own. They were so moved that they carried the infant's tiny coffin to its last resting place in Fairview Lawn Cemetery and paid for his headstone. His grave has become an icon for all the young lives lost.

J Bruce Ismay personally paid for headstones for his private secretary and a favourite steward. The latter's epitaph read: 'He remained at his post of duty, seeking to save others, regardless of his own life and went down with the ship.'

'Died 15 April 1912'

There were almost daily funerals throughout May and early June in Halifax's three cemeteries.

White Star purchased plots of land in Halifax's three cemeteries and funded the burials and upkeep of the graves. Fairview Lawn Cemetery was the last resting place for 121 victims who were believed to be Protestant. Mount Olivet Catholic Cemetery received nineteen burials and the Baron de Hirsch Jewish Cemetery ten.

White Star paid for a simple granite headstone for each of the 150 bodies that were not claimed by relatives. These were mainly Third Class passengers and crew. Each headstone gave the deceased's name if known, body number and the date 15 April 1912.

Despite photographs of missing persons being published in the press, forty-four bodies were not identified.

Families praised the orderly and compassionate handling of the remains of their loved ones. Some paid for more elaborate headstones: the families of fifty-nine wealthier victims chose to transport their bodies for burial elsewhere. Eight were shipped back to Britain.

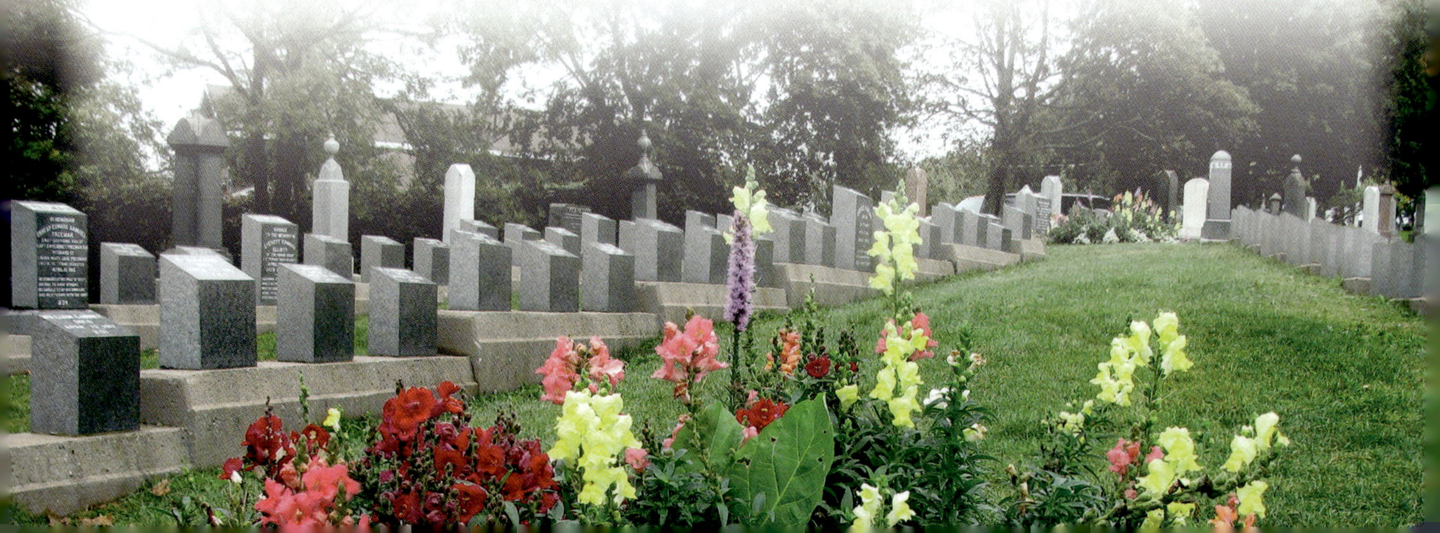

Halifax *Titanic* Graveyard, Fairview Lawn, where 121 victims were buried.

'For emergent needs – $200'

People wanted to express their grief in practical ways. They gave money towards the support of victims' families and memorials of the tragedy.

A Women's Relief Committee was set up in New York to deal with survivors' immediate needs – clothing, transport and money. One of the saddest cases was that of a young girl who had lost her brother. She refused a black dress as she had not yet given up hope.

The Red Cross dealt with loss of property and cases of hardship in North America. Newspaper magnate William Randolph Hearst launched the American *Titanic* Fund, which raised over $50,000. In Britain, the Lord Mayor's Fund cared for bereaved relatives.

The citizens of Belfast donated £12,000 to the Fund.

Harland & Wolff looked after the families of its employees. In May, the Ismays gave £55,000 to start a fund for the widows of seamen lost at sea including *Titanic*'s crew. J Bruce Ismay also raised money towards a memorial in Liverpool, one of many that soon appeared in places as far apart as Antrim and Australia.

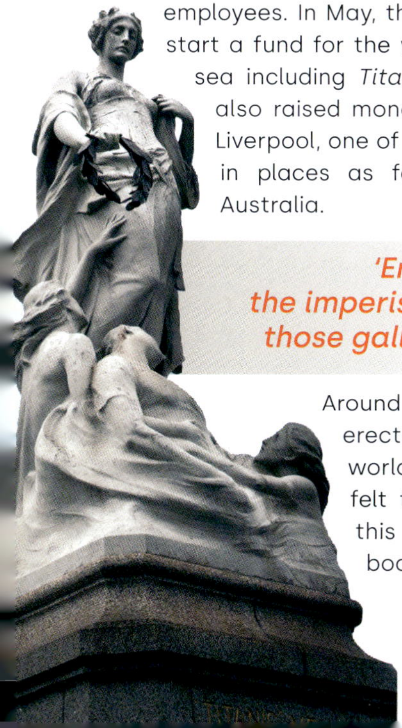

'Erected to the imperishable memory of those gallant Belfast men'

Around 400 memorials have been erected in twenty-one countries worldwide. People particularly felt the need to remember in this way because so many bodies were never found.

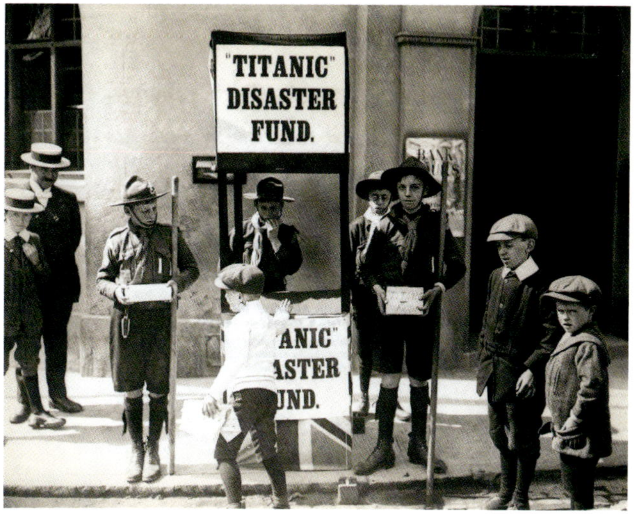

Boy scouts collect for *Titanic* Disaster Fund

Cities with strong *Titanic* associations were among the first to erect public memorials. By September 1912, Sir Thomas Brock was working on a statue of the Greek goddess of death, which now stands outside Belfast's City Hall. The engineers, so many of whom perished, were remembered in Southampton and Liverpool.

From Captain Smith to a young Swiss restaurant worker, individual crewmembers were also honoured. The leader of *Titanic*'s band, Wallace Hartley, is the most honoured individual, memorials to him including a bandstand in Ballarat, Australia.

Other communities also chose practical ways to remember individuals. Couples still renew their vows in New York's Straus Memorial Park. The Thomas Andrews Memorial Hall in Comber, County Down is now part of a primary school.

A revival of interest in *Titanic* led to new memorials. In 2002, the Addergoole Titanic Society, County Mayo commemorated the greatest passenger loss to any community in relation to its population size.

NEVER AGAIN

Apart from those on board *Carpathia*, there were no other survivors of the disaster following the loss of *Titanic*. In order to discover the cause of the tragedy, two investigations were initiated just a few days later.

'You have had a large experience of ice?'

The British Wreck Commissioner's Inquiry was longer and more formal than the American Investigation. It relied more on experts than the memories of survivors. Lawyer and former MP Charles Bigham, Lord Mersey chaired the British Inquiry that opened on 2 May. He had maritime experts to guide him.

The investigation sought answers to twenty-six specific questions, covering construction, operation, the sinking and the rescue.

The only passengers to give evidence were J Bruce Ismay, Sir Cosmo and Lady Duff-Gordon, who proved a media sensation. The Duff-Gordons were summoned to answer allegations that they had prevented their half-empty lifeboat from turning back to look for survivors by bribing the crew.

They feared that the boat might be swamped.

Although criticising their behaviour, Lord Mersey rejected the bribery charge.

Experienced seamen supported Captain Smith's decisions. Antarctic explorer Ernest Shackleton was the one voice of dissent. From his experience of sailing through ice, *Titanic* was going too fast.

'Sufficient for all persons on board'

The British Inquiry made twenty-four recommendations to avoid such a disaster happening again. The Inquiry presented its report to both Houses of Parliament on 30 July.

It concluded the loss of *Titanic*, 'was due to collision with an iceberg, brought about by the excessive speed at which the ship was being navigated.'

It acknowledged conditions at sea were unusual and dismissed claims Third Class passengers had been treated badly.

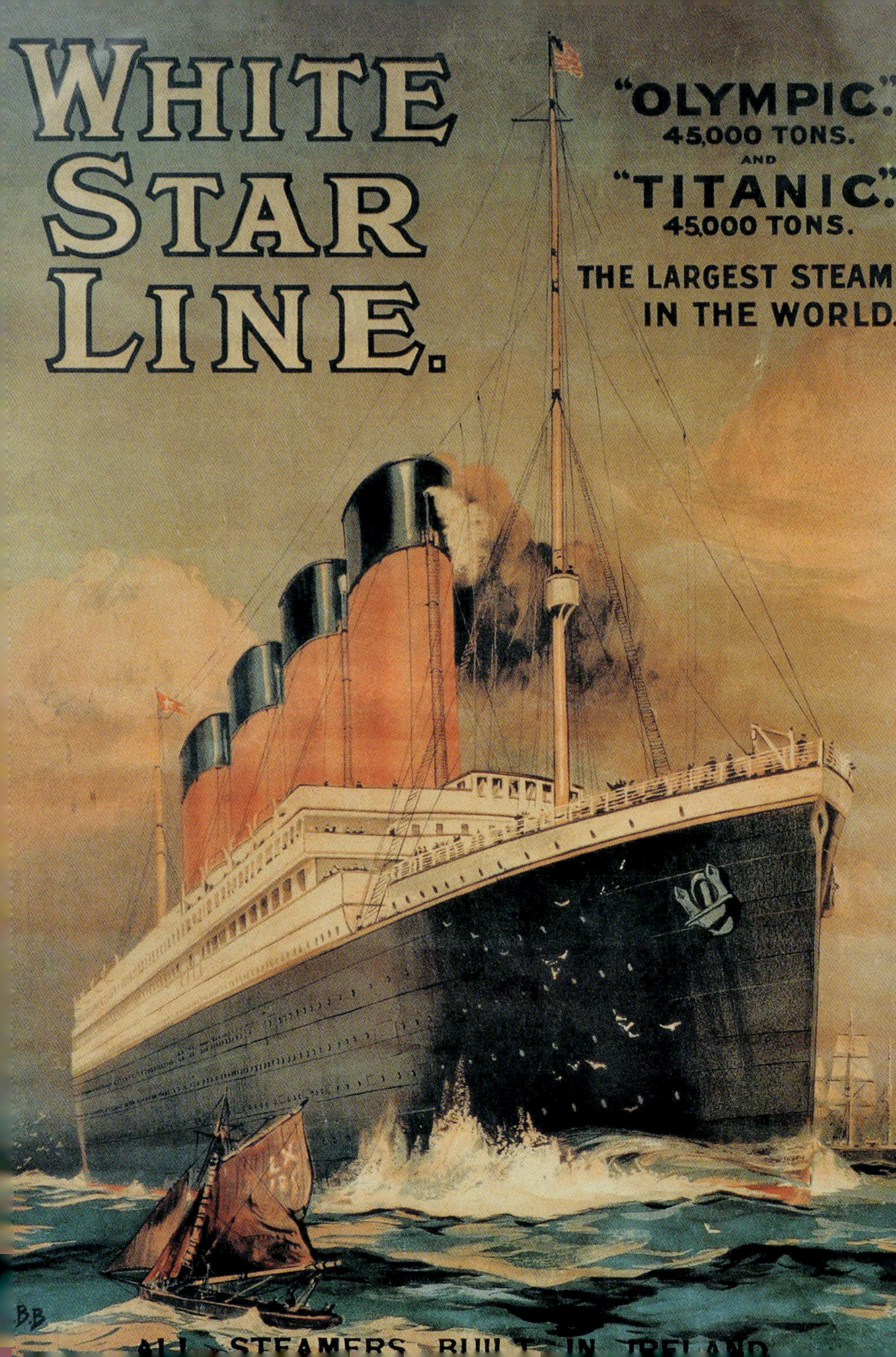

Its recommendations included:

- Lifeboat and raft accommodation to be based on the number of people carried rather than tonnage.
- More 'searching' lifeboat inspections by the Board of Trade and better training for crew.
- Ships to slow down or change course at night after ice warnings.
- All foreign-going passenger and emigrant ships to operate wireless twenty-four hours a day.
- A new Bulkhead Committee to consider design changes to aspects of ship construction.

'Strange Questions at the *Titanic* Inquiry'

Only two days after the disaster, Republican Senator Alden Smith demanded an inquiry. He persuaded President Taft to send a vessel to accompany *Carpathia* into New York in case J Bruce Ismay tried to escape. Ismay was the first witness called, protected by bodyguards because of the hate campaign against him in the press.

The US Senate Inquiry began the day after *Carpathia* docked. Passengers and crew were questioned in an attempt to find out exactly what happened and why.

The Inquiry lasted eighteen days and questioned eighty-six witnesses, from the lookouts to some of the last men to jump from the sinking ship. Republican Senator Alden Smith was an enthusiastic, energetic and hands-on chairman, suspicious of big business and impatient with out-of-date laws. He claimed no experience of maritime or legal matters and some of his questions, such as 'what were icebergs made of', – were so simple that he became a figure of fun in the British press. His criticism of British ships and laws were seen as attacks on the whole nation.

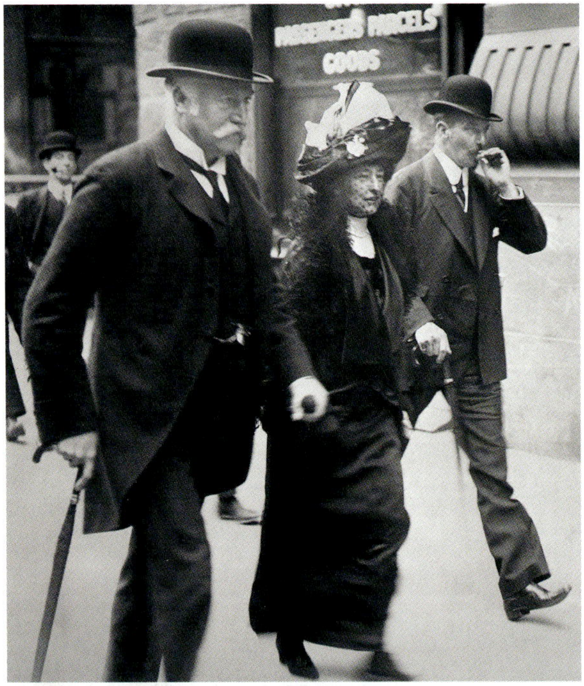

'Very few important facts escaped our scrutiny.'

As well as recommendations for safer shipping, the Inquiry provided a gripping first-hand account of the disaster. Many books and films have drawn on its evidence.

On 28 May, Senator Smith delivered his findings in a two-hour address to Congress. He could not prosecute individuals but only suggest changes to the law.

He concluded that:

- Captain Smith's indifference to danger was a direct cause of the disaster.
- More Third Class passengers died because they were given no warning.
- Loading the lifeboats was poorly organised with many not being full.
- Some crew did not report to their lifeboat stations and watched others drown.
- The lifeboats were badly crewed and ill-equipped.
- Wireless stations should be manned 24 hours a day.
- Operators' wages should be increased to discourage them from making money out of tragedies.
- Captain Lord of Californian did not assist the stricken ship.
- Captain Rostron of Carpathia deserved an honour.
- Although Ismay was not to blame for *Titanic*'s speed, his presence on board encouraged it.

J Bruce Ismay, his wife and Harold Arthur Sanderson, Vice President of International Mercantile Marine Company, on their way to the British Inquiry.

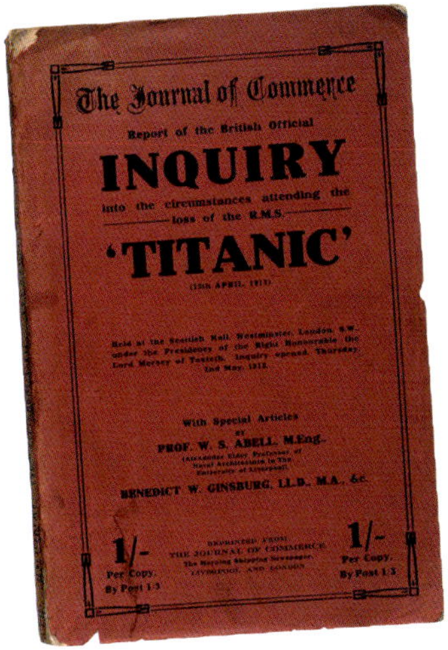

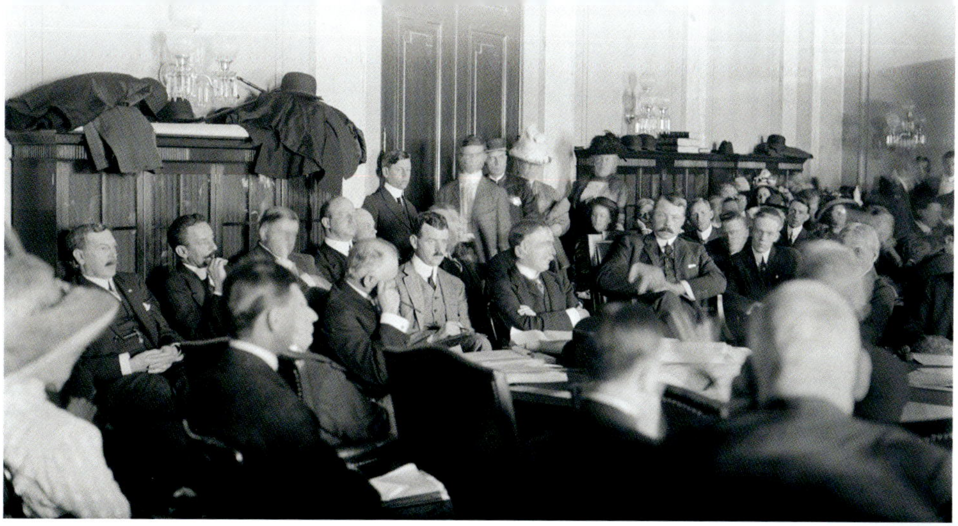

Courtroom scene for the *Titanic* Inquiry

Making the seas safer

Following the Inquiries, new laws were passed to improve safety at sea.

New laws included:

- Everyone was guaranteed a place on a lifeboat. Passengers were advised of their lifeboat station and crews received regular training in lifeboat drill. All lifeboats carried food and water, a compass and other equipment.
- All ocean-going vessels had to have a radio room manned twenty-four hours a day. Wireless operators reported directly to the captain as crewmembers.
- Safety and navigation signals took priority over commercial radio traffic. A quiet time was set aside every hour to give distress calls a better chance of being picked up. SOS became the standard emergency call. Firing rockets at sea was banned except in emergencies.
- The southern of the two North Atlantic shipping lanes was moved to avoid icebergs. An international ice patrol still monitors the shipping lanes for icebergs.
- Passenger ships are now required to be evacuated within thirty minutes in the event of an emergency.

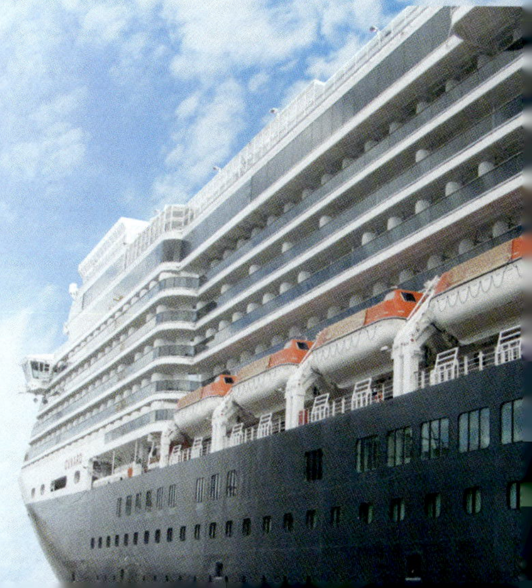

The cruise ship *Queen Victoria* docked at Belfast Harbour in 2010 is well-equipped with safety equipment

Titanic's sisters *Olympic* and *Britannic*

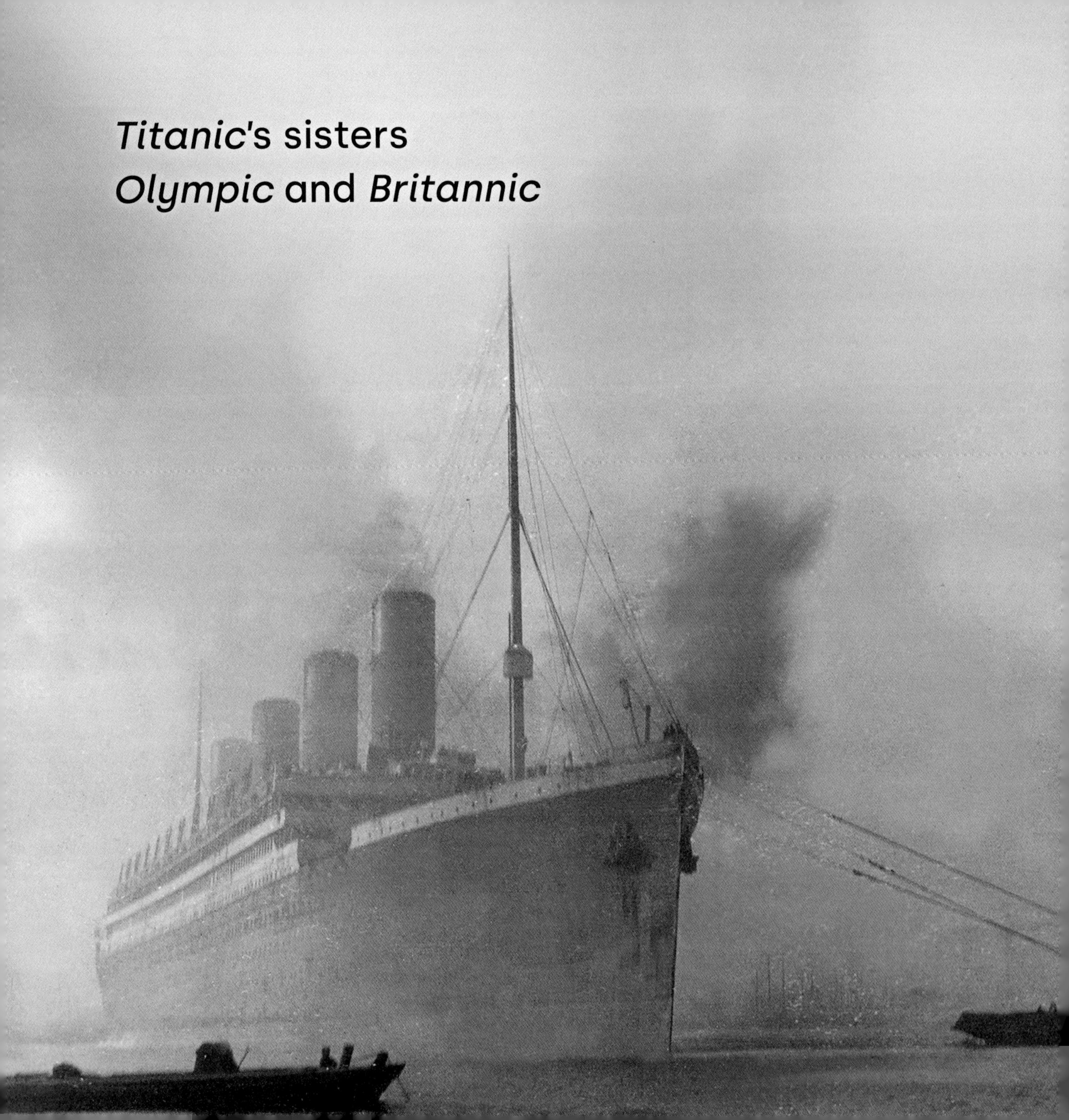

'*Britannic* goes down in 55 minutes'

Britannic, White Star's third Olympic-class liner, never sailed as a passenger ship. She is now a war grave.

During *Olympic*'s maiden voyage, J Bruce Ismay sent a Marconigram confirming the order for *Britannic*. Work stopped on Harland & Wolff's job number 433 when *Titanic* sank, and *Britannic* was redesigned with a stronger hull.

As *Britannic* was being fitted out at Queen's Island, the First World War began. On Admiralty orders, she was converted into a hospital ship and painted white with large red crosses.

Disaster struck on the morning of 21 November 1916. *Britannic* was in the Aegean Sea bound for Salonika in northern Greece to pick up war wounded. On board were 625 crew and 500 medical officers. She struck a mine and sank within an hour.

Only thirty people died thanks to better lifeboat drill, and the ship carrying three times more lifeboats than *Titanic*. Nurse Violet Jessop, a stewardess on *Titanic*, survived the sinking of *Britannic* as well.

French underwater explorer Jacques Cousteau discovered the wreck in 1975.

'Old Reliable'

Olympic had a long and eventful life. Built to outclass Cunard's super-liners, she joined her rival's fleet when White Star and Cunard merged in 1934.

After *Titanic* sank, *Olympic* returned to Belfast for a refit, not only to strengthen her hull, but to reassure the public that she was safe. When passenger numbers dropped on the outbreak of the First World War, White Star decided to mothball her in Belfast. The government had other ideas. Stripped of her finery and dressed in dazzle paint to confuse submarines, she carried up to 7,000 American troops to Europe per crossing. After returning Canadian soldiers at the end of the War, she was back in Belfast to be converted from coal to cheaper, cleaner oil.

Popular with passengers, she regularly came back to Belfast to be fitted with the latest improvements, from additional bathrooms to a dance floor. In 1935, Cunard finally retired her. She sailed to the Tyne where her fittings were sold off. Two years later her hull was towed into the river Forth to be scrapped.

Samson and Goliath

Harland & Wolff did well in the decades after *Titanic*. It remains a significant Belfast engineering business. After the *Titanic* disaster, the yard won orders to bring passenger ships up to the new safety requirements and later to build warships.

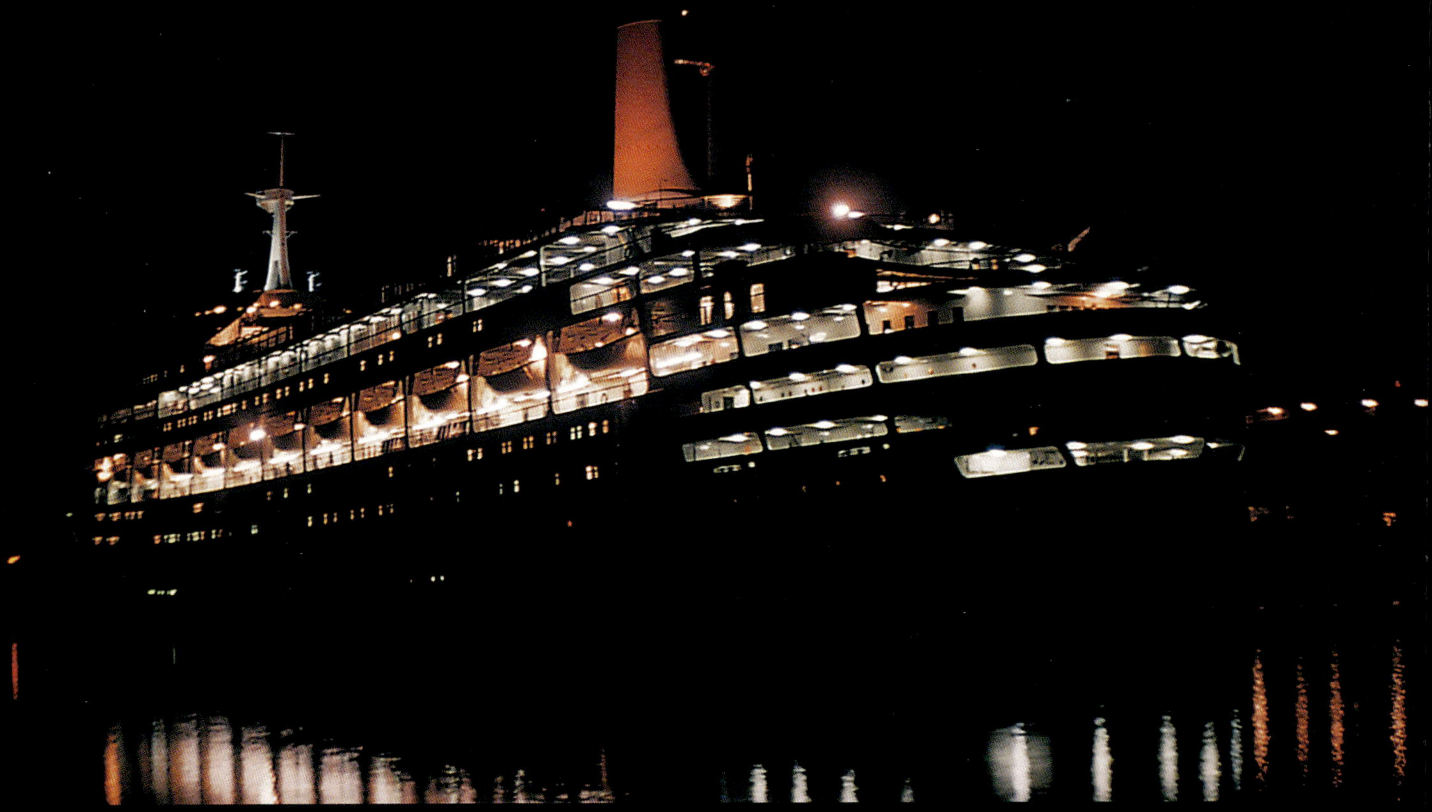

P & O passenger liner *Canberra*, 1961

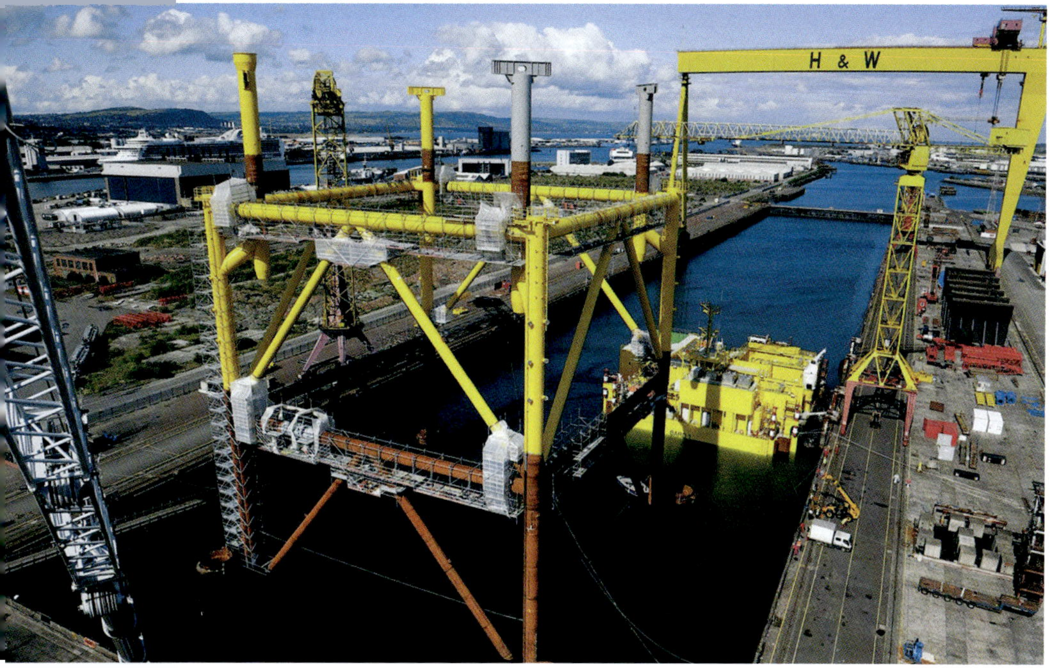

Diversification from shipbuilding into renewable energy, such as wave power generation. A transformer-jacket is being fitted under one of the cranes.

By the 1920s, Harland & Wolff employed 65,000 people at five British yards. In Belfast it had massive engine building and iron casting works and a new yard to mass-produce ships to a standard design.

The Depression and the end of the relationship with White Star were offset by a growing naval order book and a joint venture with Short Brothers to build bombers. During the Second World War, the yard built over 130 warships, repaired many more and manufactured armaments.

Air travel and overseas competition led to the decline of British shipbuilding. In the 1960s, Harland & Wolff concentrated its operations in Belfast. It has since moved into new markets from offshore oil to renewable energy. The gantry cranes Samson and Goliath still dominate the Belfast skyline.

In 2023, Harland & Wolff were selected by the Ministry of Defence to build support ships for the Royal Navy in a contract worth £1.6 billion.

BALLARD'S QUEST

'Let's go find the *Titanic*.'

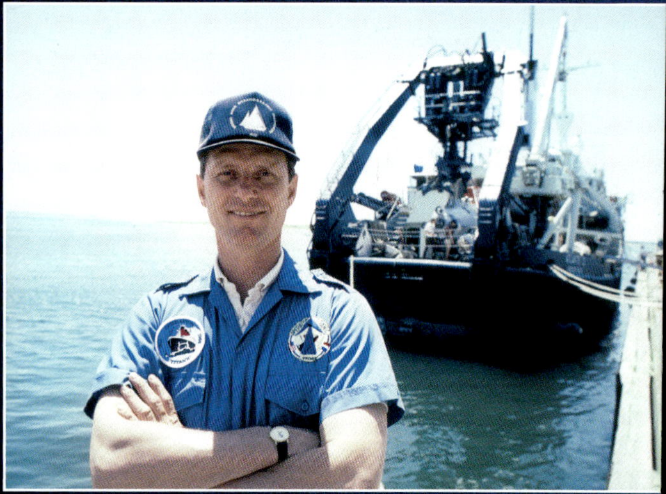

Dr Robert Ballard on the Woods Hole Oceanographic Institution dock with *Atlantis II*, the research vessel, and Alvin, a 3-man submersible, on Operation *Titanic*, 1986.

Renewed interest in *Titanic* and improved technology led to the quest to find the wreck. US underwater explorer Dr Robert Ballard discovered it in 1985.

How do you find a 52,310 ton wreck lying two and a half miles below the North Atlantic? Wealthy survivors first suggested raising the wreck. Other ideas over the decades owed much to science fiction.

Texan oil millionaire Jack Grimm funded the first serious attempts in the early 1980s. Hindered by bad weather, his expeditions failed. In 1985, French and American underwater experts took up the challenge. Dr Robert Ballard, the chief scientist of the American team, had spent years developing state-of-the-art imaging equipment.

On 1 September 1985, equipped with sensors, lights and cameras, Ballard's unmanned vessel Argo found the wreck. Images proved that *Titanic* had broken in two. Ballard returned in 1986 to explore and photograph the wreck in his submarine, Alvin on which was mounted a small remotely operated vehicle or ROV called JASON, Jr. that could actually go inside *Titanic*.

Although Dr Ballard believes the wreck site should remain undisturbed as a mark of respect, it has become a mecca for treasure hunters and tourists.

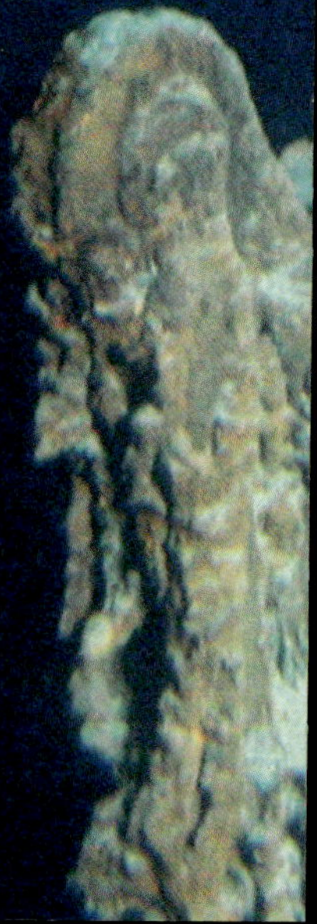

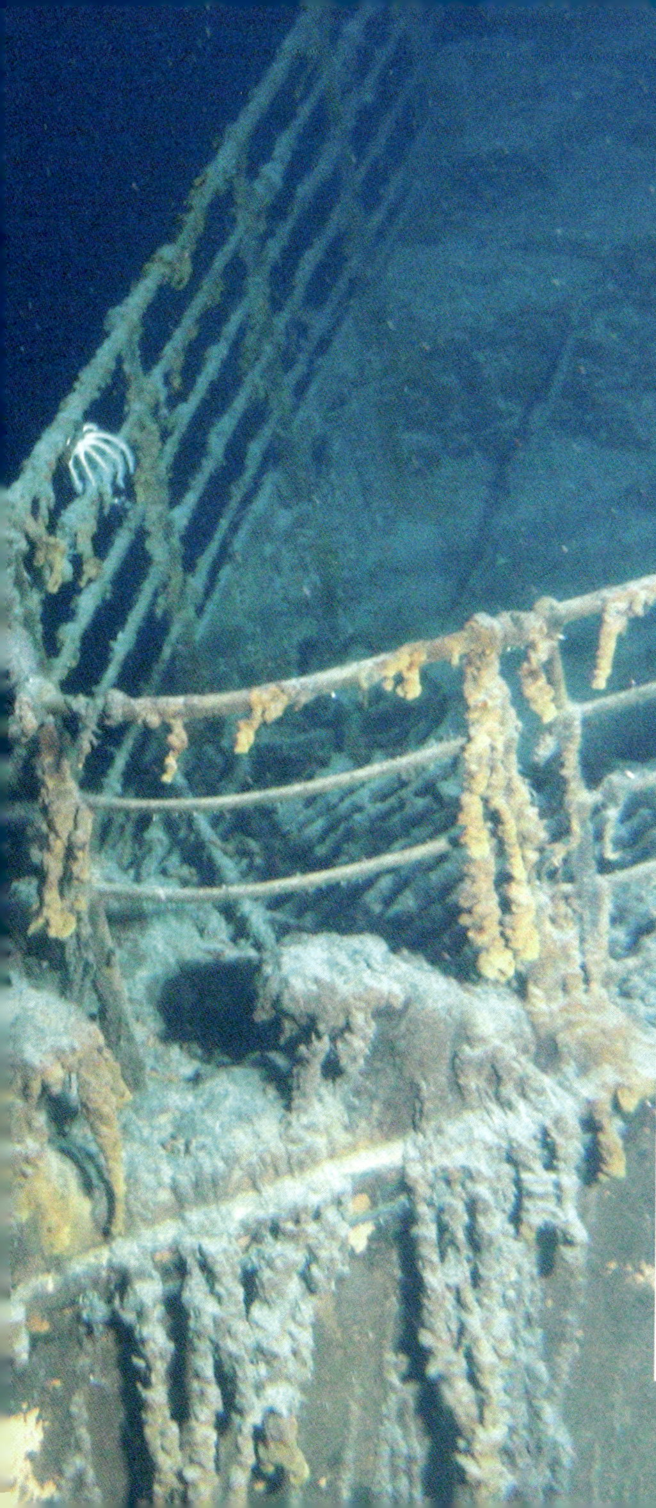

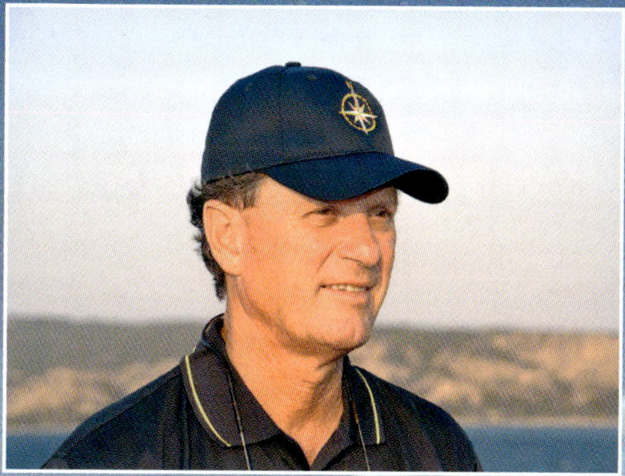

Dr Robert Ballard, ocean explorer

President of the Institute for Exploration, scientist emeritus from the Woods Hole Oceanographic Institution, has given his support to the Titanic Belfast Project.

'What strikes me most ...'

'I thought I knew all there was to know about *Titanic*, but that was until I became involved in Titanic Belfast. What strikes me most is that the people of Belfast who built this amazing ship are finally coming forth to tell their stories, to proudly embrace what they did, and make their peace with this historic moment in time.

Titanic belongs to Belfast. I'm very pleased that the city which gave *Titanic* to the world will now be able to welcome that world to Belfast.

Titanic's story is infused with romance, pathos and glory, there is no better place to tell it than Belfast.'

THE SHIP OF DREAMS

One of the reasons the Titanic story endures today is due to the emotive human stories of those whose lives were impacted by the ship. From the pride of the Belfast shipyard workers who built the Olympic-class liners, to the hopes and dreams of those embarking on a journey to start a new life, each unique story touches hearts and minds, captivating as much today as it did in 1912.

Robert Douglas Spedden

The boy who slept through the sinking

Six-year-old Robert Douglas Spedden was the only child of Frederic and Daisy Spedden, a wealthy couple from New York who were returning home after a long vacation. Douglas was cared for by his nanny Margaret Burns, whom he called 'Muddie Boons' because he could not quite pronounce her name.

Following the collision with the iceberg, Douglas was woken and dressed by Muddie, who told him that they were 'taking a trip to see the stars'. The Spedden party made their way to the boat deck where they boarded lifeboat no.3. After all the available women and children had been loaded, Frederic and about twenty other men were also allowed to board.

As they rowed to safety, Douglas slept through the night with his beloved teddy bear 'Polar' by his side. When he woke up, he saw the icebergs around and exclaimed: 'Oh, Muddie, look at the beautiful North Pole with no Santa Claus on it.'

Although the Speddens survived *Titanic*, tragedy struck two years later when nine-year-old Douglas was playing football near the family summer home in Maine and his ball went into the road. He ran out

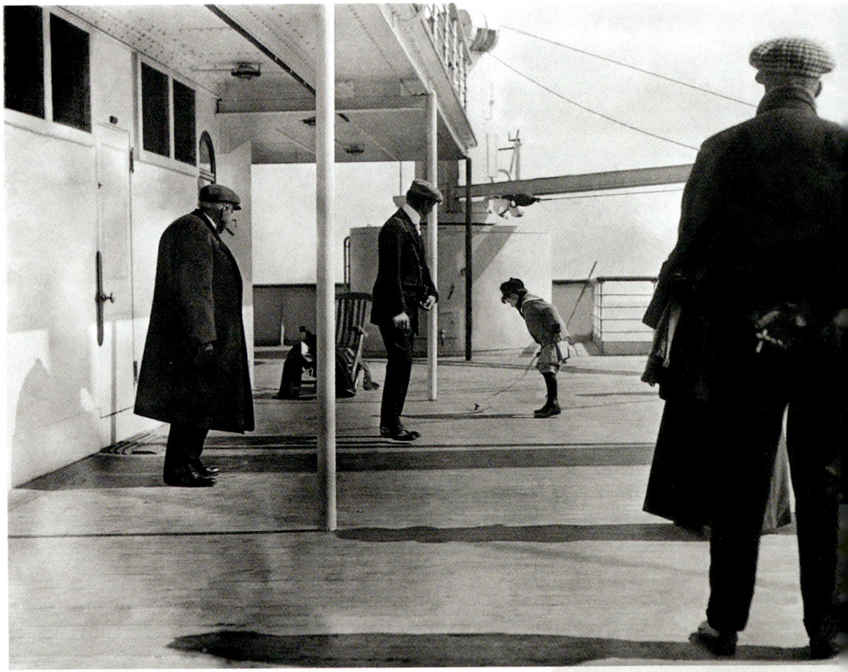

Father Browne's iconic photo of young Douglas Spedden playing on board *Titanic*.
Credit: Davison Photo.

to retrieve it but was hit by a speeding car driving on the wrong side of the road. It was one of the first recorded road accidents in the state. He died two days later from the concussion he sustained - a victim of modern transportation after all.

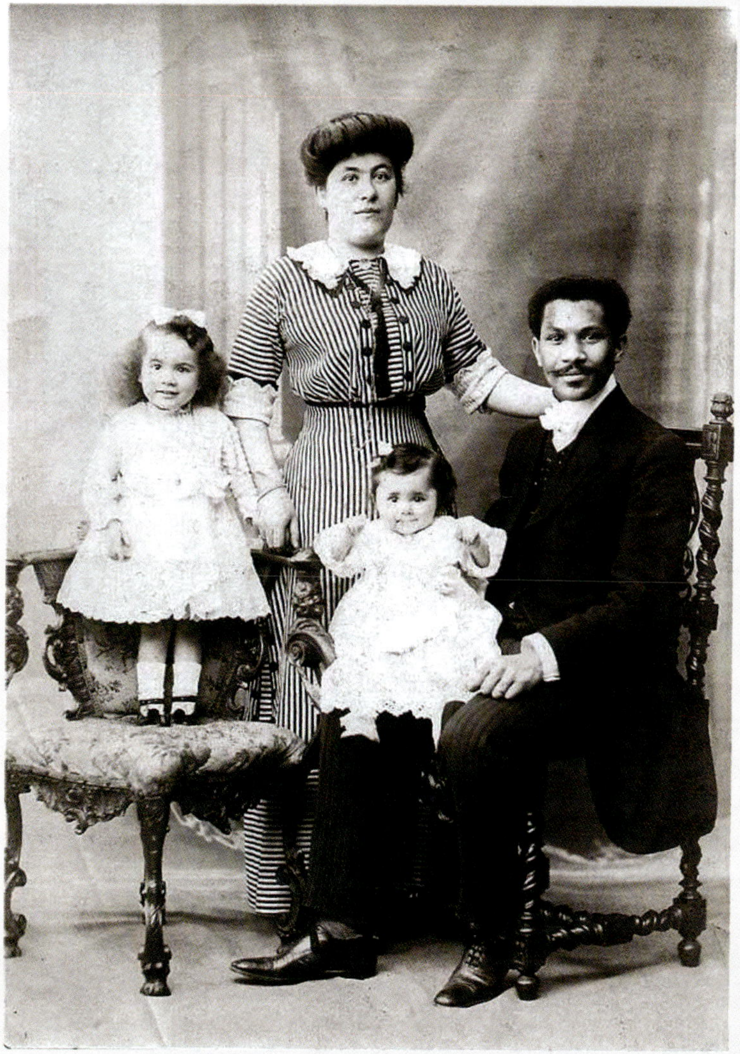

Joseph Philippe Lemercier Laroche

Racial discrimination prevented him from finding well-paid work

Haitian-born Joseph Laroche emigrated to France to study engineering when he was fifteen. Although he was a bright student and graduated as an engineer, racial discrimination prevented him from finding well-paid work.

Joseph married a local Frenchwoman, eighteen-year-old Juliette Lafargue, and a year later the young couple celebrated the birth of their first daughter Simonne.

However, their second daughter Louise was born prematurely, and suffered from ill-health in her early years.

To support his family, Joseph persuaded Juliette to relocate to Haiti where he might find a better-paying job as a qualified engineer. Their travel plans were hastened by the news that Juliette was pregnant for a third time, and in April 1912 they boarded *Titanic* at Cherbourg with Second Class tickets paid for by Joseph's mother - a welcome present for the new family.

Joseph, the only black man on board *Titanic*, died in the sinking, but his family was saved. Juliette returned to her native France with her daughters and gave birth to a baby boy whom she named Joseph, in honour of his late father.

The Goodwins

The entire family was lost in the sinking

Britons Frederick and Augusta Goodwin were crossing the Atlantic to start a new life with their six children, including 19-month-old Sidney.

Several of Fred's relatives had already emigrated to America, settling in Niagara Falls where they found work at the hydro-electric power station. Fred decided to join them and borrowed money from his siblings to pay for the fare. They boarded *Titanic* at Southampton as Third-Class passengers with a ticket that cost £46 18s (approximately £4000 in today's money).

By the time the Goodwins knew anything about the collision with the iceberg, all the lifeboats had been launched. Tragically, the entire family of eight perished in the sinking and only the body of baby Sidney was recovered.

When no relative came forward to claim the child, the crew of the *Mackay-Bennett* personally escorted the child's coffin to Fairview Lawn Cemetery in Halifax and paid for a large monument in memory of the 'unknown child'. (Sidney's body was finally identified by DNA analysis in 2008).

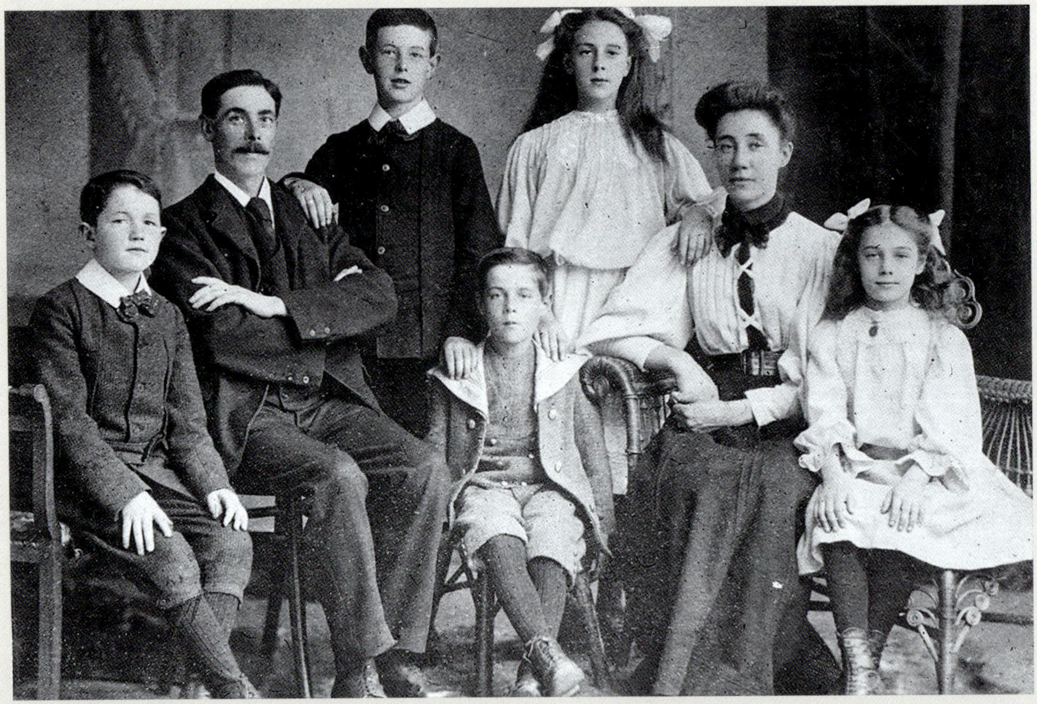

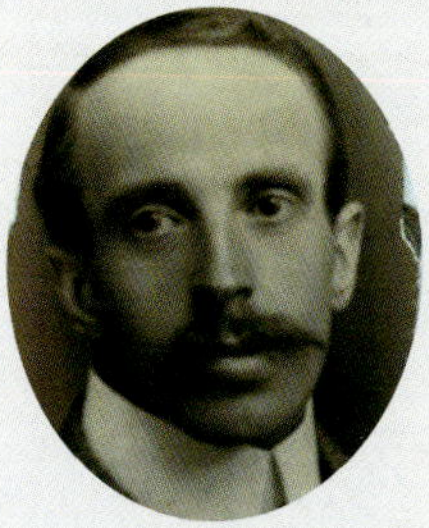

Roderick Chisholm

The skilled draughtsman and devoted family-man

Roderick Chisholm was born in Dumbarton, Scotland in 1868. He moved to Belfast in 1892 and over the next twenty years rose to become Harland & Wolff's chief draughtsman.

He worked closely with Thomas Andrews on the design of *Olympic* and *Titanic*. Being an expert in the structural detail of the ship, Chisholm was chosen for the Guarantee Group – the nine-strong team selected to oversee the smooth running of the vessel on her maiden voyage.

Apart from being an accomplished draughtsman, Chisholm was a loving husband and father. Before *Titanic* left Southampton, Roderick purchased a gift of three vases to send home to his beloved wife Susan in Belfast. Sadly, these would be the last gifts he would ever give her.

The vases remain in the family to this day. According to Chisholm's great granddaughter they remind them that: 'He was not just the Best of the Best in work, but much more importantly, he was the Best of the Best at home, where it counts most of all.'

John and Nelle Snyder

A Titanic honeymoon couple

Wealthy Minnesotans John Snyder and his new bride Nelle spent the last days of their honeymoon as First-Class passengers on *Titanic*.

After the collision, they made their way to the boat deck just as the evacuation was beginning. Passengers were reluctant to get into the lifeboats at first, unaware of the impending danger. The Snyders found themselves being physically pulled into the lifeboat by crewmembers who lowered the boat and rowed away.

From their vantage point, the urgency of the situation dawned on them: 'We first knew the steamship was sinking when we saw one row of porthole lights disappear, leaving but two, then one row, then none. ... Then, we watched the green light go down and we realized there was nothing between us and a watery grave but the frail boats into which we were crowded.'

After a harrowing night on the frigid North Atlantic, the honeymoon couple and their fellow passengers were rescued by *Carpathia*. Following the disaster, John and Nelle returned to Minnesota where they raised three children.

THE LASTING LEGACY

'I'll never let go, Jack.'

The way that films have presented *Titanic*'s last hours has shaped how we think and feel about what may have happened on board.

Titanic is a story of heroes and villains. In 1943, the Nazis made *Titanic* showing the British as greedy cowards and the Germans as brave. The hero is a German officer who rescues passengers from Third Class. The villain is J Bruce Ismay who wants to break the speed record to profit from a share swindle.

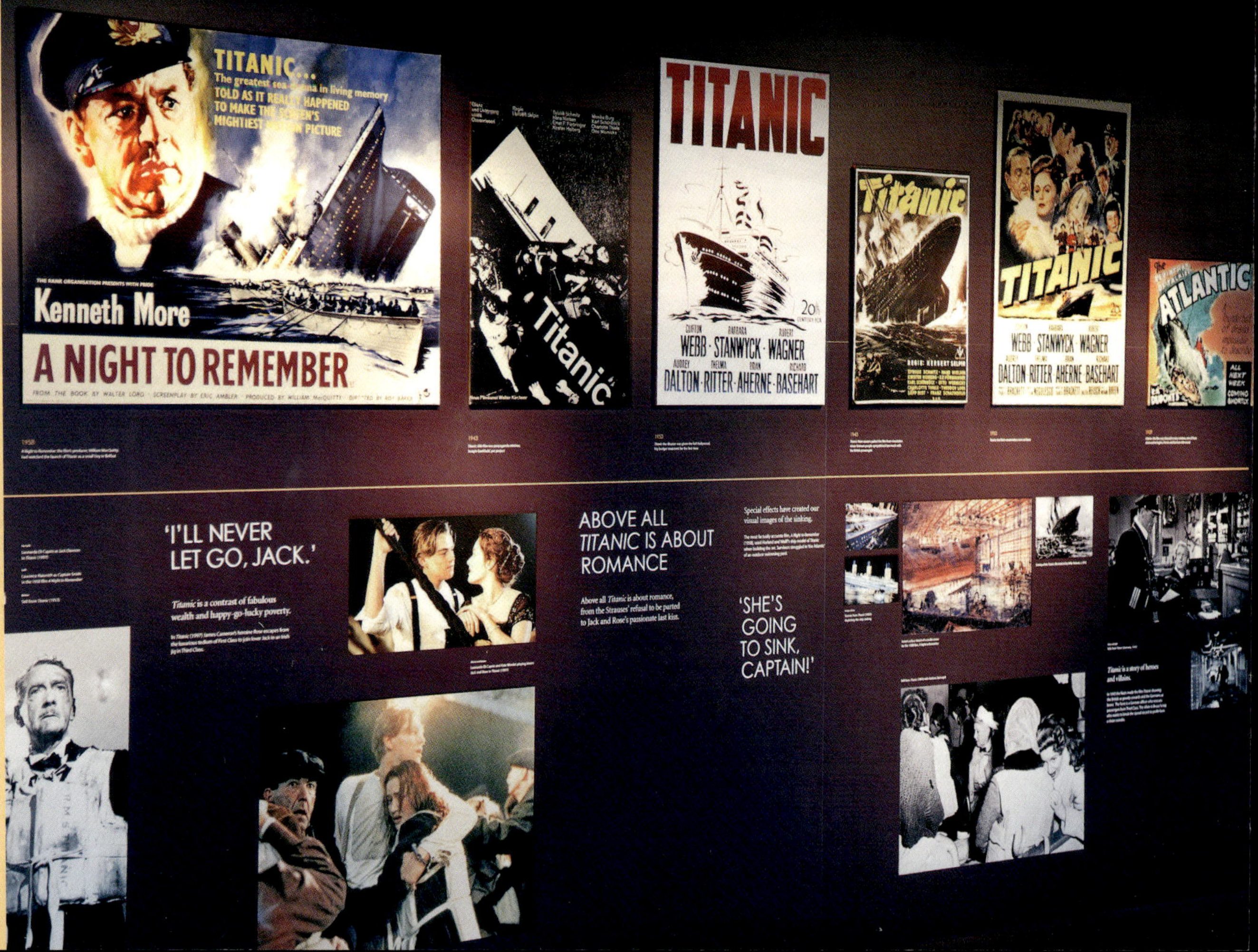

Titanic is a contrast of fabulous wealth and happy-go-lucky poverty.

In James Cameron's *Titanic* (1997) heroine Rose escapes from the luxurious tedium of First Class to join lover Jack in an Irish jig in Third Class.

Special effects have created our visual images of the sinking. The most factually accurate film *A Night to Remember* (1958) used Harland & Wolff 's ship model of *Titanic* when building the set. Survivors struggled in 'the Atlantic' of an outdoor swimming pool.

Above all *Titanic* is about romance, from the Strauses' refusal to be parted to Jack and Rose's passionate last kiss.

'She's going to sink, Captain'

How actors have presented key characters in *Titanic* films has influenced whether we see them as heroes or villains.

James Cameron created Jack Dawson, the hero of *Titanic* from his own imagination. After the film was produced, he discovered that there was a real-life Joseph Dawson on the ship.

Irishman Joseph Dawson was a coal trimmer who died in the sinking.

As in real life, Thomas Andrews has always been presented as popular, caring and deeply affected by realising the fate of his ship before anyone else.

Film has treated J Bruce Ismay less kindly. He is shown as putting himself before other passengers and profit before safety.

Second Officer Charles Lightoller has appeared in most *Titanic* films. Although he was the hero of *A Night to Remember*, James Cameron's *Titanic* questioned his competence over the loading of the lifeboats.

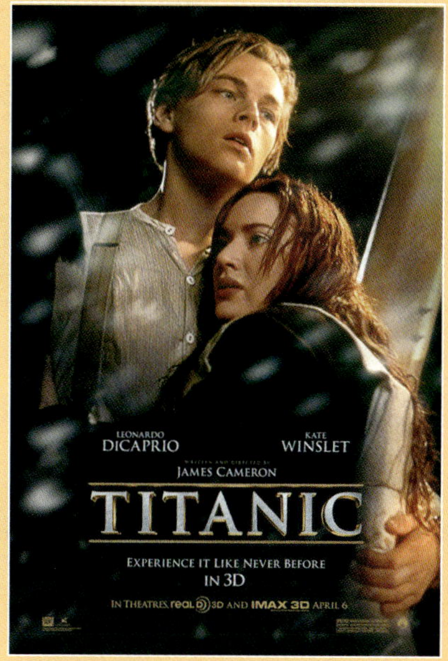

James Cameron created Jack Dawson, the hero of *Titanic* from his own imagination. After the film was produced, he discovered that there was a real-life Joseph Dawson on the ship. Irishman Joseph Dawson was a coal trimmer who died in the sinking.

The romantic last moments of the Strauses were made for film.

They first featured in *Atlantic* (1929) as the elderly Rools who refuse to be parted when the women are ordered to the lifeboats.

An unthinkable story?

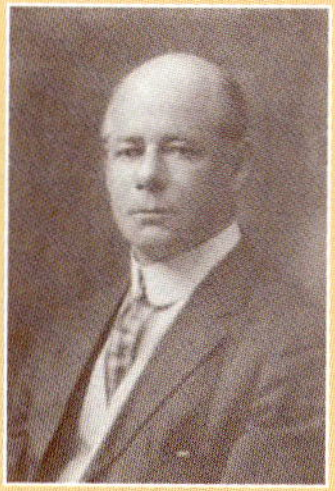

Morgan Robertson was an American novelist who, in 1898, wrote a short story, *Futility*, in which a very large unsinkable ship called *Titan* (nearly as big as *Titanic*) hit an iceberg on its side and sinks in the Atlantic at high speed, one April night. Only a few passengers and crew survive because there are not enough lifeboats. This story was published fourteen years before *Titanic* sank!

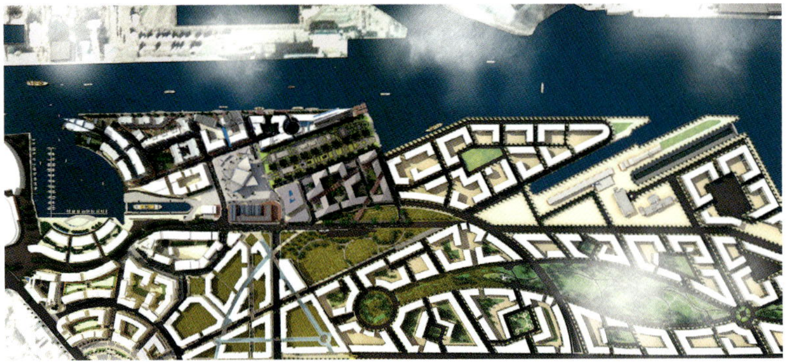

Titanic Quarter and the Maritime Mile

A new community

In October 2003, Harcourt Developments entered into a partnership with the Belfast Harbour Commissioners to redevelop the former shipyards of Queen's Island. Seeking to breathe new life into the historic waterfront, Harcourt engaged CivicArts / Eric R Kuhne & Associates in 2005 to create a vision plan that explored the island's full potential.

The result was Titanic Quarter: a mixed-use masterplan that recast Queen's Island as a home for 28,000 people, spread across seven village neighbourhoods. The design's elegant geometry of radiating boulevards, avenues and orbital promenades was stitched together with a pattern of parks and garden squares that placed every home within two blocks of a green space or the water's edge. The emphasis was on creating a sustainable model of social integration, with homes, shops and places of employment all within easy walking distance.

Titanic Belfast assumes the role of the city's long-lost Crystal Palace, providing the focus for this quarter's cultural activity.

Just a stones' throw from Titanic Belfast dive into the city's seafaring history and discover the Maritime Mile. Along the 10,000 heritage steps, you'll discover Belfast's iconic waterfront and its local neighbourhoods, historic docks and vibrant quaysides.

There's plenty to explore along the Maritime Mile, from the historic giants dominating the city skyline and public art dotted along the waterfront, to heritage attractions, top notch eateries and first-class accommodation – perfect for walking, cycling or running!

The Maritime Mile is an award-winning initiative developed by Maritime Belfast Trust.

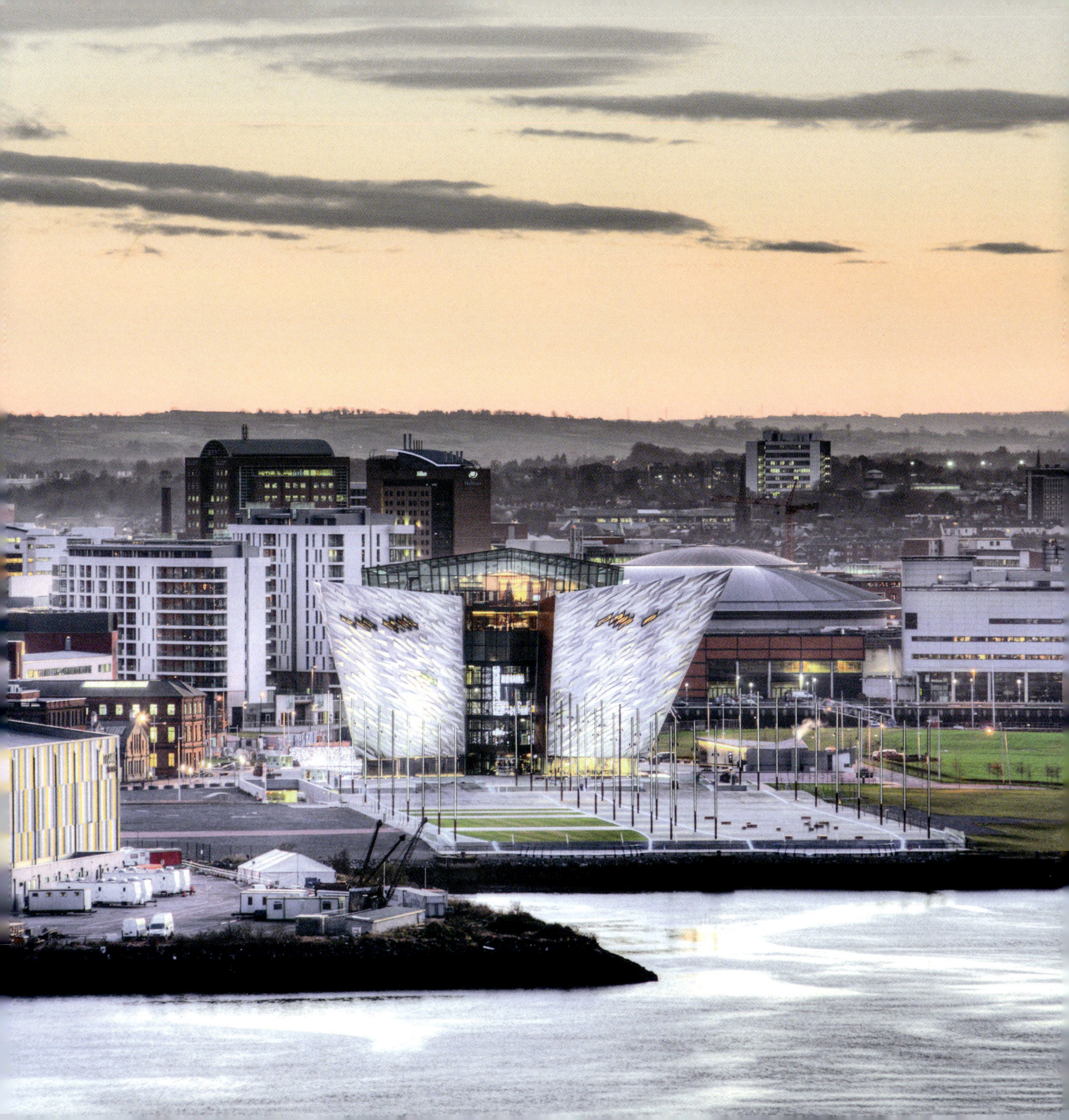

ACKNOWLEDGEMENTS

Teamwork is defined as a group of people working collectively in the interests of a common goal. The creation of Titanic Belfast is a fine example, and a large number of people have worked effectively for several years to bring about its existence. Several thousand people were involved in the planning, design and construction process and many hundreds more continue to make Titanic Belfast an international success story.

This souvenir guidebook is a humble tribute to their enthusiasm and commitment.

Published by Cadolux Ltd & Titanic Belfast Publications
Cadolux Ltd - 1a Castleview Road - Belfast, BT5 7AX

Edited by Claude-Bernard Costecalde and John Paul Doherty

Design, Cadolux, 2023
Design by Dunbar Design & Sylvie Tusinski

Printed in Slovenia
ISBN 978-0-9576300-1-7 (paperback)

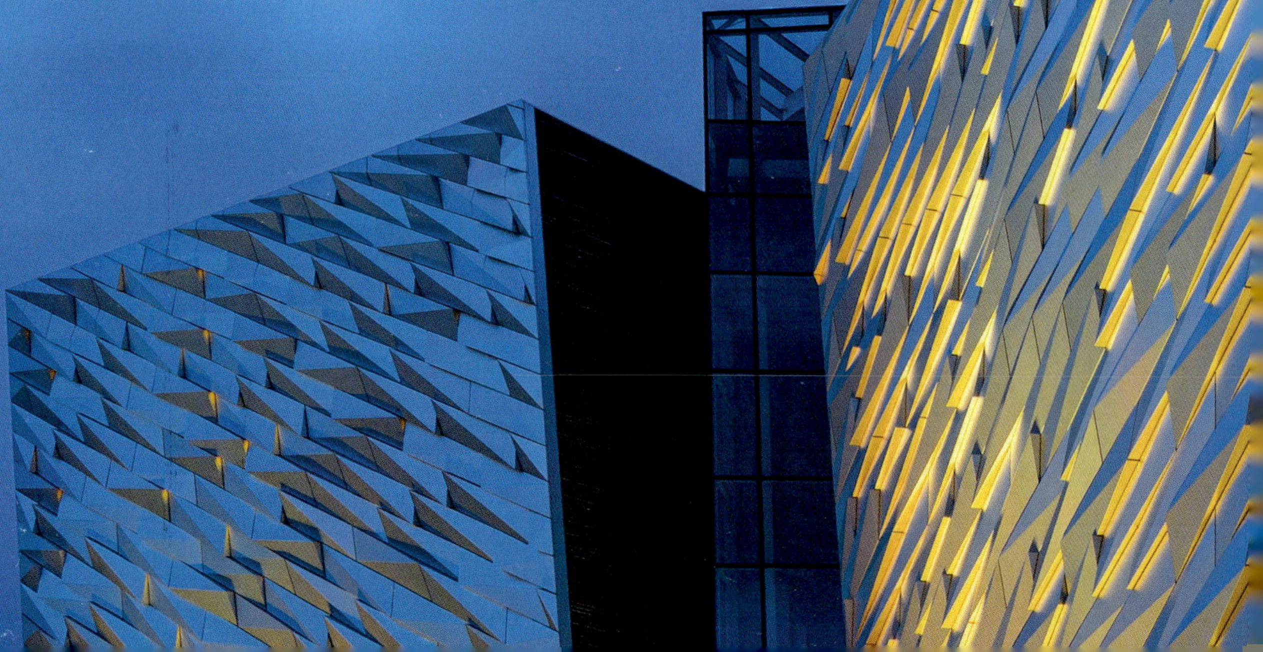